In
Search
Of
Cumorah

In Search of Cumorah

New Evidences
for the
Book of Mormon
from
Ancient Mexico

David A. Palmer

Sixth Printing: May 1999

International Standard Book Number
0-88290-169-9

Library of Congress Catalog Card Number
80-83866

Horizon Publishers' Catalog and Order Number
1063

Printed and distributed
in the United States of America by

Horizon Publishers
& Distributors, Incorporated

Mailing Address:
P.O. Box 490
Bountiful, Utah 84011-0490

Street Address:
50 South 500 West
Bountiful, Utah 84010

Phone and Fax:
Local Phone: (801) 295-9451
WATS (toll free): (800) 453-0812
FAX: (801) 295-0196

Internet:
E-mail: horizonp@burgoyne.com
Home Page: http:// www.horizonpublishers.com

DEDICATION

Appreciation is expressed to my children
Michelle, Laura and Angela;
to my wife, Gayle;
and to my parents, Delbert and Mable Palmer.
They have given me
inspiration,
sincere interest,
physical support,
and even ideas necessary to bring this research to fruition.

Gratitude is also expressed to
Bruce W. Warren,
Mr. V. Garth Norman,
Mr. Tim M. Tucker,
and Dr. John L. Sorensen
for tremendous aid
and technical assistance over many years.

Acknowledgments

In Search of Cumorah was first published in 1981. It was the product of substantial library and field research. If that research had not received guidance, orientation, ideas, and direct assistance from others, it would not have been productive. Members of the staff of the Department of Archæology and Anthropology at Brigham Young University have been particularly helpful and encouraging. They include Dr. Bruce W. Warren and Dr. John L. Sorensen. Tim M. Tucker convinced me that archæology could be truly exciting. A Uruguayan archæologist, Rafael Romano, motivated my study of the tapestry of Jucutácato by pointing to Book of Mormon parallels.

In 1977, I received an unpublished manuscript written by Dr. John L. Sorenson, *An Ancient Setting for the Book of Mormon*. After seeing favorable reviews by competent scholars, and after personally visiting most of the important locations mentioned in that manuscript, I concluded that it offered an acceptable and quite possibly correct model of Book of Mormon geography. Therefore, I have used that model as a framework within which I could present my own ideas concerning Cumorah and the events which surrounded it. My maps include only a few of Sorenson's identifications, and I have taken the liberty of making several changes. Therefore, the validity of the Sorenson geography should only be based on examination of Dr. Sorenson's own presentation, which he published in 1985.

There are several concepts developed in his model that I have utilized which bear special mention:

1. Identification of the Central Depression of Chiapas as the land of Zarahemla, and identification of cities within the land of Zarahemla.

2. Recognition of the gravelly ridge through the Isthmus of Tehuantepec as the narrow pass spoken of in the Book of Mormon.

3. Identification of the Papaloapan Basin as the Waters of Ripliancum, and

4. the Cerro Vigía as the Hill Cumorah.

I also appreciate the many comments, and assistance rendered by Dr. Sorenson during the writing of this book.

I am indebted to the Society for Early Historic Archæology. They joined me in sponsoring an expedition to acquire a comprehensive set of photographs of Preclassic ruins and artifacts in Mesoamerica. Many of the photographs in this book were taken during that expedition by Daniel Bates. His perseverance in taking and developing pictures during an extremely rigorous travel schedule is very much appreciated.

Dr. Bruce Warren, an expert in analysis of Mesoamerican ceramics and ancient historical accounts, accompanied the expedition. He was for three weeks an amiable and patient instructor. Subsequent to the trip, he has collaborated with me in studies on the tapestry and has contributed many ideas, pointed out many references, and reviewed the manuscript for this book. He is primarily responsible for discovery of the archæological data which support the theory that there were volcanic eruptions in several places in Mexico about the time of Christ.

The Foundation for Ancient Research and Mormon Studies funded my trip to the Isthmus/Gulf of Mexico region in 1990. It is believed that the trip may have been successful in identifying the ruins of the city of Bountiful. this is at a village called Tonalá at the mouth of the river.

Notwithstanding the assistance of these qualified individuals, I take full responsibility for what is written in this book. The book has not been officially endorsed by The Church of Jesus Christ of Latter-day Saints or any other organization or individual.

The personnel at various museums in Mexico and Guatemala have been helpful in obtaining photographs of their artifacts. I especially wish to thank Fernando Bustamante of the Museum Tuxteco in Santiago Tuxtla.

The assistance of personnel at various libraries is also acknowledged. These include the Newberry Library in Chicago, the University of Chicago Regenstein Library, the Olin Library of Washington University in St. Louis, the Tozer Library of the Peabody Museum at Harvard University in Cambridge, the archæological library of the University of Pennsylvania in Philadelphia, and the Harold B. Lee Library at Brigham Young University in Provo.

Appreciation is also expressed to Duane S. Crowther, President of Horizon Publishers, who edited the manuscript and prepared it for publication, and to the staff at Horizon Publishers for their efforts in producing and publishing the book in its various editions.

CONTENTS

1

WHY SEARCH FOR CUMORAH?

> *It would not be a bad plan to compare Mr. Stephens'*
> *ruined cities with those in the Book of Mormon. Light cleaves*
> *to light and facts are supposed by facts. The truth injures no*
> *one. . .*
>
> **Joseph Smith, Jr.**
> **Times and Seasons,** *Vol. 3, No. 23, p. 927*

The Hill Cumorah figures prominently in Book of Mormon history. Two civilizations were destroyed there, and the prophet Mormon hid a large collection of ancient records in that hill. A great deal of the Book of Mormon history is tied in some way to the geography of the Hill Cumorah. Where, then, do we go to find it?

A standard response might be that it is located near Palmyra, New York. Is this presumption correct? Certainly there is a hill by the same name in that location, the hill where Joseph Smith received a set of metal plates from the Angel Moroni. How did the New York hill come to be named "Cumorah," and why have many authors equated it with the Book of Mormon hill?

This book presents the theory that there are two Cumorahs. The original Cumorah, which relates to Book of Mormon history, will be called **Mormon's Cumorah** because Mormon hid there the large Nephite record library. A location for Mormon's Cumorah in the state of Veracruz, Mexico is proposed and will be defended. The hill in New York State will be called **Moroni's**

Cumorah, since Moroni placed a small set of plates there for eventual delivery to Joseph Smith. (The locations of these two hills are shown on Map #1, page 253.)

The text of the Book of Mormon will be examined and used to develop sets of criteria by which the validity of the two-Cumorah theory can be judged. Also, thirteen geographical and fifteen archæological-cultural criteria will be presented. It will be shown that the proposed hill in Mexico meets these criteria. By contrast, it will be shown that the hill in New York meets only a few of the screening criteria.

The impact of placing Mormon's Cumorah in the State of New York is to grossly distort the geography of the Book of Mormon. Doing this makes it impossible to reconcile the internal geography of the Book of Mormon with actual maps. Without a valid geography of the Book of Mormon there cannot be any serious studies of the correlation between archæology and the Book of Mormon. In fact, the traditional view that there is just one Cumorah has proved a stumbling block to development and publication of serious contributions to Book of Mormon archæology. It appears that there is no scriptural justification for placing Mormon's Cumorah in New York, and there is no evidence that Joseph Smith ever said it was there. The location of Mormon's Cumorah is, therefore, an open question which should be approached analytically.

Mormon's Cumorah In An Ancient Mexican Content

Mormon's Cumorah was a focal point of Book of Mormon history. We will show that it was in the heartland of the Jaredite civilization, and that it was surrounded by cities (Ether 14:17; 15:11).[1] The **Jaredites** were part of a group which came to America in the third millennium B.C. They were destroyed in battles near the Hill Cumorah[2] in approximately 550 B.C. (Ether 15:10-11. We will see that there is an excellent correlation between Jaredite history and the cultural history of the archæological Olmecs.

A survivor of the Jaredite battle was found by a new group, called **Mulekites**, who migrated from Palestine in the sixth century B.C.. Various ancient documents and archæological data enlarge on the information given about the Mulekites in the Book

---

1. This form will be used for references to the Book of Mormon, giving the book, then chapter and verses.

2. Called "Ramah" by the Jaredites.

of Mormon. This information ties in directly to the theory that Mormon's Cumorah was a hill called the Cerro (Hill) Vigía (pronounced Vee-HEE-ah), which is located along the Gulf Coast in southern Veracruz State.

We will look at Cumorah from the perspective of the **Nephites** as well. The important Guatemalan ruins of Kaminaljuyú (Kah-me-nahl-hoo-YOO) and the Mexican ruins at Teotihuacán are discussed in detail. These often-visited ruins appear to figure into the strategies which led to the defeat of the Nephites at Cumorah. Areas in between these two important cities are also significant, and the fact that they were abandoned at the time of the Nephite retreat to Cumorah is examined.

THE MORMON CHURCH'S POSITION ON GEOGRAPHY

The Church of Jesus Christ of Latter-day Saints has no official position on Book of Mormon geography. In fact, the Church-sponsored New World Archæological Foundation (NWAF), which for two decades has been conducting excavations in the state of Chiapas, Mexico, has steered away from direct Book of Mormon studies.

The NWAF has gained respect as one of the best organizations doing field archæological research in Mexico. (*Weaver*, 1972: 301)[3] Thus, in a wise manner, the Church has been helping to provide raw data from which others might find parallels with key events in the Book of Mormon. The Church thus avoids being drawn into speculation concerning the relationship between archæology and the Book of Mormon.

WAS MORMON'S CUMORAH THE PLACE SHOWN TO JOSEPH SMITH?

BOOK OF MORMON STATEMENTS

It is commonly believed that Moroni buried the metal plates in his care in the Hill Cumorah. However, the Book of Mormon does not tell us where Moroni hid the records.

Mormon said that he buried in the hill Cumorah (speaking of the Nephite battleground) all the sacred plates in his possession, except those given to Moroni and subsequently delivered to Joseph Smith. This seventy-four year old prophet-leader said:

---

3. All bibliographical references are given at the end of the book arranged by author. The form of reference cited in the text is author, publication date, and page number, in that order.

I Mormon, began to be old; and knowing it to be the last struggle of my people, and having been commanded of the Lord that I should not suffer the records which had been handed down by our fathers, which were sacred, to fall into the hands of the Lamanites, (for the Lamanites would destroy them) therefore I made this record out of the plates of Nephi, and *hid up in the hill Cumorah all the records which had been entrusted to me by the hand of the Lord, save it were these few plates which I gave unto my son Moroni.* (Mormon 6:6)

Moroni made additional entries on the plates given him by his father subsequent to the destruction of his people. One entry was made thirty-six years after the destruction. In the intervening time his father, and other Nephite survivors whom he knew, presumably had been killed.

Several times Moroni mentioned burying the plates. He said, "Therefore, I will write and hide up the records in the earth; and whither I go it mattereth not." (Mormon 8:4) He also said, "I am the same who hideth up this record unto the Lord; . . ." (8:14). It is significant that he did not mention Cumorah. Since he reports on continuing wars, it appears that he stayed in the general vicinity of his homeland for the first fifteen years after the last battle. After that period of time he could have gone anywhere.

I speculate that Moroni carried the plates by himself up to the Palmyra, New York area and buried them there. One purpose of Mormon's compiling and abridgement in the first place may have been the need to have a set of records that were lightweight enough to be portable. It is also possible that Moroni placed the Book of Mormon plates in the New York hill hundreds of years later, as a resurrected being—the same physical status as he held when he appeared to Joseph Smith.

DESIGNATION OF THE HILL IN NEW YORK STATE AS CUMORAH

There is no record of Moroni having told Joseph Smith that the place where the abridgement was buried was Cumorah, or that the hill was once a great battleground. If this had been the place of those great final battles, it would be rather surprising that it was not mentioned. The first record we have that identifies the hill in New York with the last Nephite and Jaredite battleground was written by Oliver Cowdery (1835:77). In a revelation given seven years later there was a hint of a possible connection. "And again, what do we hear? Glad tidings from Cumorah! Moroni, an angel from heaven declaring the fulfillment of the prophets—the book to be revealed." (D&C 128:20)

MEANING OF "CUMORAH"

We may be comfortable applying the name "Cumorah" to both the hill where Mormon buried the large Nephite library and to the hill where Moroni hid up the plates, which he later gave to Joseph Smith. One Near-Eastern student (Urrutia, 1983:40) has pointed out that Isaiah 60:1 begins with this command to Zion: "Arise, shine." The male version of that would be "kum orah." Urrutia states, "If my understanding is correct, this must be the meaning of Cumorah: "Arise, shine."

A "two-Cumorah" theory is thus most appropriate, since records were hidden in both Mormon's Cumorah and Moroni's Cumorah. Therefore, it matters little whether it was Joseph Smith or one of his associates who called the hill in New York "Cumorah."

JOSEPH SMITH'S CHALLENGE

It has been suggested that questions of Book of Mormon geography will be settled by revelation. Perhaps in that regard we should consider the Lord's reprimand of Oliver Cowdery, "Behold, you have not understood; you have supposed that I would give it unto you when you took no thought save it was to ask me. But, behold, I say unto you, that you must study it out in your mind; then you must ask me if it be right . . ." (Doctrine and Covenants 9:7-8) It seems unreasonable to expect that the Lord would want to concern the prophet and leaders of his church with such mundane details as to whether or not such things as the monochrome pottery with everted rims and mammiform supports in mound "X" at a particular ruin (and similar to pottery from a distant ruin), related to a Nephite migration. Certainly we would not expect this to happen. Furthermore, since the Restoration of the Gospel, the geography of the Bible lands has been quite satisfactorily developed without any revelation through the prophets.

The prophet Joseph Smith has stated very clearly that the approach to Book of Mormon geography must be primarily of an intellectual nature. In 1842, while serving as editor of the Nauvoo newspaper, *Times and Seasons*, he used the paper to educate the people and turn Nauvoo into a cultural center of the west.

One of the books which the prophet publicized was a national bestseller written by John Lloyd Stephens (1841). Stephens wrote a colorful description of his adventures as an emissary of the United States government to Guatemala while that country was in the throes of revolutions and counterrevolutions. Somehow emerging unscathed from very dangerous situations, he managed to explore a number of ruins. His companion, Frederick Catherwood, executed amazingly accurate line drawings of the ancient Mayan temples and stelae (carved stones with figures and writing). The reports and drawings in that book helped to reverse the general opinion that ancient Americans had been little more than savages.

Likeness of John Loyd Stephens. Reproduced with permission by Dover, New York.

After reprinting lengthy portions of Stephens' book, Joseph Smith editorialized, *"It would not be a bad plan to compare Mr. Stephens' ruined cities with those in the Book of Mormon:* Light cleaves to light and facts are supported by facts. The truth injures no one . . . ."* (*Times and Seasons,* Vol 3, No. 23, p. 927.) He went on to hypothesize that the ruins of Quirigua in Guatemala could have been those of Zarahemla, but pointed out that his identification was not conclusive. From our perspective of time we can appreciate the true brilliance of these statements. The proposed correlation of an ancient text's geography with ancient ruins had not yet developed as a proven technique, but soon would. The idea that we should make Book of Mormon geography the object of study rather than waiting for a revelation is a point which unfortunately has been forgotten by many in the intervening years.

Any attempt to make the prophet's suggested comparison without an overall geography of the Book of Mormon is almost meaningless. Those who write about Book of Mormon archæology should first commit to a definite Book of Mormon geography. There can only be one correct geography, so the scholars must eventually be able to arrive at a concensus which can be tested. Within the confines of the geographical area selected, the emphasis must be on the ruins dating to the Jaredite and Nephite time periods. While this may all seem obvious, many writers have ignored such simple prerequisites.

GEOGRAPHY BY TRADITION

Unfortunately, a tradition has developed and has been perpetuated which gives a geographical orientation to the Book of Mormon covering all the North and South American continents. It is based on statements made by some authorities of the Church, and especially upon one statement of dubious authenticity attributed to Joseph Smith.

That statement is a supposed revelation to "Joseph the Seer" which states that Lehi landed at thirty degrees south latitude on the coast of Chile. The piece of paper with that notation is in the handwriting of Frederick G. Williams. After an analysis of the facts concerning it, a famous Mormon leader and Church historian, B. H. Roberts, concluded that the evidence for the quote actually being attributable to Joseph Smith "rests on a very unsatisfactory basis . . . ." Roberts, a truly honest scholar, suggested that he should therefore abandon the geography he had previously published which placed Zarahemla in South America, and locate the Book of Mormon lands in Mexico and Guatemala. (Roberts, 1951) John A. Widtsoe also questioned the validity of the document since it was not found in the prophet's history.

By contrast with that apocryphal statement, we have a number of statements which can be more certainly attributed to Joseph Smith. A study by Lawrence Anderson (1963) showed that in the *Times and Seasons* articles Joseph Smith apparently gave his opinion that the land southward was north of Panama, in the area of Guatemala or Mexico. This would make the Isthmus of Tehuantepec the "narrow neck of land" spoken of in the Book of Mormon (*Times and Seasons* Vol. 3, No. 23, p. 927). The hypothesis was presented as his own personal idea rather than as revelation. These statements were subsequently forgotten, and the tradition which built up was inconsistent with them.

We will make no attempt to resolve statements of Book of Mormon geography by other Church authorities, but will only try to reconcile the text of the Book of Mormon itself with physical geography and archæological findings. The statements of Church leaders do not necessarily represent church doctrine. There is no doctrine of infallibility in the Church. If two Church leaders make conflicting statements concerning nondoctrinal matters, it is not a negative reflection on the Church. It is simply a reflection of the open spirit of inquiry and search for knowledge which was preached by Joseph Smith.

Joseph Fielding Smith once wrote,

> You cannot accept the books written by the authorities of the Church as standards in doctrine, only in so far as they accord with the revealed word and the standard works. Every man who writes is responsible, not the Church for what he writes. (Smith, 1956:203)

We have made reference to the tradition of Book of Mormon geography. To allow the reader to assess the extent of influence of that tradition on his or her thinking, the following quiz has been prepared. It should be taken without reference either to the Book of Mormon or to the indicated chapters where the questions are discussed.

QUIZ ON THE BOOK OF MORMON

	Yes	No	Chapter
1. Were great distances sufficient to encompass both continents covered in the described Nephite and Lamanite travels?			2
2. Does the "narrow neck of land" have to be at Panama?			2
3. Did the land configurations change so completely at the time of the Savior's crucifixion that all geographical references in the Book of Mormon are meaningless in the context of current geography?			2
4. Did the winters work a great hardship on the Nephites as they later would upon the Mormon pioneers?			2
5. Did many years elapse from the time of the final battles at the narrow neck of land to the time of the battle at Cumorah?			2
6. Does the Book of Mormon say that the land of Cumorah was at a great distance north of the narrow neck?			2
7. Following the last battle, did a few Nephites escape northward?			2
8. Is there any reason to believe that the Nephites would leave their cultural area and go into strange territory to stage their last battle?			2
9. Does the Book of Mormon suggest that the Jaredites inhabited a large portion of the North American continent?			2
10. Were there advanced civilizations in upstate New York at the time of the destruction of the Jaredites and the Nephites?			4
11. Have many advanced weapons and ceramics dated to Jaredite and Nephite times been found in upstate New York?			4
12. Does the geography of the Hill Cumorah in New York agree with the requirements imposed by the Book of Mormon?			4

In the next few chapters I will attempt to demonstrate that the answer to every one of these questions is "no," contrary to popular belief. Fletcher Hammond (1959) has stated, "Many Book of Mormon scholars assert that the Hill Cumorah is in what is now New York state. To justify that assertion disrupts and confuses the entire concept of the Book of Mormon geography." The reader will have the opportunity of evaluating that assertion during study of the next three chapters.

GEOGRAPHY FROM RECONSTRUCTION, COMPARISON, AND EVALUATION

Not surprisingly, the location of Mormon's Cumorah has been a prime subject of debate during attempts to move towards a concensus on Book of Mormon geography. Early contributors to the "Two Cumorah" theory were Col. Willard Young, J. W. Washburn (1939), M. Wells Jakeman, and Thomas Stuart Ferguson (1947). In contrast, several books discussed in Chapter 4 were written to discredit the two-Cumorah theory.

It is interesting to note that the eminent Book of Mormon scholar, Sidney Sperry, originally thought that Mormon's Cumorah was in New York. Nevertheless, he challenged generations of students at the Brigham Young University to check out that theory. The late Dr. Sperry eventually concluded, with most of his students, that there were indeed two Cumorahs (Sperry, 1968).

In the last forty years there have been great advances in archæology. These include the discovery of radiocarbon dating and its calibration, the publication of scores of detailed archæological field reports, linguistic advances, native calendar studies (Edmonson, 1988), publication of popular books, and the decipherment of the previously enigmatic Maya writing (Schele and Freidel, 1990). There have also been advances in the interpretation of the text of the Book of Mormon in light of these findings. Major books published since the first publication of this book include those by Sorenson (1985), Warren and Ferguson (1987), Allen (1989), and Huack (1988). An extensive critical review of Hauck's book by John Clark (1989) and a completely internal textual analysis by Sorenson (1991) developed carefully considered internal geographies that are in essential agreement with the geographical plan presented herein.

Since the first publication of this book and others, beginning in 1981, opinion of many thoughtful members of the Church has shifted to acceptance of Mesoamerica as the land of the Book of Mormon. Furthermore, the specific hill proposed as the last battleground for Nephites and Jaredites has won widespread acceptance.

Sorenson's geography (1985), has been carefully reviewed by a number of scholars. Not all agree with it, but some very knowledgeable people do. This book presents the rationale for the location of Cumorah. However, for a thorough evaluation of the many other facets of the geography and the cultural detail associated with it, the reader should study the works of Sorenson and others as they are published.

When Joseph Smith presented his geographical theories, he did not do it dogmatically. He used the phrase, "I will not declare positively that . . . ." In the same spirit, I recognize that this book cannot be the last word. New information is continually coming forth. Only discovery of Mormon's record repository will prove definitively which hill was the scene of the last battles. However, any viable candidate for Mormon's Cumorah must pass all the tests provided by the Book of Mormon. The only hill of which I am presently aware, that passes all those criteria, is the Cerro Vigía in the state of Veracruz.

SUMMARY

1. There are two hills called Cumorah. The one in the state of New York was where Moroni buried the plates later given to Joseph Smith. The original hill Cumorah is in Mexico. It was the place where Mormon buried the Nephite library and where the Nephites were destroyed.

2. The word "Cumorah" may mean, "arise, shine."

3. The hill in New York probably was given the name "Cumorah" by Oliver Cowdery. There is no significant evidence Moroni ever called it thus. The Book of Mormon does not say where Moroni buried his set of plates.

4. The Cerro Vigía in the southern part of the state of Veracruz, Mexico, is proposed as the location of Mormon's Cumorah.

5. It is speculated that following the Nephite battles, Moroni carried his records from Mexico northward to New York and

buried them in the spot where they were later delivered to Joseph Smith.

6. The Church of Jesus Christ of Latter-day Saints has no official position on Book of Mormon geography, but it finances fundamental archæological research in Mexico and Central America.

7. Joseph Smith encouraged correlation of archæological discoveries with Book of Mormon geography. He did not indicate that the matter would be resolved by revelation. He said, "It would not be a bad plan to compare Mr. Stephens' ruined cities with those in the Book of Mormon."

8. Without definition of the geography of the Book of Mormon there can be no meaningful correlation of its history and archæology.

9. Tradition is an unreliable source of information of Book of Mormon geography.

10. The theory presented here for Cumorah fits into the overall Limited-Tehuantepec correlation, and follows some of the specific correlations developed by John L. Sorenson.

2

WHAT DOES THE BOOK OF MORMON REQUIRE FOR GEOGRAPHY OF THE JAREDITE AND NEPHITE BATTLEGROUND?

> And it was in a land of many waters, rivers, and fountains.
>
> Mormon 6:4

Mormon's Cumorah (Ramah) is a spot of central importance in the Book of Mormon geography because its location is described in both the Jaredite and Nephite accounts. In this chapter a list of thirteen specific criteria given in the Book of Mormon for the location of Ramah/Cumorah will be developed. But first we shall consider more general aspects of the geographical setting. In doing so we will give rationale for negative answers to the first nine questions posed in Chapter 1.

An understanding of the geography of the Book of Mormon requires knowledge of topography, dimensions, directions, configuration, climate, plant and animal life, plus archæology. Any attempt to superimpose a conceptualization of Book of Mormon geography on a simple map of the New World is doomed to failure. Vertical projections of that landscape were an extremely important aspect of Jaredite and Nephite histories. This is perhaps not as obvious today with modern transportation, but to a Nephite *up* meant *up in elevation* and *down* meant *down in elevation,* with a substantial difference in effort required to go in one direction or the other.

GENERAL GEOGRAPHICAL ORIENTATION

There are forty-eight references in the Book of Mormon to a general land northward and/or a general land southward. These lands were located between "east" and "west" seas, and connected by a narrow neck of land (Jakeman, 1963). There are forty-four statements indicating that the city or land of Nephi was located in a region of hills or mountains, being "up" from the land called Zarahemla. Nephi was also in a southerly direction from Zarahemla. A river called Sidon flowed in a northerly direction past the city of Zarahemla. Its "head" was near the border between the land of Zarahemla and the land of Nephi. There is strong internal evidence for the authenticity of the Book of Mormon in the fact that in all these statements of relative topography there is no apparent contradiction.

DISTANCES

Were great distances, sufficient to cover both continents, covered in the described Nephite and Lamanite travels? A careful reading of the text convinces me that the distances were never very great in modern terms. From the land of Nephi to the city of Zarahemla was only a twenty-day journey for men, women, children and flocks. It took forty days for Ammon's expedition, but only because they were wandering and going uphill. (Mosiah 23:3, 24:25, 7:4) Fifteen to twenty kilometers per day is a reasonable estimate for movement of a large group herding animals over mixed mountainous and flat terrain. Thus, we can estimate an approximate distance of 300-400 kilometers from somewhere near the city of Nephi in the Lamanite heartland to the city of Zarahemla in the Nephite heartland. Later journeys by Alma in which he traveled throughout the land of Zarahemla were measured in days, not months (e.g. Alma 8:6).

Distances travelled in the land northward are not specified and can only be inferred. The land northward is described as being covered with inhabitants from sea to sea (Helaman 11:20). That seems feasible demographically, but only if the land northward was inhabited for only a few hundred kilometers northward from the isthmus.

THE NARROW NECK OF LAND

Does the narrow neck of land have to be at Panama?

There are a number of reasons to think not. One key reason is that the Book of Mormon makes clear that south of the isthmus there is a division between the Nephites and Lamanites which runs from the sea on the west to the sea on the east (Alma 22:27, Alma 50:8). The South American continent spreads out east and west just south of Panama, so that in a Panama correlation the Lamanite-Nephite kingdoms must be presumed to be spread out across the entire continent.

Nephite Lamanite Battles

A reading of Alma 22 and accounts of the subsequent wars between Nephites and Lamanites during the first century B.C. indicates very strongly that such a division would have been out of the question. The king of the Lamanites had control or at least some influence over that territory from one sea to the other. This is evident later on when the Lamanite armies were fighting first near the east sea, and then quickly move to the head of the River Sidon (e.g. Alma 43). In Chapter 56 we read of the big impact that the 2,000 young warriors of Helaman had in defending the entire border from the head of Sidon to the west sea. It is most difficult to envision these battles in dimensions of thousands of miles, especially when one examines a topographic map of South America.

Joseph Smith's Statements

Joseph Smith made one statement which suggested his thinking at that time to the effect that Panama (formerly, the isthmus of Darien) was the narrow neck (*Times and Seasons*, Vol. 3, No. 22, p. 922). In the very next issue, however, he modified his position after having studied further the writings of Stephens.

> Since our "extract" was published from Mr. Stephens' "Incidents of Travel" and etc., we have found another important fact relating to the truth of the Book of Mormon. Central America or Guatemala, is situated north of the Isthmus of Darien and once embraced several hundred miles of territory from north to south. The city of Zarahemla, burnt at the Crucifixion of the Savior, and rebuilt afterwards, stood upon this land as will be seen from the following words in the Book of Alma—"And now it was only the distance of a day and a half's journey for a Nephite, on the line Bountiful, and the land Desolation, from the east to the west sea; and thus the Land of Nephi, and the land of Zarahemla was nearly surrounded by water: there being a small neck of land between the Land Northward and the Land Southward."

(*Times and Seasons* Vol. 3, No. 23, p. 927, cited in Anderson, 1963). Joseph Smith was suggesting that the city of Zarahemla was north of Panama. Later, in the same article, he tentatively correlated the city of Zarahemla with the ruins of Quirigua, Honduras. According to the Book of Mormon, Zarahemla is in the land southward, so Panama could not have been Joseph Smith's "narrow neck" candidate. (Map #4, pp. 256-257 shows the Isthmus of Tehuantepec and associated ruins discovered to date which date to Book of Mormon times.)

The reason for introducing Joseph Smith's statements is not to settle the issue by authority. The very way in which he approached the problem showed quite clearly that he viewed it as one that would be solved by investigation and intellectual effort. His arguments, however, are sound. The area of southern Mexico and Guatemala is indeed nearly surrounded by water and fits the description given in Alma 22:32.

Distance Across the Narrow Neck

One objection to consideration of Tehuantepec as the narrow neck of land is distance, since it is about 230 kilometers across. Mormon said it was "a day and a half's journey for a Nephite, on the line Bountiful and the land Desolation, from the east to the west sea . . . ." It should be noted that the passage does not read "from the east sea to the west sea." The journey may have been from some strategic point within the isthmus to the west sea. The idea that this could be the case is reinforced by another passage in which the order of phrasing is reversed. "And they did fortify against the Lamanites, from the west sea, even unto the east; it being a day's journey for a Nephite, on the line which they had fortified and stationed their armies to defend their north country" (Helaman 4:7).

It is hypothesized that this defense line stretched from the Pacific Ocean to the continental divide. Fortifications between the ocean and the mountains would have served as a barrier preventing movement along the narrow coastal plain towards the isthmus from Guatemala.

A Narrow Pass on the Gulf Coast Side

Movement through the isthmus on the Gulf of Mexico side of the divide is extremely difficult unless the ridge running from Acayucan past Minatitlan is followed, as shown on Map #4. Elsewhere the area is too swampy for travel. In fact, going back through time, it appears that there never have been trade routes crossing the isthmus in a true east-west direction except along that ridge and along the Pacific side. Modern roads are shown on the map since their routes are not dissimilar from ancient trade routes. According to Zeitlin (1979:168), both the Pan American and Trans-Isthmian highways ". . . closely parallel ancient paths of trade and communication . . . ."

There are some Nephite-period ruins overlooking the road between Acayucan and Minatitlan. One such mound can be seen along the highway twenty-five kilometers from Acayucan. There are many such ruins which have never been documented due to inadequate archæological surveys in this area of the lower Coatzacoalcos River basin. For example, Francisco Pereau (1972:90) has published an aerial photograph of a very impressive mound group next to a river. It is close to the important ruins of San Lorenzo and on ground owned by a former governor of the state of Veracruz (Pereau, 1978). However, as recently as 1978 no archaeologist had apparently ever set foot on the site. Informal reports of ruins across the river from Minatitlan have been received from employees of the PEMEX oil company.

It seems likely that the gravelly ridge crossing this swampy area and ending at the major ford on the Coatzacoalcos river could be the narrow pass at which Teancum was able to stop the flight of the people of Morianton.

> Therefore, Moroni sent an army, with their camp, to head the people of Morianton, to stop their flight into the land northward. And it came to pass that they did not head them until they had come to the borders of the land Desolation; and there they did head them, by the narrow pass which led by the sea into the land northward, yea, by the sea, on the west and on the east. (Alma 50:33-34)

The "borders" of the different lands appear to have been rivers in many cases, which suggests that the encounter took place near the Coatzacoalcos River.

During seasons of flooding, approximately half of the year, it would indeed appear that there are seas on each side of the ridge. In fact, when we crossed it at the height of the dry season, we still saw large expanses of water on the Gulf Coast side which was exposed to our view from the road.

The idea that this ridge was the narrow pass spoken of in the Book of Mormon finds further support in this passage:

> And he also sent orders unto him that he should fortify the land Bountiful, and secure the narrow pass which led into the land north ward, lest the Lamanites should obtain that point and should have power to harass them on every side. (Alma 52:9)

The reference to a "point" emphasizes the fact that the entire isthmus was not being spoken of.

A NARROW PASS ON THE PACIFIC COAST SIDE

There is another passage which speaks of a "pass" but it might be on the Pacific side of the isthmus. In the series of final Nephite battles around the narrow neck of land, Mormon and his armies defended a pass:

> I did cause my people that they should gather themselves together at the land Desolation to a city which was in the borders, by the narrow pass which led into the land southward . . . therefore we did fortify against them with all our force. And it came to pass that in the three hundred and sixty and first year the Lamanites did come down to the city of Desolation to battle against us;   (Mormon 3:5-7)

It seems to me quite likely that this was a different pass because vertical topography was a factor which had no role in the battles of some centuries previous that we have just referred to. Notice that the Lamanites came *down* and when the Nephites counter-attacked they went "*up,* out of the land of Desolation."

Examination of Map #4 shows that there are no elevated areas within a hundred kilometers of the ridge near the mouth of the Coatzacoalcos, on the eastern side. By contrast, the Sierra Madre reaches close to the shoreline on the Pacific Side, where a city located near the present town of Juchitan could control travel both towards the Tuxtlas and towards the valley of Oaxaca. Could this not be the specific land of Desolation spoken of? If so, it would seem likely that the city Desolation was Laguna Zope,' a very large center during both Jaredite and Nephite times. It was in an exceptionally good location to benefit from trade through the isthmus. It had to be near the seashore because " . . . the city Teancum lay in the borders by the seashore; and it was also near the city Desolation." (Mormon 4:3)

If near the sea, then which one? This is suggested, though not definitively, by the following passage:

> And it came to pass that Hagoth, he being an exceedingly curious man, therefore he went forth and built him an exceedingly large ship, on the borders of the land Bountiful, by the land Desolation, and launched it forth into the west sea, by the narrow neck which led into the land northward.   (Alma 63:5)

Either one of the two inland lagoons shown on the Pacific Ocean side of the map would have been ideal launching points for such a vessel.

---

1 Laguna Zope is located 1 kilometer from Juchitan, to the west of the barrio of Chiguigo. It straddles the Pan American Highway

Map #4, pp. 256-157, shows a number of the ruins which definitely date to the Nephite period located in the general area of these lagoons. The NWAF has reported many other sites without a description of their age. They also reported a number of sites dating to the early Classic time period which begins in 300 A.D. Such sites were not included though they might, but don't necessarily, go back to the time of Mormon. (Delgado,1965)

FORTIFICATIONS IN THE NARROW PASS

Some of the most impressive fortifications that have been discovered were built at the site of Horcones. There is a very large hill, about ten kilometers south of Tonalá, which divides the coastal plain. Some of the mounds are visible from the stone road which leads up to the transmission tower. They are nestled on an escarpment about half way up the slope. Other ruins can only be reached by climbing on foot. Engravings were found on some of the stones used in the road construction. This was due to utilization of stone from the ancient building platforms. In some cases the road was built directly over the top of the ancient road which connected causeways and fortifications on the hill. With construction beginning at least as early as the time of Christ, the Horcones defenses must have been an important factor in the Nephite strategy. It could have served as a key roadblock to Lamanites trying to reach the land northward via the strip of wilderness which was "on the west of the land of Zarahemla, in the borders by the seashore . . ." (Alma 22:28)

ORIENTATION OF THE ISTHMUS

An obvious problem with identification of Tehuantepec as the "narrow neck of land" is that it runs north-south, not east-west as would be expected if it were to separate the land "northward" from the land "southward." However, this is only one part of the larger problem of Book of Mormon geography. If one assumes that the Book of Mormon "north" is actually true north, one has the same problem as Hammond (1959), who placed his map of the Book of Mormon in Mesoamerica generally but was unable to develop a specific correlation with present topography of the area. The solution, which is now agreed upon by many serious students of this subject, is that the **Book of Mormon north was west-north-west in our coordinate system**. This is the reason for the orientation of some of the maps presented in this book which have west-north-west at the top.

NEPHITE COORDINATE SYSTEM

We will begin with the bold statement that with a few exceptions, the *Nephites never used true north to represent their direction for north*. A preliminary documentation for that statement is given in Appendix A. Here we will lay out some of the key arguments for that position.

DIRECTIONS FROM THE STARS

Any mariner of the Atlantic or North Pacific would immediately say that north can be taken by a sighting on Polaris, the one star in the sky that is virtually immobile. However, that would not have been possible in the days of Lehi and Nephi. Because the earth has a wobble in its spin, the direction of the pole describes an imaginary circle in the sky of about 47 degrees over a period of 25,695 years. At the time of Lehi, the circle was about 24 degrees. There was no obvious replacement at that time.

DIRECTIONS FROM THE SUN

Directions from the sun's rising and setting would have been difficult, since the places of rising or setting vary by fifty degrees over the course of a year. However, the Nephites did pay some attention to directions. Basically, they appear to have used two and possibly three different systems. Only one was based on the sun: measurement of solstitial directions. Many ruins were located near mountains which facilitated sightings which had that direction.

DIRECTIONS FROM THE SEAS

Along the coast of the Gulf of Mexico, east of the Coatzacoalcos River, there are no visible mountains with which to obtain directions. In Appendix B some evidence is presented which indicates that the Gulf of Mexico was called the "East Sea" by the natives even down to the time of Conquest.

One reason for this may have been cultural, but it exactly fits within what appears to be a complete ninety-degree change in directions in that zone. That then explains the directions spoken of during the Book of Mormon wars in that area. Further, it agrees with positions of major sites spoken of such as La Venta and Bountiful. That latter site was recently discovered, taking advantage of their insight.

MULEKITE DIRECTIONAL SYSTEM

There is one other factor which could have reinforced the west-north-west orientation. As will be shown in Chapter 7, the Mulekites crossed the east sea, or Atlantic Ocean. Most of their early activity was probably centered about the Isthmus of Tehuantepec, where the sea was actually on the north. Thus viewing the Gulf of Mexico as the sea east, the Pacific must have been the sea west. That orientation would also have required a change in coordinates such that **north in their system was actually closer to west in our system.**

NATIVE MAPS

The famous Mayan archæologist, J. Eric Thompson, gives reinforcement to the idea that the Hebrew directional systems may have been transmitted to America. "I am inclined to think that south originally was called 'on the right hand,' and this it would be when one faces the east, which to the Maya is the most important direction. Indeed, east is at the top of the two native maps accompanying the land treaty of Mani." (Thompson 1960:249) Though by the relatively late time period of the treaty of Mani there may have been a shift to a solar orientation, the basic idea of "forward" being east was still in effect.

ARCHÆOLOGICAL VERIFICATION

Archæological data tend to corroborate the coordinate shift of the Nephites. If their "forward," based on a landing on the coast of Guatemala, was north-north-east, then we might expect to find a similar alignment of some of the Nephite archæological sites. The geographical model used here would suggest that we look to the valley of Guatemala for the first settlements of the Nephites, and the Grijalva basin for settlements subsequent to about 250 B.C.

At the Guatemalan site of Kaminaljuyú, the first construction of temple mounds was in the period from approximately 500 B.C. to 200 B.C. (the period known as Providencia or Late Formative). There were five groups of mounds, and in all cases they were aligned towards the north-north-east (Michels, 1979). That type of alignment was no longer used in later periods.

In the Central Depression of Chiapas there is even more evidence. Based on his survey of hundreds of sites, Lowe (1959:70) reported that the Preclassic ruins are consistently oriented in a north-north-easterly direction. That is exactly what we would expect if there were a coordinate shift such as the one we have postulated.

There are indications that in making the abridgment of Ether's Jaredite history, Moroni used his own geographical definitions and directions. Therefore, throughout this book we will attempt to consistently give directions in the Nephite coordinate system when speaking of Nephite or Jaredite events. In other words, if we say that Alma went north, the reader can translate that to west-northwest in modern terms. When not speaking of the Book of Mormon text, conventional directions will be used.

CHANGES IN THE LAND AT THE TIME OF THE CRUCIFIXION

One argument made against attempts to correlate Book of Mormon geography with the modern map is that land configurations changed drastically at the time of the crucifixion, thus, geographical references in the Book of Mormon should no longer be relevant. Is this correct? Are we wasting our time digging into details and looking for specific Book of Mormon cities?

To answer this question we must examine the authorship of the Book of Mormon. The record of the Nephites from about 600 B.C. to about 130 B.C.[2] was primarily a religious and ancestral record kept on the Small Plates of Nephi. It contains very little geographical information, except for the notation that the land of Nephi was at a higher elevation than was Zarahemla (Omni 13,

---

2. Studies indicate that Christ was born sometime between 10 B.C. and 1 B.C. Further, the Nephites may have used a 360-day lunar calendar during the first 600 years of their history. Therefore, all quoted dates as taken from the Book of Mormon are subject to some error. That error is neglected here because it is well within the statistical limits of error and of radiocarbon dating.

27). The Large Plates of Nephi were kept by the kings, who recorded both historical and religious events. These latter records were abridged by the prophet Mormon in the middle of the fourth century A.D. His abridgment, known as the "Plates of Mormon," was translated by Joseph Smith. The translation of the more complete history up to 130 B.C. was lost by a scribe, Martin Harris. It was never retranslated since the Small Plates of Nephi covered the same time span.

Mormon quotes from the plates he was abridging, but most of the record is in his own words. This is especially true for geographical descriptions. A good example is the section in Alma 22:27-34 where Mormon interrupts his narrative to give an overall geographical orientation to the lands of his people. At no place in the narrative is anything ever said which would indicate that the topography being described was no longer the same at the time of writing, centuries after the destruction at the time of Christ's death.

Since all the geography presented for the Nephites was given by Mormon himself, we don't have to worry too much about supposed great changes in the map. While much destruction may have taken place on the ground, I speculate that satellite pictures taken before and after that destruction (had it been possible) would have shown only minor changes in the courses of rivers and in the shape of the coastline.

VOLCANOES AND THE GREAT DESTRUCTION

An examination of the destruction and its causes is helpful in developing a topographic criterion for the Nephite lands—they must be in an area of volcanoes.

The Book of Mormon description of the destruction will be cited directly:

> . . .There arose a great storm, such an one as never had been known in all the land. And there was also a great and terrible tempest; and there was terrible thunder, insomuch that it did shake the whole earth as if it was about to divide asunder. And there were exceeding sharp lightnings, such as never had been known in all the land. (III Nephi 8:6-7)

The city of Moroni "sank into the sea", some cities were burned, and others were covered with earth. In addition:

> . . .there was a great and terrible destruction in the land southward. But behold, there was a more great and terrible destruction in the land northward, for behold, the whole face of the land was changed,

because of the tempest and the whirlwinds and the thunderings and the lightnings and the exceeding great quaking of the whole earth; And the highways were broken up, and the level roads were spoiled, and many smooth places became rough . . . And thus the face of the whole earth became deformed, because of the tempest, and the thunderings, and the lightnings and the quaking of the earth. And behold, the rocks were rent in twain; they were broken up upon the face of the whole earth, insomuch that they were found in broken fragments, and in seams and in cracks, upon all the face of the land
(3 Nephi 8:11-13, 17, 18)

Almost immediately after this the entire land was covered with a thick darkness, so bad that the survivors ". . . could feel the vapor of darkness." Many people were ". . . overpowered by the vapor of smoke and darkness." (3 Nephi 10:13) This effect was so pervasive that they could see no light for the space of three days, being completely enveloped throughout the land in "mists of darkness".

Historical research into the causes of catastrophes gives some strong indications of what happened to the Nephites and Lamanites at that time. There was obviously a devastating earthquake, and its aftershocks lasted for three days. Simultaneously, it appears that there was eruption of at least one and probably several volcanoes. They probably erupted with deafening explosions, spewing smoke, noxious gases, and volcanic ash into the air. Lava probably covered some cities built on their fertile slopes.

Eruptions of several volcanoes in recent times have had similar results. The volcano Tambora in Indonesia erupted in 1815, releasing six million times more energy than an atomic bomb (Press, 1977). "For three days it spread almost absolute darkness over an area extending nearly 300 miles from its crater" (Burtin, 1974). Similarly, when Mount Katmai, Alaska erupted in 1917, "dust fell for three days." About twenty miles from the mountain the deposit of volcanic ash was three to four feet thick.

The 1980 eruption of Mt. St. Helens, Washington, also spread darkness and destruction. Though reported to have released the equivalent power of only five hundred atomic bombs, the results were significant. An ash cloud and great mud flow were immediate consequences. Mudflows are produced by the mixing of water and hot volcanic ash. By contrast with the rather slow flow of lava, these boiling cauldrons of ash can flow at up to one hundred kilometers per hour. In 1877 an eruption in Ecuador created a mudflow that travelled 250 kilometers, killing about a thousand people.

The 1991 eruption of Mount Penatubo near U.S. bases in the Phillippines spread a cloak of ash-induced darkness that lasted for several days.

Hot gases can flow out after an explosive eruption and travel at great speed, destroying all life. These "glowing clouds," as they are called, are a mixture of gas, ash and dust. One such cloud killed about 38,000 people within minutes when Mount Pelee exploded on the island of Martinique.

The exceedingly sharp bolts of lightning mentioned in the Book of Mormon would be directly related to the eruptions. The tremendous amounts of heat and explosive energy released during a volcanic eruption create massive atmospheric convection. The result can be an almost continual display of lightning (Warrick, 1975). It would have been observed prior to the time that the volcanic ash cut off vision of the violent display of nature. One photograph has been published showing an enormous lightning bolt over Mount Mesuvius at the time of its 1947 eruption (Leet, 1948). The turbulence could also create the "whirlwinds" (3 Nephi 8:12).

Erupting volcanoes can emit very large quantities of carbon oxides and sulfur compounds. These can easily exceed the limits of human tolerance. Thus we can understand why many were overcome, and I suspect, died of asphyxiation. Sulfur dioxide and carbon dioxide tend to retard combustion, possibly explaining problems experienced in lighting fires. In 1948 there was considerable volcanic activity in Iceland. The composition of carbon dioxide rose so high in some areas that cars stalled from lack of oxygen. (Thorarinsson, 1979; 150)

The simultaneous eruptions and earthquakes can be understood by reference to the theory of plate tectonics. According to this theory, the earth's crust is divided into a number of rigid sections of rocks called plates, which slide over a layer of partly-melted rock. Interactions at the interface between plates creates a light magma, which rises. If it reaches the surface, a volcano is formed. There is a string of volcanoes along the western portion of North and South America, most of which are very close to a major plate boundary. The description given in the Book of Mormon suggests an abnormally-large shift in the plates at the time of the Crucifixion. That would have caused the earthquakes and simultaneously send magma to the surface in several places, unleashing terrible destruction.

Based on the preceding data, I propose that a combination of earthquakes and volcanic eruptions were the natural forces unleashed on the Nephites and Lamanites. (The resulting tidal wave which would have destroyed coastal cities was a consequence of the earthquakes.) Therefore, we conclude that the Nephite heartland was encompassed by volcanoes. Their entire cultural area was affected by the destructions (3 Nephi 8:17). Since a period of "three hours" in Nephite reckoning was required for the ash to reach at least one observer, areas over two hundred kilometers from each volcano could have been affected. Mormon notes that there was a disparity of opinion on how long it took before things got pitch black (3 Nephi 8:19). The amount of time would obviously vary, depending on one's distance from the nearest erupting volcano. Mormon did not understand the primary cause of the darkness, but certainly reported on it as well as he could from the documents in his possession.

In summary, we should expect to find volcanoes in the general vicinity of the Nephite heartland, which was centered about an isthmus. There is some possibility that remains of the ash layer might be found in the vicinity, at levels in the ruins which date to the time of Christ.

CLIMATE AND THE BATTLE AT CUMORAH

What the record does not mention with respect to climate is just as important as what it does say. This comes to the point of the next question. "Did the winters work a great hardship on the Nephites, as they later would upon the Mormon pioneers?" The journals of the Mormon trek west are filled with stories of hardship and death caused by the cold winters.

If the last battles of the Nephites or Jaredites were in upstate New York, the journeys to that area by hundreds of thousands of people in each case would have been migrations of enormous proportions. As will be shown, the Nephite journey had to be made in less than ten years from the time they left the narrow neck of land. The travellers would have had to cross innumerable rivers, plus deserts and mountains. The fact that cold or snow is not mentioned even once is strong evidence that no part of the Nephite history took place as far north as New York. By contrast, a temperate, tropical or sub-tropical climate is suggested. The Nephite problem was (tropical) fevers (Alma 46:40), not harshness of the weather.

DISTANCE OF MORMON'S CUMORAH FROM THE NARROW NECK

This book will show that Mormon's Cumorah was probably within a few days journey of the isthmus of Tehuantepec. In the New York theory, by contrast, it is a distance from Tehuantepec that is at least twice the distance travelled by the Mormon pioneers. This can be seen quite clearly on Map #1, p. 253. The difference is so great between these approaches that certainly we should be able to find some information in the text to help decide between them.

We will approach this problem by first examining the chronology and geography of events surrounding the last Nephite battles. The geography of the Jaredite battles which culminated at the same spot will also be considered. Finally, the Limhi expedition which related the two cultures geographically will be discussed. For further analysis of these events the reader is referred to Washburn (1974), Chapter 32.

CHRONOLOGY OF THE LAST NEPHITE BATTLES

The first five chapters of Mormon give an account of the series of final battles, which I will now summarize. Nephites were attacked in the land southward in A.D. 322 (Mormon 1:8-12). Five years later, Mormon was made general of the Nephite armies. He presided over a great retreat into the land northward (Mormon 2:3). After motivating his army, Mormon led them to victories in which the Nephites regained control of all the land north of the isthmus. This was accomplished in A.D. 350 (Mormon 2:29), following which there were ten years of semi-peace.

The Lamanites carried out a major attack in the year A.D. 360 (Mormon 3:7) Seven years of bitter fighting went on around the cities by the narrow neck of land, especially the city of Desolation. Mormon resigned as the Nephite general during this war. There was an eight-year lull in the fighting, but in A.D. 375, the Lamanites attacked again at the narrow neck (Mormon 4:19). There was a fierce battle for the city of Desolation, which the Nephites lost. After one more city was taken, Mormon concluded that his cache of records in a hill called Shim was endangered. Therefore, he retrieved them, and whether he kept them with him, or moved them quickly to the hill he called Cumorah, we are not told (Mormon 4:23).

Mormon resumed command of the Nephite forces at this point in time. Because of the strength of the Nephites in the cities beyond the narrow neck, the Lamanites were repulsed. Certain areas, especially small villages and towns, were abandoned and the people gathered to make their defense in the larger cities (4:22, 5:4). It was possibly during this time that the atrocities mentioned in Moroni 9 were committed. Nothing is said here about directions. In fact, there is not one single directional statement given, from the time of the battles at the city of Desolation to the battle at Cumorah. There is nothing to suggest that they were not still within a few hundred kilometers of the Isthmus. This consolidation phase in which the Nephites gathered at their strong cities in the land northward consumed five years.

In A.D. 380, there was another onslaught by Lamanites which put the Nephites to flight. Mormon's description suggests that he had lost control of his people (Mormon 5:6-7). He wrote to the Lamanite king and won a truce so that he could gather his people for a final battle in the "land of Cumorah." This gave him time to regain control of the situation. "And it came to pass that we did march forth to the land of Cumorah, and we did pitch our tents around about the hill Cumorah . . . . And when three hundred and eighty and four years had passed away, we had gathered in all the remainder of our people unto the land of Cumorah." (Mormon 6:4-5)

The Nephites thus had four or five years in which they gathered at Cumorah. Only ten years had passed since they lost control of key cities at the narrow neck of land. If those battles were on the Pacific side of the isthmus, and the cities used as havens were on the route from the modern city of Tehuantepec through Oaxaca and possibly on up to Puebla, then there would have been a substantial distance to travel in order to congregate at Cumorah, which will later be shown to be near the "eastern" seashore. Nevertheless, a "march" is very different than a migration, with its attendant logistics and food-supply problems. Also, the implication made by Mormon is that he was familiar with the land of Cumorah already.

The reader is advised to reread the first six chapters of Mormon to verify that what has been said here is consistent with the text. Particularly important is the short length of time between the battles at the narrow neck and the last stand at Mormon's Cumorah. Directions and distances can only be inferred, since nothing is said concerning them.

THE NEW YORK THEORY

In attempts to defend the New York theory, some unwarranted liberties have been taken, to the point of actually contradicting what has been said. For example,

> After a series of protracted retreats, ever northward, Mormon was in the vicinity of the hill Shim, where he recovered the records Ammaron had buried there, and this hill was near the place where the Nephites were destroyed. Mormon's forces were traveling in reverse practically all the time from the 326th year until the 380th. Land after land they traversed . . . As soon as the Lamanites could muster reinforcements they were on the march again, following the fresh trails of the Nephites—ever northward. The mad pursuit did not end until the Lamanites overpowered the foe in the land of many waters, far to the north. (McGavin, 1949, p. 39)

This statement grossly exaggerates the time used for gathering to Cumorah and suggests directions which can only be inferred because they are not made in the text. Furthermore, nothing is said in the text regarding changes in climate, great migrations, or moving to strange lands.

THE ESCAPE ROUTE

Following the last battle Mormon mentioned " . . . a few who had escaped into the south countries" (Mormon 6:15). This suggests that there was an escape route, possibly going as far as the land southward. Nearness to the narrow neck is implied. Other evidence to support that view will be presented later in this chapter.

NEPHITE SPECIFICATIONS FOR THE LAND OF CUMORAH

Mormon listed a few significant factors concerning the land of Cumorah, which must be met by any candidate area.

> And it came to pass that we did march forth to the land of Cumorah, and we did pitch our tents around about the hill Cumorah, and it was in a land of many waters, rivers, and fountains; and here we had hope to gain advantage over the Lamanites.   (Mormon 6:4)

The terminology "many waters" could either be generic, or it could be used to refer to the sea, as in 1 Nephi 17:5. The need for nearby rivers is evident, but what about "fountains"? Water springing from under the earth was viewed with special significance by ancient peoples, particularly in Mesoamerica. Since fountains are less prevalent than rivers, this is an important criterion.

What did all that water have to do with gaining advantage over the Lamanites? This ties to a related question asked in Chapter 1. Is there any reason to believe that the Nephites would leave their cultural area and go into strange territory to stage their last battle?

I propose that Mormon chose an area for the last battle with which he was thoroughly familiar, and chose it on the basis of potential for food production. In his statements concerning the last battles, Mormon emphasizes the importance of numbers of people in winning the battles (Mormon 4:17, 5:6). The best way to attract people to his side was to have plenty of food. Choice of a particularly productive area in which to concentrate his people would help him to gather in the largest possible army. This approach stands in contrast to the idea of taking his people on a great march into unfamiliar territory where provision of food would be the single greatest problem. In fact, such a trek would have been suicide.

Therefore, we have as criterion that there was an abundance of water, and can deduce that it helped provide a military advantage. I further suggest that this advantage was related to food production.

NATURE OF THE HILL CUMORAH

The hill Cumorah must have been a significant landmark, because the surrounding area was named after it. Further, Moroni was able to identify it as the same hill where the Jaredites had previously been destroyed (Ether 15:11). The hill may have had a cave which served to hide Mormon's extensive collection of records.

The hill must have been large enough to sustain a battle of major proportions. It is quite clear that the battle took place on that hill and the plain leading up to it, for the following day Mormon was able to survey the entire scene of carnage from the top of the hill. Two hundred and thirty thousand Nephite men, plus their women and children, were destroyed. It would seem that a hill of 500-1000 meters in altitude would be required. A major mountain would be out of the question, because it would not have been possible on such a mountain to conclude the battle in a single day. Furthermore, the elderly and wounded Mormon had to be able to climb to the top of the hill during the night, from wherever he fell in battle.

Another point which relates to size and shape is the fact that the Nephites camped "round about the hill." The hill must therefore have been free-standing, rather than just another peak abutting a chain of hills or mountains.

LOCATION OF RAMAH/CUMORAH FROM THE JAREDITE POINT OF VIEW

THE FLIGHT OF KING OMER

The early settlements of the Jaredites were in a dry highland area called Moron. During an early part of Jaredite history King Omer was involved in civil strife, and his life was placed in jeopardy. We are told that

> The Lord warned Omer in a dream that he should depart out of the land; wherefore Omer departed out of the land with his family, and traveled many days, and came over and passed by the hill of Shim, and came over by the place where the Nephites were destroyed, and from thence eastward, and came to a place which was called Ablom, by the seashore, and there he pitched his tent . . . "   (Ether 9:3)

Three conclusions can be derived from this account:

1.Cumorah was near the eastern seacoast.

2. The hill was a prominent landmark or it would not have been recognized by Moroni as the same spot as Cumorah when he made his abridgment of Ether's account.

3. The hill Shim, once also a record repository, was passed on the way to Cumorah.

FLIGHT OF THE FLOCKS

Some years after the Omer episode, the kingdom was once again in Moron rather than on the coast. Following a period of great wickedness, a drought came upon that land. Poisonous serpents abounded, much as they did under similar circumstances during the Israelite exodus from Egypt (Numbers 21:6-8). The "flocks" were so frightened that they " . . . began to flee before the poisonous serpents, towards the land southward, which was called by the Nephites, Zarahemla. And it came to pass that there were many of them which did perish by the way; nevertheless, *there were some which fled into the land southward*." (Ether 9:31-32) The land of Moron therefore had to be close to the narrow neck of land. Further, there could not have been large rivers, deserts, or impassable mountain ranges for the flocks to cross. A downhill flight through the valleys of Oaxaca to the area of Tehuantepec City seems within the realm of possibility.

After the snake population was brought under control, the land southward was used for hunting. (Ether 10:19-20) If enormous distances had been involved, this would not have made sense because the animals would have spoiled during transport back to the population center.

THE CITY OF LIB

The Book of Mormon describes development of a great new civilization during the time of Lib. It centered around the city of Lib. "And they built a great city by the narrow neck of land, by the place where the sea divides the land." I gather from this statement that the city was located somewhere in the isthmus, and probably near the river Coatzacoalcos. The river was viewed as an extension of the sea and also served as a geographical boundary between the two sides of the isthmus.

The city of Lib became a cultural and technological capitol for the Jaredites (Ether 10:22-28). There is nothing said in the subsequent Jaredite history which indicates radical geographical movement away from this general area. There are significant external contacts developed by trade, but all events seem to center around the heartland. This includes the final Jaredite battles.

We are now in a position to answer the question, "Does the Book of Mormon suggest that the Jaredites inhabited a large portion of the North American continent?" There is simply no textual evidence that they did, a fact which can be verified by careful probing of the Book of Ether.

FINAL WAR OF THE JAREDITES

Jaredite civilization was destroyed in a great and bitter civil war. Coriantumr fought Shared, Lib, and Shiz, respectively, in a dispute over who should rule the kingdom. It was a struggle for a life of luxury and power, with the losers becoming the slaves. The battles with Shared show that the old highland capitol of Moron was still important. (Ether 14:6, 11) Lib took the kingdom from Shared, and in the subsequent series of battles we find mentioned a coastal plain:

> . . . the army of Coriantumr did press forward upon Lib, that he fled to the borders of the seashore . . . Lib gave battle unto him upon the seashore. And it came to pass that Lib did smite the army of Coriantumr, hat they fled again to the wilderness of Akish. And it came to pass that Lib did pursue him until he came to the plains of Agosh.   (Ether 14:12-15)

It is clear from a subsequent verse that the seacoast spoken of was on the east (in Nephite coordinates—north-north-east in modern coordinates). "And it came to pass that Shiz (the brother of Lib) did pursue Coriantumr eastward, even to the borders of the seashore, and there he gave battle unto Shiz for the space of three days. (Ether 14:26)

Near the coast there was, besides a plain, some mountains or hills. We read of the valley of Corihor, the valley of Shurr, and the hill Comnor. (Ether 14:28) On the hill Comnor, Coriantumr was almost killed. This led him to consider relinquishing the kingdom. In fact, there was not much of a kingdom left by that time, with the cities destroyed and two million people killed. A period of time elapsed during which Coriantumr recovered from his wounds. No movements are mentioned, but they may have been possible. When the war resumed, Coriantumr was pursued to the "waters of Ripliancum, which by interpretation is large, or to exceed all."

The fact that Ripliancum was not called a sea, lake, or river, suggests that the body of water was both large and ill-defined. It is an important landmark, because it was apparently about a day's journey from the hill Ramah/Cumorah. Note in the following quotation the pitching of tents, which appear to delineate the days.

> Wherefore, when they came to these waters they pitched their tents; and Shiz also pitched his tents near unto them; and therefore on the morrow they did come to battle. And it came to pass that they fought an exceedingly sore battle in which Coriantumr was wounded again, and he fainted with the loss of blood. And it came to pass that the armies of Coriantumr did press upon the armies of Shiz that they beat them, that they caused them to flee before them; and they did flee southward, and did pitch their tents in a place which was called Ogath. And it came to pass that the army of Coriantumr did pitch their tents by the hill Ramah; and it was that same hill where my father Mormon did hide up the records unto the Lord, which were sacred.   (Ether 15:8-11)

After gathering into respective camps for four years, the two sides once again clashed, with destruction of every warrior except Coriantumr. A prophet named Ether observed these events, apparently from close range, and included them on a record engraven on twenty-four gold plates. Thus ended the civilization of the Jaredites and their contemporaries.

Did this battle signal the end of all human life on the continent until arrival of the Nephites? That seems most unlikely. The heart of the civilization was destroyed, but what of all the outposts and trading networks? What do we make of the use of the Jaredite word "Nehor" (Ether 7:9) among the Nephites? Also, the secret combinations of the Jaredites appear to have been transmitted to the Nephites (3 Nephi 3:9), suggesting that part of the Jaredite culture survived the last battle.

THE LIMHI EXPEDITION

A most important evidence that Ramah/Cumorah is not far north of the narrow neck of land is found in the descriptions of an expedition of 43 men sent by King Limhi.

To understand that expedition, it is necessary to briefly review some Nephite history. The Nephites originally established their homeland in the land of Nephi, a highland area in the southern extension of the cultural area mentioned in the Book of Mormon. In about 250-230 B.C., their king led them down to the land of Zarahemla to escape possible extermination by the Lamanites. One generation later a group of people left Zarahemla to go back and resettle the land of Nephi. The account of these people is contained in Mosiah, chapters 9 to 24.

The expedition, led by Zeniff, wandered many days before finding the land of Nephi. After arriving they prospered somewhat, but two generations later found themselves in bondage to the Lamanites. They were hopeful that their relatives back in Zarahemla might be able to help them to escape, but had maintained no correspondence with them and did not know the way. Therefore, an expedition was sent out by King Limhi to find it. The expeditionary force never did find Zarahemla.

> . . . they were lost in the wilderness. Nevertheless, they did find a land which had been peopled; yea, a land which was covered with dry bones; yea, a land which had been peopled and destroyed; and they, having supposed it to be the land of Zarahemla, returned to the land of Nephi . . . And they brought a record with them, even a record of the people whose bones they had found; and it was engraven on the plates of ore.   (Mosiah 21:25-27)

A second account of the same expedition gives more detail, quoting King Limhi:

> Being grieved for the afflictions of my people I caused that forty and three of my people should take a journey into the wilderness, that thereby they might find the land of Zarahemla, that we might appeal unto our brethren to deliver us out of bondage. And they were lost in the wilderness for the space of many days, yet they were diligent, and found not the land of Zarahemla but returned to this land, having traveled in a land among many waters, having discovered a land which was covered with bones of men, and of beasts, and was also covered with ruins of buildings of every kind, having discovered a land which had been peopled with a people who were as numerous as the hosts of Israel. And for a testimony that the things that they had said are true they have brought twenty-four plates which are filled with engravings, and they are of pure gold. And behold, also, they have brought breastplates, which are large, and they are of brass and of copper, and are perfectly sound. And again, they have brought swords, the hilts thereof have perished, and the blades thereof were cankered with rust;   (Mosiah 8:7-11)

A significant difference between these two accounts is that the first states their conclusion that Zarahemla had been destroyed. The second recognizes that they failed to find Zarahemla, since this is part of a statement made to Ammon who had just told the king that he was from Zarahemla.

DISTANCE TRAVELED BY THE EXPEDITION

These accounts have considerable significance when considered in the context of the geography of the area. Remember that for people knowing the way, it was an easy twenty-day journey from the land of Nephi to Zarahemla. It is hard to believe that Limhi's men would have traveled more than a month or two before turning back.

If the expedition personnel reached Ramah/Cumorah, they must have been unaware that they passed through the isthmus, and it could not have been too far beyond the isthmus. After all, they undoubtedly had some vague ideas concerning a land southward and land northward, and Zarahemla was in the heart of the land southward. Furthermore, their objective was not to explore but to find help. It strains credulity to believe that the group pushed so far up into the continent that they crossed dozens of rivers, left their own cultural area, moved into regions with completely different climates, traversed thousands of kilometers, and still returned to their homes thinking they had arrived at the land southward city of Zarahemla. Yet, that would be required of any theory which placed the last Jaredite battles in upstate New York. I believe a more reasonable conclusion is that those last Jaredite battles centered around the narrow neck of land.

POSSIBLE ROUTE TAKEN

While considering the Limhi expedition, it is instructive to consider the course that it might have taken if the isthmus of Tehuantepec was the narrow neck of land.

How would the expedition leader chart the course back to Zarahemla? He was probably aware of the following facts:

1. Zarahemla was at a lower elevation than Nephi.
2. Zarahemla was on the west bank of a major river called Sidon.
3. Sidon flowed into the east sea (this gleaned from the fact that the Mulekites apparently followed it up from the coast and they landed on the eastern side).

The leader might also have been aware of the possibility that headwaters for the Sidon began somewhere within the land of Nephi.

The effort must have seemed straightforward. They had to go in the general direction of Zarahemla, follow the tributaries until they arrived at the river Sidon, and follow it downstream to Zarahemla. What went wrong?

Examination of Map #5, p. 258, shows my hypothesis for the route actually followed by the expedition. In essence, they followed the wrong river system and missed Zarahemla entirely. This could have happened very easily because tributaries to the Grijalva and the Usumacinta rivers arise within a few miles of each other in the Guatemalan highlands. They could have thus made the same mistake made in 1840 by John Lloyd Stephens.

I believe he was traveling the same route sought after by the Limhi expedition. He came to a place above the present city of Huehuetenango. At that point he made a fundamental error which could have been the same mistake made by the explorers of two millennia before. He said:

> At half past two we reached the top of the Sierra Madre, the dividing line of the waters, being twelve miles from Gueguetenango [sic] and in our devious course making the second time that we had crossed the sierra. The ridge of the mountain was a long table about half a mile wide, with rugged sides rising on the right to a terrific peak. Riding about half an hour on this table, by the side of a stream of clear and cold water, which passed on, carrying its tribute to the Pacific Ocean, we reached a miserable rancho.
>
> (Stephens: 1969:233, V. II)

The stream which Stephens thought to be flowing to the Pacific was in fact feeding the Grijalva River which flows to the Gulf of Mexico. If the Limhi expedition made the same mistake as Stephens, they would have crossed the divide and followed the tributaries leading to the Usumacinta. This mistake would have been even more likely to occur if during isolation of their people they had reverted to a directional system closer to that which is now accepted, by contrast with the standard Nephite directional system discussed previously in this chapter.

Thus, one might speculate that they followed the Usumacinta as far as the coast, and then traveled towards the isthmus and thence the Tuxtlas, looking for signs of human habitation.

The manner in which the two major river systems south of Tehuantepec have very close headwaters gives the Limhi story more vivid meaning and helps us to understand a possible explanation of how they could have failed.

OBSIDIAN TRAILS

Another factor which must be considered here is the possibility that Limhi's expedition followed an existing trail. Going back into Early Preclassic times, there were trails from different parts of Mesoamerica which converged on the Guatemalan highlands. The reason was the need for obsidian, used for blades. This black volcanic glass is found in large nodules at a number of volcanoes, shown on Map #9, pp. 262-263. The exact source of obsidian found at faraway sites can be determined using trace element analysis, and the date of formation of the blades can be determined as well. At the time of the Limhi expedition, the obsidian used on the Gulf Coast and in Chiapas, the Isthmus of Tehuantepec, and the Guatemalan lowlands (Usumacinta basin) came almost exclusively from the volcano San Martin Jilotepeque. (Sidrys, 1976, Nelson, n.d.)

Thus, it is possible that after arriving at the vicinity of that volcano on their way to Zarahemla, the explorers came upon the obsidian trail which led down to the Usumacinta valley. They may have encountered people along the way, but could not communicate because of language differences.

There are thus two possible explanations for the manner in which the Limhi expedition failed to find Zarahemla. They may both have been factors in the choice which led the men in the wrong direction.

These are just a few of the many fascinating details which are encountered once one begins to examine Book of Mormon incidents within the context of a specific geography. Further insights to that geography will be examined later.

SUMMARY

1. There is consistency among the scores of topographical references in the Book of Mormon.

2. The area referred to in the Book of Mormon is quite limited; a few hundred kilometers in extension.

3. I agree with Joseph Smith that Tehuantepec was the narrow neck of land.

4. The Nephites may have used three different coordinate systems. None was based on modern coordinates. Significant evidence exists for primary use of solstitial directions. There was occasional complete rotation of north by ninety degrees counterclockwise near the Gulf of Mexico, which was always called the "East Sea."

5. Changes in the land at the time of the Crucifixion do not impact on the Book of Mormon geography because we owe all geographical statements in the New World to Mormon and Moroni, who wrote after those destructions occurred.

6. The great destructions may have been due to a shift in the tectonic plates, with resulting earthquakes and volcanic eruptions. The darkness which persisted for three days was probably due to fallout of volcanic ash.

7. Only ten years elapsed from the time of Nephite battles at the narrow neck to the time of their total destruction, and their gathering lasted only four to five years.

8. Part of the Jaredites or their neighbors escaped death at the last Jaredite battle.

9. The story of the Limhi expedition is strong evidence that Ramah-Cumorah must be near the narrow neck of land. The manner in which the expedition missed finding Zarahemla can be explained within the geographical and cultural setting of highland Guatemala.

TOPOGRAPHIC AND GEOGRAPHIC CRITERIA FOR MORMON'S CUMORAH

Based on direct statements from the text of the Book of Mormon, and in a few cases, strong inferences drawn from statements in the text, a list of topographic and geographic criteria for Mormon's Cumorah has been developed. These criteria are as follows:

1. near eastern seacoast
2. near narrow neck of land
3. on a coastal plain, and possibly near other mountains and valleys
4. one day's journey south (east-south-east in modern coordinates) of a large body of water
5. in an area of many rivers and waters
6. presence of fountains
7. the abundance of water should provide a military advantage
8. an escape route to the land southward
9. hill must be large enough to provide a view of hundreds of thousands of bodies
10. hill must be a significant landmark
11. hill should be free standing so people can camp around it
12. temperate climate with no cold or snow
13. in a volcanic zone susceptible to earthquakes

3

WHAT PHYSICAL REMAINS ARE REQUIRED TO IDENTIFY THE JAREDITE AND NEPHITE BATTLEGROUND?

> *. . . They did enable the people in the land northward that they might build many cities, both of wood and of cement.*
>
> *Helaman 3:11*

Within the Book of Mormon there are numerous statements concerning the physical culture of the Nephites and Jaredites. Is it reasonable to expect that we could eventually make correlations between an ancient text, such as the Book of Mormon, and discoveries made by archæologists? In this chapter I will show that such correlations are possible, explain some of the tools used by the archæologist which give us the necessary data to correlate, and then from the Book of Mormon itself I will develop lists of criteria for physical remains of the Jaredite and Nephite cultures. The lists will include specific criteria needed to identify the last battleground of the Jaredites and Nephites: Ramah/Cumorah or Mormon's Cumorah. These criteria will be added to those developed in Chapter 2 in subsequently testing the New York theory and the specific Mesoamerican theory for Mormon's Cumorah which is presented in this book.

In Chapter 1, I presented the challenge by Joseph Smith to compare Book of Mormon cities with the ruins being discovered in Mesoamerica. That he expected a positive result from that comparison is perhaps indicated by this statement: "It will be as it ever has been, the world will prove Joseph Smith a true prophet by circumstantial evidence, in experiments, as they did Moses and Elijah." (*Times and Seasons*, Vol. 3, No. 22, p. 922) The comparison Joseph Smith suggested must in retrospect be viewed as either inspiration or a stroke of genius. Until that time there had been practically no attempts to correlate ancient texts with archæological excavations. In fact, that science was just being born.

BEGINNINGS OF TEXT-CENTERED ARCHÆOLOGY

Biblical archæology is based on a geography of the Bible. It was not quite as obvious as might be thought, even though there are some points such as Jerusalem which were fixed. The identity of scores of other bible cities had been lost, and the "tells" or mounds indicating presence of ruins had for the most part lost their identity. The foundations of biblical geography were laid by Edward Robinson and Eli Smith, who made careful surveys and investigations in Syria and Palestine. The work was reported in 1841 and 1856. Without such work, there never would have developed a reputable field of scientific inquiry known as "biblical archæology."

The most spectacular of early text-centered geographical reconstructions of ancient history is due to Heinrich Schliemann, who not only located a ruin but proceeded to excavate it, layer by layer. His objective—to find the ancient city of Troy!

One of the greatest pieces of ancient literature was the *Iliad*, written by Homer in roughly 750 B.C. During the nineteenth century, skeptical literary critics believed that the Iliad's Trojan war was ". . . in the eyes of modern enquiry essentially a legend and nothing more." (Silverberg, 1962) However, Schliemann believed that Homer's story of the abduction of the Grecian beauty Helen by the young Paris of Troy, and the subsequent war between Greek cities and Troy, was a story with historical substance. He believed that if Troy really existed, remains could be found, and Homer would be vindicated as an historian.

Schliemann first used Homer's text to reconstruct the geography of the *Iliad*. In 1870 he began his search and chose to dig on a large mound which was situated in a spot consistent with his geography. He uncovered through years of work a number of superimposed cities, one of which had been destroyed by fire.

Schliemann discovered a number of treasures which he found to be like some mentioned by Homer. Though it has taken other expeditions using more sophisticated techniques to sort out the overlapping strata in the long and complex history of those ruins, it is now generally accepted that Schliemann found the site of Troy. Using the same techniques, he proceeded to discover related sites and treasures in Greece. While he did not prove that any of the characters in the poem were real, the expeditions which he initiated have certainly shown that there was such a place as Troy. It flourished and died in a cultural setting like that described by Homer.

THE NATURE OF ARCHÆOLOGY, AND BOOK OF MORMON STUDIES

It was during the lifetime of Schliemann that archæology developed as a science. Archæology is founded on the key concepts of *place, time,* and *culture.* Attempts to verify a text through archæology, without first reconstructing the geography of the text, are of little if any value. As an example, let us suppose that the entire Book of Mormon history took place in the small area now known as the country of Uruguay. Showing pictures of ruins from Peru and Central America as evidence for the Book of Mormon would then be very misleading. The importance of location to archæology cannot be denied. Therefore, I contend that no one should be writing about Book of Mormon archæology who is not willing to commit, at least tentatively, to a specific geography of the Book of Mormon that has been examined and criticized by qualified scholars. There can only be one correct geography, so the scholars must ultimately arrive at a concensus which can be tested. Differences of opinion are bound to exist, but in many cases they can be resolved by research.

The chronology of events in the Book of Mormon must ultimately be reconciled with the dating of archæological remains. Only the preclassic and early classic periods in Mesoamerica date to Book of Mormon times. Unfortunately, some authors have ignored both the geographical and time constraints imposed by the Book of Mormon, with the result that much of their material is irrelevant.

To understand what can be expected from studies into "Book of Mormon archæology" we will examine briefly the parallel but much earlier and now mature development of "biblical archæology." Atlases are published which show virtually every important journey made in the Bible. Places can be recognized and many biblical events can be correlated with events mentioned by other peoples such as the Assyrians. A number of ruins and documents have been found which confirm the existence of Israelite kings and the historical validity of their battles. Much insight has been gained into otherwise obscure biblical passages through all the cultural background data that has been developed. On the other hand, there are some discoveries which appear inconsistent with Bible history. A good summary of the role of archæology in Bible studies is as follows:

> Archæology neither proves nor disproves the Bible in conclusive terms, but it has other functions, of considerable importance. It recovers in some degree the material world presupposed by the Bible. To know, say, the material of which a house was built, or what a 'high place' looked like, much enhances our understanding of the text. Secondly it fills out the historical record. . . . Thirdly, it reveals the life and thought of the neighbors of ancient Israel—which is of interest in itself, and which illuminates the world of ideas within which the thought of ancient Israel developed . . .   (Bermant, 1979; 68)

A similar impact of archæology can be expected for the Book of Mormon. We can expect that passages which today we struggle to understand, may take on vivid meaning when cast in the light of an ancient cultural setting.

We should not expect to see an immediate and obvious correspondence between archæological data and the Book of Mormon. Our perceptions of what that Nephite record says, and what Mormon intended it to say, can be quite different. In general, I suspect that we have interpreted Mormon's record as being more comprehensive than it really was. He said it was just a "small abridgment" of the plates of Nephi. (Mormon 5:9; Helaman 3:13-14; 3 Nephi 5:8-9) Some cities are mentioned only in passing, and other cities are never identified. Therefore, some interaction between archæology and studies of the text are necessary to define the scope of the Book of Mormon culture and identify it within its ancient framework.

DATING METHODS

Development of methods for dating ancient settlements and cities is extremely important to accurate correlation of early American sites with Book of Mormon cities. Both relative and absolute dating methods have been developed.

RELATIVE DATING

Relative dating is based on stratigraphy. During excavation the archaeologist doesn't dig wantonly looking for pots or the most exciting architectural features. Rather, the strata from each successive occupation of a site is carefully studied for architectural and cultural features. The most commonly retrieved item is broken pottery. It lasts indefinitely and serves as an excellent time marker because fabrication techniques and styles changed with both time and location. Pottery can thus be used to detect ancient trade, date destructions of cities, and trace the rise and fall of cultures. Computers are now used to help relate the masses of data which accumulate from all the different ruins studied, and thus find interrelationships. (Professor Bruce Warren of Brigham Young University is the pioneer of this technique.)

Where there are dislocations between cultures and a progression of style is not evident, arguments can arise with respect to the antiquity of the various cultures. In the early 1940's the dean of the Mayan scholars made a very convincing case that the Olmecs came *after* the Maya. But the development of an absolute dating technique eventually showed that the Olmecs flourished two thousand to a thousand years *before* the Maya.

ABSOLUTE DATING

Radiocarbon dating was introduced by W.F. Libby in 1949, providing the most useful method yet discovered for establishing age of objects which cannot be dated by ancient records. (Libby, 1949, 1973) Though a number of authors have tried to discredit absolute dating techniques such as the radiocarbon method in order to justify their own views of world history, significant progress has been made in substantiation of the validity thereof. The reader is referred to articles by various authors in "Science and Religion: Toward a More Useful Dialogue" (Hess, 1979), for a discussion of this progress.

The principle of radiocarbon dating is very simple. Radioactive elements are unstable, and they decay into stable elements at a fixed rate. They have a "half-life" which means that if the half-life is a thousand years, half of the radioactivity will disappear in the first thousand years. After two thousand years, only one quarter of the original radioactivity will remain. Every living thing contains carbon, and an extremely small percentage of that carbon is radioactive. It is called carbon 14; normal carbon is carbon 12. The rate of decay of radioactive carbon 14 was first reported as 5,568 years, though the currently accepted value is 5,730 years. Published dates, which by convention still use the former figure, must be increased in age by 3% to account for this discrepancy.

Radioactive carbon is continually produced in the upper atmosphere by bombardment with cosmic rays. Within three years there is virtually complete mixing of that carbon, in the form of carbon dioxide, within the earth's atmosphere. When a tree creates its annual ring, it is doing so via a photosynthetic process which abstracts carbon dioxide from the air. Once the ring is formed, the radioactive carbon within it begins to decay. Even if the tree is burned, the charcoal which remains can be dated, by measurement of the percentage of radioactive carbon remaining.

This technique rested until a few years ago on the assumption that the amount of carbon 14 in the atmosphere had always been the same and that there was complete uniformity in the atmosphere. The mixing assumption has been proven, but the assumption of constancy of carbon 14 is now known to be only qualitatively correct. The earth's bombardment with cosmic rays varies inversely with the strength of the earth's magnetic field, which is known to have changed significantly during the last six thousand years. Therefore, some means was needed to correct for that effect.

Extremely old bristlecone pine trees have been discovered in the American Southwest. Three different laboratories have carefully dated hundreds of ring sections and have developed calibration factors. There is in fact a systematic deviation with time. The impact of applying these correction factors is to move events dated to the middle of the second millennium B.C. about two hundred years further back in time. (Ralph, 1974)

The most comprehensive tabulation of radiocarbon dates for Mesoamerica has been made by Sorenson. (1977) He has corrected all dates to the correct half-life of carbon 14, 5,730 years, and applied the tree ring correction. I have attempted to do likewise with reported dates not taken from his tabulation. Such dates will be referred to as "MASCA" corrected. Typical radiocarbon dates are accurate to within about 5%, though there is promise of reducing that to 1 % (exclusive of the dendro correction) by using a nuclear accelerator method. (Bennett, 1979)

Obsidian blade surfaces hydrate at rates which vary according to temperature and composition. (Friedman, 1978) Measurement of the depth of the hydrated layer gives an indication of the time elapsed since the blade was first flaked off the master core of obsidian. Careful calibration of the rate of hydration in the valley of Guatemala enabled excavators at Kaminaljuyú to date thousands of blades. They are found in abundance in the archæological strata. (Michels, 1973)

Other sources of absolute dates are monuments with inscribed dates. The accuracy of the dates from these sources hinges upon accuracy of the correlation developed to convert them to our modern dating system. I have followed the generally accepted Goodwin Martinez-Thompson (GMT) correlation.

An Archæological Test for Ramah/Cumorah

Archæology, with its various disciplines, can be used to establish the presence or absence of a culture, particularly if it was an advanced culture that was acquainted with pottery making and other crafts. In general terms, then, we can conceive of testing geographical theories of the Book of Mormon in an absolute manner.

Of particular consequence to the question of locating Ramah/Cumorah is this question: "Were the last battles of the Nephites and Jaredites located within their normal sphere of influence, or were they carried out far removed from their cultural centers?" If the latter possibility were correct, then an archæological test for Cumorah would be more difficult.

In the previous chapter we saw that the text gives no evidence of long marches out of the cultural area of the Nephites. In fact, it mentions no long marches and doesn't even indicate a northward direction for the gathering to the land of Cumorah. Those who survived were still surrounded and were hunted and killed. (Mormon 8:2-3) In A.D. 400, Moroni describes wars and bloodshed in the area surrounding him, but doesn't say where he went in the 21 years before the final date he puts in the record. During that period he could have traveled over much of the continent.

We gain more insight into the nearness of the battleground to settled areas by reading the story of the last Jaredite battles from the book of Ether. A very key factor in understanding these Jaredite battles is the presence of an established populace in the areas where these battles occurred. They had not gone on a great trek to some unknown area to fight their wars. In describing Coriantumr's flight to the plains of Agosh, Ether said:

> And Coriantumr had taken all the people with him as he fled before Lib in that quarter of the land whither he fled. And when he had come to the plains of Agosh he gave battle unto Lib, and he smote upon him until he died; nevertheless, the brother of Lib did come against Coriantumr in the stead thereof, and the battle became exceeding sore, in the which Coriantumr fled again before the army of the brother of Lib. Now the name of the brother of Lib was called Shiz. And it came to pass that Shiz pursued after Coriantumr, and he did overthrow many cities, and he did slay both women and children, and he did burn the cities . . . And it came to pass that the people began to flock together in armies, throughout all the face of the land.   (Ether 14:15-19)

These verses are of considerable significance as they establish that the area of the last Jaredite battleground was right in the midst of the Jaredite settlements and cities. We read further that

CULTURAL CHARACTERISTICS OF THE JAREDITES   **61**

adjacent to the hill Ramah (Cumorah) was a place called "Ogath." (Ether 15:10-11) It was most likely a Jaredite settlement. From these data we can establish as a requirement that Ramah /Cumorah must be near ruined cities dating to 550-600 B.C. (This dating will be discussed later.) If it was an area settled by the Jaredites, who lived close to the narrow neck of land, then it is most reasonable to assume that the area of Ramah/Cumorah was settled by the Nephites prior to their last battle in 385 A.D. The evidence thus indicates the probability of finding Ramah/ Cumorah within the cultural spheres of both the Jaredites and Nephites. Artifacts and ruins should be found from two different time periods, a millennium apart. In addition, there should be supporting cities from the area surrounding the hill.

Specific artifacts which should be found at the hill itself include axes, arrowheads, and other weapons of war. Some fortifications from the Nephite period might be found on the hill, but the Jaredite battle appears to have been fought on the plain in front of the hill. Weaponry is a necessary but insufficient criterion. We must expand the criteria by examining both the Jaredite and Nephite cultures. (Some of the cultural criteria involve the broader discipline of anthropology, but the reader need not be concerned here with academic distinctions.) In painting this cultural picture, a large number of references will be made to the Book of Mormon. This is done so that we may remain firmly rooted in what was said by Mormon rather than being swayed by notions and tradition concerning what he said.

CULTURAL CHARACTERISTICS OF THE JAREDITES

The Jaredites migrated to the land of America from the Near East. There is no evidence as to their race; they could just as easily have been Mongolian as Semitic. They left at the time of the confusion of tongues, when the people were "building a tower to get to heaven." (Book of Mormon preface) This is probably the same tower identified in Hebrew scriptures as being in the land of Shinar. (Genesis 11:2-9) As pointed out by Warren (1963), Shinar was part of the Mesopotamian civilization, which had a fully developed urban tradition. "Tower" building was probably the construction of stepped pyramids which were an important feature of the early Mesopotamian cities. Other elements of that culture included writing, advanced horticulture, ceramics, textiles, metallurgy, massive architecture, class structure, commerce, industry, centralized law enforcement, organized religion, and public works projects. (Lindquist, n.d.)

There is evidence in the Book of Ether that some of that culture was adapted and used when the immigrants arrived in America. If so, some parts of that cultural tradition may be manifested in archæological remains.

Efficient food production is a prerequisite to most other forms of culture. Without it, the population must spend their time hunting and gathering food. Thus, it is significant that the Jaredites brought "seeds of every kind." (Ether 2:3) Their first act upon arriving in the New World was to "till the earth." (6:13, 18) Their agriculture was eventually successful, though I suspect that there may have been some substitution of native crops such as maize (field corn) for the Old World grains. They developed special agricultural technology including the plow, which would make possible planting of grain crops by broadcasting the seed. (10:25)

Once firmly established, the Jaredites reported having "all manner of fruit, and of grain . . ." They also had success in raising domesticated animals (Ether 9:17-18), though the animals raised then may not have survived into Nephite times, much less to the time of the Conquest. With time the Jaredites probably refined their agricultural techniques through use of irrigation, and improved species better adapted to the climate. They developed special tools for working their animals. (10:26) These advances permitted part of the population to turn to other pursuits and begin developing a more advanced culture. (Ether 10:27-28)

Urbanism was a consequence of strides made in food production. During the first millennium of Jaredite culture the cities do not seem to have been large, but gradually urbanism became important. (Ether 9:23, 10:9) Of particular note is the "great city by the narrow neck of land" which provided the impetus for great cultural advances during the latter part of the Jaredite history. (Ether 10:20-28)

A **formal political state** with a succession of kings became a mark of Jaredite culture. Even when conflict could have been avoided by the simple expedient of migration to other areas, it was only used in one case. Usually, the Jaredites followed a traditional practice of defending their kings to the death, resulting in the destruction of the entire nation—the only two remaining combatants were the two claiming kingship, Coriantumr and Shiz.

There were many periods in which the ruling political state subjugated other people, especially those with competing claims to authority. When the brother of Jared led his people to the New World, he warned against the evils of establishing kingdoms, and said, "Surely, this thing leadeth into captivity." His words were amply fulfilled. A listing of the periods of one people or another being in captivity encompasses most of the Jaredite history. (e.g., Ether 10:30-32)

Laws and law enforcement were a consequence of the formal political state. The laws varied in correctness, at some times being administered well, " . . . he did execute judgment in righteousness" (7:11), and sometimes poorly, "Ethom did execute judgment in wickedness all his days . . ." (11:14). Penalties must have been prescribed because there were prisons. (7:18, 9:7, 10:6) When Shule was king, he made a law protecting the rights of the prophets who were engaged in the unpopular activity of calling people to repentance. (7:25) Most of the laws were probably unilateral decisions by the kings, which varied substantially from one king to another.

Craft specialization became an important factor in Jaredite civilization, made possible by the advances in food production. This new industry fostered interregional trade. The best example of this is the massive cultural development in the time of Lib (we will show later from internal chronological reconstruction that this was mid second millennium B.C.). A few verses will illustrate.

> And they were exceedingly industrious, and they did buy and sell and traffic one with another, that they might get gain. And they did work in all manner of ore, . . . And they did have silks and fine-twined linen; and they did work all manner of cloth . . . And they did make all manner of tools to till the earth . . . And they did make all manner of weapons of war. (Ether 10:22-27)

Of special significance, as will be shown in Chapter 6, is this statement: "And they did work all manner of work of exceedingly curious workmanship." This probably refers to development of a new art form, possibly in either stone or pottery. Many of the statements made here, including the concept of trade, can be tested archæologically.

Class distinctions developed soon after craft specialization, with its attendant wealth, changed the economy. There were competing royal lineages (of which the "Jaredites" were just one). There were secret combinations, common folk, and slaves. The bitterness of the wars may have had something to do with desire of people to either maintain or change their positions on this social scale. (Ether 10:31-32) The religion preached by the prophets would have had an ameliorating influence on the class distinctions, which may be one reason that the prophets were often rejected and cast out. (11:2, 11:20-22,13:2)

Writing was important to maintenance of knowledge and the keeping of history. The brother of Jared made an impressive written record and his skill came with him to America from the Old

World. (Ether 4:4-5) Perhaps one of the greatest miracles in the Book of Mormon is the preservation of that early record through all the dynasties and wars of the Jaredites down to the time of Ether, and then through other fortuitous circumstances into the hands of King Mosiah in about 92 B.C. That preservation may have been due to a lineage of prophets who kept the record of the brother of Jared as a sacred relic, and used it to maintain some knowledge of writing. Ether must have had records from which he compiled his history. Furthermore, the elite knew how to write, for at the very end of their civilization we find Coriantumr writing letters to his opponent, Shiz. (15:4, 5, 18) Nothing is said, however, about writing among the common people.

Altogether, the picture painted by Ether is one of a people with a substantial amount of culture. They were not nomads, as has been suggested. (Nibley, 1952) The text shows that they were city dwellers who didn't move too far away from their capital of Moron in two millennia. Such movements as occurred were probably deliberate, related to development of trading networks which all tied into the heartland of their culture.

Transition Between Jaredite and Nephite Culture

The "Nephite" civilization embodied those groups commonly referred to as Nephites, Lamanites, and Mulekites. The origin of these groups was Jerusalem, circa 600 B.C. They brought with them, apparently, a substantial amount of cultural background. However, it is not necessarily correct to assume that in 500 B.C. every person walking the Americas wore a star of David, worshiped Jehovah, and practiced circumcision.

The previous culture, the Book of Mormon indicates, was essentially destroyed in a great civil war. However, that does not mean that every last person on the North and South American continents was killed. It simply means that within a radius of perhaps two hundred kilometers from the scene of the last Jaredite battle, almost everyone was involved. Beyond the frame of reference of the last battle there is every reason to suppose that life continued on. The demise of the heartland as a cultural center would have hurt the economy of the outlying areas, with the collapse of trade. Some cultural resemblances to the Jaredites might be expected to have survived.

The Jaredite survivors (if indeed they are called Jaredite since they may have been from other lineages) would have vastly outnumbered any boatloads of people arriving from Palestine. A number of hints of such survivors are found in the Book of

Mormon. We do not expect much more than hints because when the Nephites joined with a larger group, the people of Zarahemla (Mulekites), the new group received bare mention. (Omni 12-19, Mosiah 25:2) After all, Nephi and those who followed him were writing about their people and their religion. They never claimed to be writing a general history of the New World. "Wherefore, it is an abridgment of the record of the people of Nephi, and also of the Lamanites . . ." (Book of Mormon preface)

The "Lamanites" were cursed. This is mentioned subsequent to Nephi leading his people into the wilderness away from Laman and Lemuel and their families. The first mention of the curse was also subsequent to construction of an elaborate temple, so some years may have passed. The curse, which came upon them because of wickedness was,

> . . . that they might not be enticing unto my people the Lord God did cause a skin of blackness to come upon them . . . And cursed shall be the seed of him that mixeth with their seed; for they shall be cursed even with the same cursing . . . they became an idle people, full of mischief and subtlety, and did seek in the wilderness for beasts of prey.   (2 Nephi 5:21-24)

How did this happen? Did the Lamanites all wake up one morning to find that their skin color had darkened? Certainly that's quite possible for the Lord to accomplish, but it could have also happened by natural means. Laman and Lemuel were power hungry, and if there were natives in the area they would have been prime candidates for domination. In short order there would have been intermarriage. The children would have been dark skinned if the natives were dark, a very good possibility.

Nephites usually beat the Lamanites in battle, often because of superior weaponry, protection, and strategy. The Lamanites were killed by the thousands. However, the Nephites were always outnumbered and were usually surrounded by Lamanites and under pressure from them. In 400 B.C. the Lamanites were . . . exceeding more numerous than were they of the Nephites." (Jarom 6) We also read that in about 122 B.C. the combined total of Nephites and Mulekites did not equal even half the number of Lamanites. (Mosiah 25:3)

These facts could be explained by the theory of survival of many natives after the last Jaredite battle at the hill Ramah. The relevance of this theory is that eventually the old native traditions, culture patterns, and methods of food production would have had large impact on the Lamanites, perhaps more so than the culture brought from Palestine. The Nephites may also have received some native influence, and Nephi may have used some of the natives to help build his temple. (2 Nephi 5:16)

CVLTVRAL CHARACTERISTICS OF THE NEPHITES

Metallurgy had been developed in Palestine which was in an "iron age" at the time of Lehi's departure. However, evidence for iron and steel may be very hard to find, both because of deterioration and loss of the technique. The Nephites were using iron when they were in the highlands. (2 Nephi 5:15, Jarom 8) However, it was not mentioned after the Nephites were forced out of their highland home down to the land of Zarahemla. Later on, the emphasis was on precious metals (Helaman 6:9) and one could almost infer that the knowledge of iron working had been lost. Thus, finding iron or steel is possible but is not a necessary criterion for locating the Book of Mormon cultures.

Precious metals, by contrast, were worked throughout the Nephite period. Though most certainly used for jewelry, the most important use from our perspective was in manufacture of metal plates. They were used for permanent record keeping whereas the native paper they used (Alma 14:8) permitted widespread dissemination of the knowledge of writing and reading. The early prophet Nephi appears to have used the naturally occurring ore, (1 Nephi 19:1) rather than refining it to get "pure" gold. The ores available were composed of gold, silver, and copper. (1 Nephi 18:25)

An alloy of gold and copper called "Tumbaga" was in use at the time of the Conquest. It had the advantages of gold while weighing only half as much. (Putnam, 1966) Addition of silver would lower the melting point and give the plates increased hardness. Perhaps the ore deposit found by Nephi had just the right combination of elements to give a reduced weight, permanence, and good engraving properties. It is interesting that Joseph Smith said that the plates had the "appearance" of gold.

There is uncertainty as to the amount of precious metal objects that might be recovered from Nephite ruins. When Limhi's people abandoned the city of Nephi, they took "all their gold, and silver, and their precious things, which they could carry." (Mosiah 22:12) They may have also passed objects down from one generation to another instead of burying them with their dead.

Wheels receive far less attention in the Book of Mormon than we might expect. Aside from a quotation from the Brass Plates, the word is not used at all. The use of wheels *might* be inferred from a number of references to chariots. (e.g. Alma 19:6, 3 Nephi 3:22) However, there is no reference to carts or wagons. In detailed accounts of movements during the wars, the mode of transportation implied is foot travel. Was the "horse," mentioned in several places, unsuitable for riding, or was it rare, as the horse neared extinction? If wagons were built, they would have been made from wood and could not survive in most climates for two thousand years. Without an abundance of draught animals, carts would not have been very useful and would have been scarce at that time. Thus, we may expect the possibility of some small evidence for the wheel, but it cannot be used as a criterion for location of Nephite lands.

Urban life should certainly be found in Nephite lands and in later years among the Lamanites. The wars centered around cities, the preaching was carried from city to city, and the whole framework of Nephite life was tied to cities. The list of cities destroyed in A.D. 34 is impressive in length. (3 Nephi 8:8-14, 9:3-10) Most of the ruined cities tied to the Nephites should date from 100 B.C. to A.D. 400, with a few cities going back as far as 600 B.C.

Nephite cities were centers for industry and trade, having markets and other elements of well-organized urban society. Take Zarahemla for example. It had at least one major highway, probably more than one marketplace (Helaman 7:10) and walls. (Helaman 13:4)

Towers were constructed by the Nephites, apparently for several purposes. King Benjamin, for example, had one constructed from which he could speak to his people. (Mosiah 2:7) Two towers are mentioned in the land of Nephi (Mosiah 11:12-13, 20:8) which permitted Nephites to observe the war preparations of neighboring Lamanites. Of even more significance is the tower in the garden of Nephi (the son of Helaman). Was it commonplace for important households to have towers? They must have had some religious significance for Nephi did his praying on top of it, in full voice, even though it was in a very public spot. (Helaman 7:10) Sorenson (1975) has documented a case for considering that the Nephite "towers" were really pyramids or tall mounds.

Governmental structure among the Nephites evolved from kingdoms to a system of judges. (Mosiah 29:38-42) Eventually the chief judge took on administrative duties, and came to be known as the governor. (3 Nephi 1:1) An important factor in that system was the fact that such judges were elected democratically. Complexity of the Nephite legal system is suggested from development of a class of lawyers. (Alma 10:14-15) However, central governmental control was usually weak. (e.g. Alma 46)

Cement was used, in addition to wood, in construction of houses, temples, and synagogues. It is mentioned as far back as the first century B.C. (Helaman 3:9-11)

Shipping was carried on to facilitate communications and trade. There must have been knowledge of how to construct fairly large vessels. (Alma 63:5-8, Helaman 3:10) This cannot be used as a test, however, because the vessels themselves could not survive this long and the probability of finding paintings of them is slim.

Long distance trade by whatever means can be tested archæologically. It can only be inferred during long periods of Nephite history, when in fact there may have been little organized trade. The Book of Mormon does talk of movements of people, and armies marching from one place to another within the restricted area south of the narrow neck of land. Up to the time shortly before the birth of Christ, there was little communication with the land north of the isthmus. In fact, they believed that the land northward was cursed. (3 Nephi 3:24) Organized trade really became an important fact of life (insofar as the text tells us) in about 27 B.C. (Helaman 6:7-8, 4 Nephi 46)

Agriculture was the foundation of all other cultural advances of the Nephites. Many crops are mentioned, but the principal crop was corn (likely the native variety known as maize). (Mosiah 7:22, 9:9) In one instance we read, "a numerous host of Lamanites came upon them and began to slay them, and to take off their flocks, and the corn of their fields." (Mosiah 9:14) Other references to agriculture and its importance are numerous within the record.

One criticism of the Book of Mormon is that it mentions the use of wheat and barley, Old World crops not grown at the time of the Conquest (Mosiah 7:22, Mosiah 9:9, Alma 11:7, Alma 11:15). However, there should remain some evidence of their use.

Science 83 reported the discovery by professional archæologists of what is apparently pre-Columbian domesticated barley. It was found among the ruins of the Hohokam civilization near Phoenix, Arizona. The very important Hohokam culture existed in southern Arizona from about 300 B.C. to 1450 A.D. The research was done during emergency surveys prior to construction work. This barley, found in copious amounts, is apparently a "naked" type. It appears from comparing this barley with that found at the Snaketown excavations that the barley samples date no later than 900 A.D.

The Hohokam apparently moved into the area from Mesoamerica. They soon began constructing a vast irrigation network using water from the Gila and Salt Rivers. That network eventually covered about 10,000 square miles of the desert and served about 22 cities. They served a population of about 100,000 to a million, with about 40,000 people living in the vicinity of Phoenix. Later Pima Indians and then Mormon settlers took advantage of some of the Hohokam canals (*FARMS Insights*, March 1984).

The discovery of barley in Arizona, where none has been found in Mesoamerican ruins, is probably due to the far superior preservation factor of the desert. Elsewhere, the grains would have quickly decomposed due to moisture. This is apparently the first direct New World evidence for cultivated pre-Columbian barley. In Mesoamerica it may be necessary to use phytolith analysis. That approach was first suggested by Treat (1978). It could also be used to discover wheat. Probably the best site for such soil samples would be at the ruins of Kaminaljuyú, Guatemala.

Some knowledge of **astronomy** is indicated by Mormon's statement ". . . surely it is the earth that moveth and not the sun." (Helaman 12:15) Nephites were also acquainted with the regular motion of the planets (Alma 30:44). They also noted a new star that appeared as a sign of the Savior's birth (3 Nephi 1:21). They developed good calendar systems based on this knowledge as well as movements of the sun. It is likely that the Solstice measurements were used for corrections to the length of the year in their calendars.

Writing and reading were apparently widespread among the Nephites. After explaining that the abridgement he was making contained less than a hundredth part of the Nephite records, Mormon went on to state, "But behold, there are many books and many records of every kind, and they have been kept chiefly by the Nephites. And they have been handed down from one generation to another by the Nephites, . . ." A dissemination of information in those records to the populace is indicated also. "Now behold, all those engravings which were in the possession of Helaman were written and sent forth among the children of men throughout all the land . . ." (Alma 63:12)

The Nephites used a form of writing described as "reformed Egyptian." Moroni said:

> And now behold, we have written this record according to our knowledge, in the characters which are called among us the reformed Egyptian, being handed down and altered by us, according to our manner of speech.   (Mormon 9:32)

It is improbable that we will find an exact duplication of the Nephite writing system elsewhere in the world, since Moroni said, "none other people knoweth our language."

Organized religion was of course the heart of Nephite culture. It began with Nephi building a temple, (2 Nephi 5:18) developed into an organized church structure some centuries later with growth of the population, (Alma 4:4-5) reached a spiritual culmination with the appearance of Christ (3 Nephi) and finally went into an apostasy phase in about 300 A.D. when religion was used as a focal point for economic growth. (4 Nephi 26-41)

SUMMARY

1. Joseph Smith expected proof for the Book of Mormon to evolve from correlation of Book of Mormon geography with archæological discoveries in Mesoamerica.

2. Elucidation of ancient texts such as the Iliad and the Bible began with internal reconstruction of their geographies. Troy and other important ancient cities were discovered as a consequence.

3. Archæology can flesh out the material world that is presupposed by ancient texts and help us to understand the context of otherwise obscure passages in the Bible and Book of Mormon.

4. The radiocarbon dating method, recalibrated by testing of very old tree rings, is considered generally reliable and is used as a basis for chronologies given herein. It gives absolute dates to chronologies developed in a relative manner through stratigraphic techniques. Obsidian dating is also useful.

5. An archæological test for Ramah/Cumorah is possible since the hill should be found in the context of two cultures dating to about 600 B.C. and A.D. 385.

6. Discovery of weaponry at Mormon's Cumorah is a necessary condition, but the other cultural characteristics of both Jaredite and Nephite peoples must also be found in the vicinity.

7. The Jaredites had a reasonably advanced culture with some characteristics brought from the Old World and others presumably developed independently in America.

8. There is evidence in the Book of Mormon for survival of some people from Jaredite times into times of the Nephites. Subjugation of some of them by the Lamanites is a possibility which would explain some of the Lamanite history.

9. The Nephites developed an impressive society with organized agriculture. They had centralized government with an early

type of democracy, organized religion, and some advanced technology including writing.

10. Evidence for domesticated barley has been found in the dry climate of Arizona.

Summary of Identifiable Physical Remains Required to Identify the Jaredite and Nephite Battleground

Criteria applicable to both Jaredite and Nephite cultures: Some can be fulfilled not only from the hill itself but also from the surrounding cultural area.

1. cities in the vicinity of the hill

2. towers or stepped pyramids for religious purposes

3. efficient agriculture

4. metallurgy

5. formal political states

6. organized religion

7. idolatry at certain times

8. craft specialization

9. trade

10. writing

11. weaponry in immediate vicinity of hill

Criteria applicable only for the Nephites:

12. astronomy

13. calendar system

14. cement

15. wheels

(The absence of mention of these four traits for the Jaredites does not preclude their presence during those times.)

In Chapter 2 we developed a set of geographical criteria for Ramah/Cumorah from the Book of Mormon. Those criteria, combined with the archæologically related criteria listed above, provide a model against which theories for location of Ramah/Cumorah can be tested.

In Chapter 4 we will compare the model developed from the text of the Book of Mormon with the theory that Mormon's Cumorah (Ramah/Cumorah) is in Palmyra, New York. In Chapter 5 the same criteria will be applied to test the theory that Mormon's Cumorah is in Mesoamerica at the Cerro Vigía.

**Hill in New York where Joseph Smith
received the metal plates from Moroni.**

4

AN ARCHÆOLOGICAL AND GEOGRAPHICAL TEST OF THE NEW YORK/CUMORAH THEORY

> *Omer departed out of the land with his family, and traveled many days . . . and came over by the place where the Nephites were destroyed, and from thence eastward, and came to a place which was called Ablom, by the seashore . . .*
>
> *Ether 9:3*

Early associates of Joseph Smith appear to be responsible for equating "Mormon Hill" near Palmyra, New York, with Mormon's Cumorah. Orson Pratt wrote that the hill in New York was the scene of the last battles of both the Nephites and Jaredites. To explain the resulting confusion of record repositories he postulated two separate compartments for the different plates hidden within the hill. He said, "Cumorah was the name by which the hill was designated in the days of the Prophet Moroni, . . ." (*Millennial Star*, 28:417)

Notwithstanding Orson Pratt's reputation as a scholar, one can search in vain in the Book of Mormon or Joseph's record of visits by Moroni for any substantiation of Pratt's assertion. Thus, there is no theological requirement that the hill in New York be regarded as Cumorah. However, since the word Cumorah means "arise revelation," there is no harm in calling it Moroni's Cumorah. The extrapolation by which Moroni's Cumorah is equated with Mormon's Cumorah is the theory we shall now test.

A set of geographical criteria were developed in Chapter 2, which laid a foundation for identification of Mormon's Cumorah. A parallel set of archæological criteria were developed in Chapter 3. Both sets of criteria were carefully documented from the text of the Book of Mormon. In this chapter the New York theory will be tested, using both sets of criteria. Before beginning that comparison, however, we shall examine some of the more popular arguments for linking the hill near Palmyra with the last Nephite battleground.

Arguments for The New York Theory

The City of Manti

The exposition of arguments for the one-Cumorah view in *Doctrines of Salvation* includes several references to the march of Zion's camp. It was an expedition led by Joseph Smith from Kirkland, Ohio, to western Missouri in 1834. During the march, one of the mounds observed was identified as the ". . . ancient site of the City of Manti, which is spoken of in the Book of Mormon . . . ." This incident was cited to substantiate the idea of Book of Mormon cities in North America. Aside from the fact that such statements were completely unsubstantiated, it is instructive to consider whether the idea is even feasible.

There is only one City of Manti referred to in the Book of Mormon. It was by the "head of the river Sidon," which was near the strip of "wilderness" separating the Nephites from the Lamanites. (Alma 22:27) That strip ran from the sea east to the sea west, dividing the land of Zarahemla from the land of Nephi. Both of those lands were southward from the narrow neck of land. Since advocates of the New York theory would agree that the northernmost possible isthmus separating the land northward from the land southward is Tehuantepec, there is no possible way for a site up in the United States to have been the Book of Mormon City of Manti.

The Zelph Incident

A second argument made is that Joseph Smith identified the New York area as the last battleground. Joseph Fielding Smith says, "Moreover, the Prophet Joseph Smith himself is on record, definitely declaring the present hill called Cumorah to be the exact hill spoken of in the Book of Mormon." Reference was made to the (Documentary) *History of the Church*, 1948 edition, Vol. 2, pp. 79-80. This is an account of the "Zelph incident," which also occurred during the march of Zion's camp. A mound covered with bones was discovered. The men dug into it and found a skeleton with an arrowhead between its ribs, which apparently was the cause of the man's death. Various reports of Joseph Smith's reaction to the scene have been the cause of considerable confusion. The citation given in the 1948 edition of the *History of the Church* does indeed appear to support Smith's contention. However, the first edition gives an entirely different version, which definitely does not support that contention. Since both were supposedly taken from the prophet Joseph Smith's hand-written journal, which one is more correct?

The 1948 edition will be quoted, with words italicized which were not in the 1904 edition.

> During our travels we visited several of the mounds which had been thrown up by the ancient inhabitants of this country—Nephites, Lamanites, etc., and this morning I went up on a high mound, near the river, accompanied by the brethren. From this mound we could over-look the tops of the trees and view the prairie on each side of the river as far as our vision could extend, and the scenery was truly delightful. On the top of the mound were stones which presented the appearance of three altars having been erected one above the other, according to the ancient order; and the remains of bones were strewn over the sur-face of the ground. The brethren procured a shovel and a hoe, and removing the earth to the depth of about one foot, discovered the skeleton of a man almost entire, and between his ribs the stone point of a Lamanitish arrow, which evidently produced his death. Elder Burr Riggs retained the arrow. The contemplation of the scenery around us produced peculiar sensations in our bosoms; and subsequently the visions of the past being opened to my understanding by the Spirit of the Almighty, I discovered that the person whose skeleton was before us was a white Lamanite, a large, thick-set man, and a man of God. His name was Zelph. He was a warrior and chieftan under the great prophet Onandagus, who was known from the *Hill Cumorah, or* east-ern sea to the Rocky Mountains. The curse was taken from Zelph, or at least, in part—one of his thigh bones was broken by a stone flung from a sling, while in battle, years before his death. He was killed in battle by the arrow found among his ribs, during the last great strug-gle of the Lamanites and Nephites.
>
> (*History of the Church*, Vol. 2, pp. 79-80, 1948 edition)

I have obtained a photostatic copy of the original handwritten account, and the reason for the discrepancy between the editions is clear. Within the manuscript there are numerous insertions and deletions, just what one would expect when the history was being written by a scribe, subject to review and later correction. The 1904 edition included most corrections, while the 1948 edi-tion ignored most but not all of the corrections. Due to copyright restrictions the original cannot be reproduced here, but the added and deleted parts of the text are shown in typed form. All the insertions were in the same handwriting, which differed from that of the main body of the manuscript.

> During our travels we visited several of the mounds which had been thrown up
>
> by the ancient inhabitants of this country, Nephites,~Lamanites,~etc, and this
>
> several
> morning I went up on a high mound, near the river, accompanied by the brethren.
>
> From this mound we could overlook the tops of the trees and view the prairie
>
> on each side of the river as far as our vision could extend, and the scenery was
>
> truly delightful.
>
> On the top of the mound were stones which presented the appearance of three
>
> altars having-been-erected one above the other, according to ancient order, and
> the remains of
> ^xxxxxx- bones were strewn over the surface of the ground. The brethren
>
> procured a shovel & hoe, and removing the earth to the depth of about one foot
>
> the stone point of
> discovered the skeleton of a man, almost entire, and between his ribs was a
>
> Burr Riggs
> Lamanitish arrow, which evidently produced his death. Elder Brigham-Young
>
> retained the arrow, and-the-brethren-carried-some-pieces-of-the-skeleton-to
>
> around
> Clay-County. The contemplation of the scenery before us produced peculiar
>
> subsequently
> sensations in our bosoms: and , the visions of the past being opend to my
>
> understanding by the Spirit of the Almighty I discovered that the person whose
>
> we had seen
> skeleton was-before-us was a white Lamanite, a large thick set man and a man
>
> His name was Zelph.   and chieftan
> of God. ^ He was a warrior under the great prophet Onandagus who was known
>
> from the hill-Cumorah-or eastern sea to the Rocky Mountains. His-name-was-Zelph,
>
> Zelph
> The curse was taken from him or at least, in part. One of his thigh bones was
>
> broken by a stone flung from a sling while in battle, years before his death. He
>
> was killed in battle by the arrow found among his ribs, during a last great
>
> Elder Woodruff carried the thigh bone to Clay County.
> struggle with the Lamanites and-Nephites.

The foregoing typeset reconstruction of the Prophet's history of the Zelph incident clearly shows that all reference to "Nephites," "Cumorah," and "last" battle were stricken when the manuscript was revised. Who was responsible for the alterations? According to the Church Historian's office, the first draft was written by Willard Richards and the corrections were in the handwriting of

Thomas Bullock. Both were scribes employed in the writing of the *History of the Church*.

The sequence of events surrounding the writing of the history has been summarized by Dean Jessee (1971) of the Church Historical Department. Due to a variety of problems, the writing of the history did not begin in earnest until the Nauvoo period. During that time, Willard Richards worked rapidly to complete the history, but was only able to bring it up to 1838 before the martyrdom of Joseph Smith. In February, 1845, the work on the history continued under the direction of the Council of the Twelve, with Thomas Bullock now employed to work directly with Willard Richards. Bullock had a major role in the writing of the remaining history.

The history had been written from other existing records and contained a few errors. Therefore, before his death the Prophet had gone through and revised forty-two pages. Subsequent to the death of Joseph Smith, the Council of the Twelve directed the work of revision. In the presence of Brigham Young, Heber C. Kimball, Willard Richards, and George A. Smith, Thomas Bullock read the history out loud, and presumably corrected it, based on their comments as first-hand observers of many of the important events in church history. (See Jessee, 1971:473, note 108.) From this I would conclude that the corrections were made based on the first-hand knowledge of Brigham Young and Heber C. Kimball. Note that two of the changes involved the Twelve. Furthermore, the changes make the account agree with the account in Elder Kimball's journal which states that the vision was not given until after the camp had departed from the mound.

Neither edition of the Documentary History is completely consistent in using the corrections, but the first edition in 1904, edited by B. H. Roberts, was unquestionably the more accurate rendering.

Preston Nibley, then the assistant church historian, examined the same page of the manuscript on August 29, 1957. Fletcher Hammond, who accompanied him, reported, ". . . Brother Nibley has authorized me to say that the 1904 edition of the Documentary History of the Church Vol II at pages 79 and 80 correctly reports the "Zelph" incident; and that the part of the 1934 (and the 1948) edition of the same history which differs from it is erroneous." (Hammond, 1959)

While this discussion may seem to have become somewhat technical, there is a very important point to be made. The original corrections made to the Documentary History were done under the direction of the Council of the Twelve, with those present actually being parties to the event spoken of. Thus, the corrections must be considered accurate. This leaves us, to the best of my knowledge, without a single recorded instance of Joseph Smith saying or inferring that the last Nephite battles and Jaredite battles were near Palmyra, New York.

LAND "FAR TO THE NORTH"

McGavin and Bean (1949) argue that Cumorah is a great distance north. "Whenever the Book of Mormon writers describe Ramah-Cumorahland, it is always described in a similar tone— a land far to the north, a land richly endowed with all the natural bounties; a land of many waters, fountains and streams." (p. 21) What does the Book of Mormon really say?

"Therefore, Morianton put it into their hearts that they should flee to the land which was northward, which was covered with large bodies of water, and take possession of the land which was northward." (Alma 50:29) Now two questions can be posed: (1) how far northward was it, and (2) was it the same area where the land of Cumorah was located? Those are open questions at this point. A clue to the first question is in the next verse. "And behold, they would have carried this plan into effect, (which would have been a cause to have been lamented) but behold . . ." Why would it have been lamentable for that group of contentious people to exile themselves by several thousand miles from the land of the Nephites? That would have been advantageous to the Nephites.

The insertion by Mormon suggests that they would still have been close enough to cause shifts in the strategic balance in the area of Bountiful. Otherwise, the Nephites would have said, "Goodbye! Good riddance," instead of sending a key army to head them off at the narrow pass which led through the isthmus.

The second Book of Mormon account is similar. About twenty years after the first incident, there were planned migrations into the land northward, possibly due to tensions arising from overpopulation in the land southward. (Helaman 3:1-5)

> . . . there were an exceeding great many who departed out of the land of Zarahemla, and went forth unto the land northward to inherit the land. And they did travel to an exceeding great distance, insomuch that they came to large bodies of water and many rivers. Yea, and even they did spread forth into all parts of the land, into whatever parts it had not been rendered desolate and without timber, because of the many inhabitants who had before inherited the land.

It is unlikely that they would go so far as to cut off all kinship ties, and they apparently didn't go beyond the land inhabited previously by the Jaredites and Mulekites.

Were the bodies of water mentioned the same as those mentioned with respect to Cumorah (Mormon 6:4)? The text does not say. In Mesoamerica there are two possible areas this could have referred to. One was in the valley of Mexico, where there was a very large inland lake (Texcoco). The other area is the large region of lagoons forming the Papaloapan basin in Veracruz. Either could be referred to, and would be acceptably close to the land of Zarahemla. It would be fruitless to argue over how far an "exceeding great distance" was to a Nephite. That must remain a matter of opinion.

THE LIMHI EXPEDITION

A second argument by McGavin and Bean is that "The description these pioneers [the men of the Limhi expedition] gave of the country is typical of the Book of Mormon description of Cumorahland." They, of course, meant upstate New York. Actually, the only description of the land itself was that it was "among many waters." That description is so vague as to fit many areas in Middle and North America. In fact, as pointed out in Chapter 2, the account of the Limhi expedition is one of the good, strong arguments against the New York theory. The expedition's goal was to find Zarahemla and get help for their families back in the highlands, not to go exploring. How could they possibly have crossed the River Coatzacoalcos, traversed the rivers feeding into the Papaloapan lagoon system, the rivers flowing out to the port at Tampico, crossed the great Mexican desert and subsequently the Rio Grande, thence northward further still, crossing innumerable rivers such as the Mississippi, and still think they were heading towards their home of Zarahemla, an easy twenty-days walk from Nephi? They would have had to hunt for food, suffer through the seasons, and endure untold hardships. They could have done all that, but it would have taken many years. They returned thinking they had found the land of Zarahemla which is in the heart of the land southward! It is extremely difficult to accept, on that basis, such a trek as would have been required to reach upstate New York.

Evaluation of The New York Theory with Geographical Criteria

In Chapter 2, thirteen geographical and topographical criteria were listed based on statements from the Book of Mormon. Let us now compare the New York model against them.

There are a few criteria which appear to be satisfied by the New York model. These are:

- one day's journey south of a large body of water—Lake Ontario
- in an area of many rivers and waters—the finger lakes area is a possibility (but water in the immediate vicinity of the hill is not abundant and may pose a problem to the theory)
- the hill must be free standing

On the other hand, there are a number of other criteria which are definitely not satisfied:

- near a narrow neck of land
- the presence of fountains
- in a land of volcanoes susceptible to earthquakes
- in a temperate climate with no cold or snow
- the hill must be a significant landmark (it only stands out because of the monument of Moroni on top)
- the abundance of water must provide a military advantage
- near the eastern seacoast
- on a coastal plain, and possibly near other mountains and valleys
- there is an escape route to the land southward
- the hill must be large enough to provide a view of hundreds of thousands of bodies

The hill Cumorah described by Mormon must have been an elevation of sufficient prominence to have commanded attention. When the Lamanites agreed to meet the Nephites there for battle, it is unlikely that they were given a detailed topographic map. The size of "Mormon Hill" in New York is only about fifty meters, which makes it suitable for the stage of a pageant but hardly for an enormous battle. In fact, it is rivaled in size by a number of pyramids built in Mesoamerica. The 1000 B.C. pyramid at La Venta is 31 meters high, with a volume of 99,000 cubic meters, and the "Pyramid of the Sun" at Teotihuacán is over sixty meters high, with a volume of 840,000 cubic meters.

McGavin and Bean try to sidestep this issue by assuming that the battles took place on the surrounding drumlin hills. "It seems utterly impossible to visualize the final battles in Cumorahland without assuming that every important hill in that neighborhood was fortified as the Nephites are said to have fortified other battlefields." (p. 47) This is a far different picture than that painted by Mormon. At Cumorah he speaks of no fortifications, and he speaks of only one hill, Cumorah. It was large enough for his whole army to camp around, and that also means there was enough water right there to sustain them. Nowhere is more than one hill mentioned by Mormon in connection with that battle, though the prophet Ether spoke of several nearby hills and valleys. At the end of the battle Mormon and Moroni were among the few survivors. They viewed the bodies of all their people, a terrible scene of carnage. That would not have been possible if the battle had been spread around throughout the vicinity as suggested by McGavin and Bean.

COMPARISON OF NEW YORK MODEL WITH CULTURAL TRAITS AND PHYSICAL REMAINS

McGavin and Bean presented significant amounts of data on antiquities of New York state in support of their position. From that I conclude that there must have indeed been some wars in western New York among the Indians. I will also grant that there might have been scores or even hundreds of drumlin hills with stoneworks that might have served as fortifications.

What I am not prepared to accept is an age for those remains going back to Nephite times, much less Jaredite times. McGavin and Bean (1949) did not have the advantage of modern dating techniques when they published. Radiocarbon dating was just around the corner, but in its absence even the best of the archæologists made gross errors in assigning dates to early American cultures. Today, we are in a much better position to evaluate the archæological data from the state of New York. In doing so, we will first look at the archæology of the eastern half of the United States, and then will examine the specifics of archæology in New York to see whether there is consistency with the Book of Mormon model.

THE MOUNDBUILDERS

Prior to 1000 A.D., the most advanced culture in the United States was that of the "moundbuilders." Their very impressive mounds throughout the eastern United States were the subject of curiosity, looting, and debate from the time of the colonists to the time of Joseph Smith. As previously mentioned, they figured into Mormon church history during the march of Zion's camp through Ohio and Illinois. Though Joseph Smith took an interest in them, he never equated them with Book of Mormon cities or events, as he later would do with ruins in Mesoamerica.

Fawn Brodie and the Moundbuilders

One of the most influential critics of Joseph Smith felt that in the mounds she had found the answer to the history contained in the Book of Mormon, which she believed he had invented. "It was a common legend," says Brodie, "that western New York and Ohio had once been the site of a terrible slaughter and that the mounds were cemeteries of an entire race." Her thesis was that Joseph Smith decided to write a story of the moundbuilders, which would terminate in a final battle on a hill near his home. (Brodie, 1945)

This misconception has persisted to the present, leading many authors of books and articles on North American archæology to make either direct or, as in the following citation, indirect disclaimers relative to what they suppose is in the Book of Mormon.

> The story of prehistoric North America is one of steady progress over thousands of years, studded by singular achievements. There are no lost tribes or boatloads of sailors from the Old World in this story, no superior visitors, either natural or supernatural. There are only the American Indians, and the events that transpired as a natural consequence of their humanity, their imagination, and the culture they carried with them when they arrived.   (Snow, 1976)

To the extent that Snow was correct in this disclaimer, it should not have any direct bearing on the Book of Mormon history, which I maintain occurred elsewhere on the continent.

Explanation of the Mounds

It may be surprising to learn that the beginnings of the archæological method can really be credited to Thomas Jefferson. He was attempting to settle the dispute over whether the mounds were used for burials after great battles, or were built up for burials over a long period of time. To settle the question, he made a vertical cut through the mound and examined the strata that were exposed. This was the advent of stratigraphy, a cornerstone of the archæological method. Jefferson observed that the bodies were in different strata, and the different strata were distinct from each other. He observed that the skeletons on the bottom were the most decayed, those on the top the least. This suggested to him different times of inhumation. He also found infant bones in the mound. From these data he arrived at his conclusion, "Everyone will readily seize the circumstances above related, which militate against the opinion that it covered the bones only of persons fallen in battle . . ." (Ceram, 1971) Subsequently, it has been verified that the majority of the mounds were used for elaborate burial rites, and that their construction extended over centuries.

EXTENT OF THE MOUNDBUILDER CULTURE

There are reported to be over 10,000 mounds in Ohio and Illinois. (Temple, 1977) Two classifications have developed. The earlier group is called the Adena, and the more advanced later culture is called the Hopewell. The beginning of the Hopewell culture was sometime between A.D. 200 and A.D. 500. Some mounds built after about 1000 B.C. were temple mounds, rather than burial mounds. They were associated with development of fairly complex social structures. Ceram (1971:194) states that construction of so many large mounds by a "primitive people" goes "far beyond the Egyptian achievement in its totality." Note, however, that the time when this occurred was after the Book of Mormon time period.

The Hopewell artisans produced very fine prehistoric art. They worked copper imported from Lake Superior into a variety of ornaments and jewelry, even creating two-dimensional drawings on copper plates. Meteoric iron was beaten into a foil.

Joseph Smith's statements about Zelph coincide with what we know about the Moundbuilders. The descriptions of the location of the Zelph mound by members of Zion's camp were sufficiently precise to permit its identification with Mound PK-5 on the archæological survey by the Illinois State Museum. (Wittorf, 1970) The mound is on the Illinois River about two and a half miles south of Valley City in Pike County, Illinois. It pertains to the Hopewell culture. It will be recalled that following a visit to this site Joseph Smith is reported to have said that Zelph was a ". . . warrior and chieftan under the great prophet Onandagus, who was known from the eastern sea to the Rocky Mountains . . . ." This statement was indeed prophetic, for it has now been proven that the Hopewellians did have trade contacts reaching from the Rockies to the Atlantic Ocean. Mica was imported from New England and shells came from the Gulf Coast. Their obsidian used for blades came from Yellowstone, a fact now established by activated neutron analysis of trace element distribution.

Despite the large amount of mound construction activity, the Hopewellians did not organize into cities until 1000 A.D. Their largest city appears to have been Cahokia, Illinois, which had 100 mounds and a population of 10,000 to 15,000. As a point of comparison, five centuries earlier Teotihuacán had a population on the order of 200,000.

Throughout most of the moundbuilding tradition there were no large communities and there was no intensive agriculture. Some farming, especially of corn, does appear to have been practiced, and hunting was still important, as evidenced by the large number of arrowheads and knives left behind.

EARLIER CULTURES

Prior to the Hopewell culture was the Adena, whose antiquity is now estimated to go back as far as 1500 B.C., and which survived until Hopewell times. The Adena people, centered in Ohio, were not numerous. Their creative energy seems to have been devoted almost exclusively to the cult of the dead. They had a mediocre pottery tradition and the beginnings of agriculture. They did not have the bean, as did peoples in Mesoamerica, so hunting was required to provide protein. The most well-known Adena mound is the "serpent mound." Built about two thousand years ago, it winds for half a kilometer on an Ohio hilltop. Though some Adena burial mounds are found in the state of New York, Snow is of the opinion that those mounds are a result of adoption of the burial cult by local tribes influenced by traders.

Prior to the Adena culture there were several small culture centers. The "Red Paint" and "Old Copper" cultures go back in time before 2000 B.C. The latter of these were a group of prehistoric Algonquins who found lumps of native copper on the shores of Lake Superior. They worked the metal, never casting it, but learning to anneal it. No cultures similar to these developed in the lower Great Lakes region.

ARCHÆOLOGY OF NEW YORK STATE

A definitive study of the archæology of New York state was published in 1965 by William Ritchie, which serves as the basis for the subsequent discussion. Though the archæology of related states is interesting, a New York Cumorah theory must satisfy archæological and cultural criteria in its own territory. In examining New York state's archæology, we will begin with the archaic culture and move forward in time, reversing the direction previously taken in examination of the moundbuilders.

ARCHAIC CULTURE (3000 B.C. TO APPROXIMATELY 1300 B.C.)

The archaic cultures were mobile and without much, if any, social structure. Their sites were small and their dwellings were insubstantial. The largest village had about 100 people. They left no traces of agriculture or pottery. Though they obtained some copper tools, they had no ornaments. They selected their sites according to fishing potential, but they also hunted deer, turkey, and pigeon. There was some gathering of vegetable foods. The males are described as being about five feet five inches tall, of slender build, and having long, narrow and oval-shaped faces with narrow noses. During the latter half of this phase, the "Laurentian tradition," the people were heavy boned, and again stood at a height of about five and a half feet. They had broad, round heads, with short and broad noses. This physical type persisted down to about A.D. 1000, notwithstanding traditions of "giants."

TRANSITIONAL STAGE (1300 B.C. TO 1000 B.C.)

The transitional phase saw introduction of pots made of soapstone, plus some early ceramics. Little of this cultural tradition is found in the western part of New York, however.

EARLY AND MIDDLE WOODLAND STAGE (1000 B.C. TO APPROXIMATELY A.D. 900)

During this stage there was a gradually-increasing emphasis on agriculture. Burials were mostly cremations. There was the beginnings of a pottery tradition and small copper ornaments were developed. Trade developed with the Upper Great Lakes area, Quebec, and Pennsylvania. There were also some contacts with the Adena culture.

Ritchie has developed a picture of the life of these people based on archæological data. In the winter they probably ranged the forests in small groups. No campsites have yielded any post molds, so the shelters must have been quite temporary. In the summer they used ". . . a flimsy wigwam affair of poles with bark or mat covers, which rested almost upon the surface of the ground." Overall, the picture we gain of these people, who overlapped Jaredite and Nephite time periods, is one of small bands of semi-civilized people with little social organization.

The simple fact is, they still did not have agriculture, but subsisted by hunting and gathering. "Projectile points, chiefly of large size, probably for arming javelins and hand-held spears, and bone fish hooks, proclaim the already ages-old basic hunting-fishing economy in our area, which however, has as yet supplied no trace of cultigens, although maize horticulture is now definitely established for the Hopewell culture of Illinois and Ohio."

LATE WOODLAND STAGE (A.D. 900 TO A.D. 1600)

Finally in this late phase, especially after A.D. 1100, the Owasco people in New York began to show signs of moving out of the cultural backwater in which their ancestors had been mired. The bow and arrow came into use—arrowheads from the Palmyra area probably are no older than A.D. 1100. The villages developed in size up to 300 people. Pottery was still very crude; the vessels didn't even have supports. The Owasco is the earliest culture in New York state for which the cultivation of corn and beans can be substantiated.

INTERPRETATION OF THE ARCHÆOLOGICAL DATA

The hazards inherent in assigning a Book of Mormon provenance to every arrowhead or mound in view is evident from this review of the archæology of the moundbuilders, and especially those in the State of New York. This point will be emphasized by returning to the list of criteria at the end of Chapter 3. Since the cultures in New York and the moundbuilders areas were different, I will consider them separately.

		Moundbuilder Area	Palmyra Area
1.	cities in vicinity of Ramah-Cumorah	too far	no
2.	towers or stepped pyramids for religious rather than burial purposes during Book of Mormon times	no	no
3.	efficient agriculture	beginnings	no
4.	metallurgy	some	no
5.	formal political state	no	no
6.	organized religion	yes	no
7.	idolatry	yes	?
8.	crafts beginnings	yes	very little

	Moundbuilder Area	Palmyra Area
9. trade	yes	very little
10. writing	no	no
11. weaponry near hill		*
12. astronomy	no	no
13. calendar system	no	no
14. cement	no	no
15. wheels	no	no

We need feel no embarrassment concerning the archæological data presented here. The Book of Mormon requires no battles in New York, and Joseph Smith didn't either. Joseph's only definitive statement on the moundbuilders did not involve the Book of Mormon directly. As we have seen, however, he prophetically made an accurate assessment of the scope of the territorial connections of a people now known as the Hopewellians.

There are two key facts which must be taken into account by anyone who still thinks that book of Mormon culture ever extended up into New York state: (1) archæological evidence is overwhelmingly in contradiction of such a view, and (2) there is almost no evidence in New York of contact with Mesoamerica, which had much superior technology. If the Nephites had part of their territory up in the United States, cultural contacts would have been so direct that North American civilization would have been very similar to that in Mesoamerica. That did not happen, as the great Mexican desert proved a barrier through which culture diffused only with great difficulty.

SUMMARY

1. There are no known statements by Joseph Smith connecting the Cumorah near Palmyra with the Nephite/Jaredite battleground.

2. Suggestions that Joseph Smith did make such a reference in connection with the Zelph incident are erroneous. Examination of the original manuscript shows that the 1948 edition of the *History of the Church*, which contains that account, is incorrect and the original 1904 edition gave a more accurate rendering.

---

*There appears to be evidence for battles on hills near to "Mormon Hill" but not on the hill itself. Presumably the greatest collection of artifacts would be on the hill where the last battle occurred.

3. Key geographical arguments presented for the New York theory apply better to Mesoamerica. The account of the Limhi expedition actually gives strong evidence that Mormon's Cumorah could not have been in New York state.

4. Only three out of thirteen of the geographical criteria developed in Chapter 2 are satisfied by the hill near Palmyra.

5. Archæological information on northeastern United States and New York in particular shows that the Book of Mormon people did not live there and had very little, if any, contact with those who lived in New York.

6. Until A.D. 1100 there were no settlements in New York state greater than 300 people, and the use of the bow and arrow was unknown.

5

A Mesoamerican Model for Location of Mormon's Cumorah

Since our "extract" was published from Mr. Stephens' "Incidents of Travel," and etc. we have found another important fact relating to the truth of the Book of Mormon. Central America, or Guatemala, is situated north of the Isthmus of Darien and once embraced several hundred miles of territory from north to south. The city of Zarahemla, burnt at the Crucifixion of the Savior, and rebuilt afterwards, stood upon this land . . .

Joseph Smith
Times and Seasons, *October, 1842*

In this chapter I propose a location in Mesoamerica for Mormon's Cumorah, and will show that it fits both the geographic and archæological criteria established in chapters 2 and 3, respectively. The accompanying maps (#2, p. 254, and #3, p. 255) show most of the area encompassed by Mesoamerica. It extends about half way up from the Isthmus of Tehuantepec towards the Rio Grande. At the northern limit is an arid semi-desert which served as a barrier to both settlement and travel. On the other side of the isthmus is the rest of Mexico, plus Guatemala, El Salvador, and parts of Nicaragua, Honduras, and Costa Rica.

Mesoamerica is a land with a variety of climates, due to the mountain ranges and proximity to two different oceans. The large amount of volcanic dust dispersed through the region has made it very fertile.

Within Mesoamerica there were several dozen shared cultural traits. They formed part of a rich ceremonial complex among different groups which traded goods and ideas with each other. The term "Mesoamerica" thus relates to a pattern of civilization, the extent of which varied with time. It was smaller during certain periods of the Book of Mormon than it was at the time of the Conquest.

MESOAMERICA AND BOOK OF MORMON GEOGRAPHY

One is led naturally to look to Mesoamerica as a possible choice for the Book of Mormon lands because it is here that a large number of ruins dating to the Book of Mormon time period have been found to exist. Most of the scholars who place the Book of Mormon lands in Mesoamerica agree that (1) Tehuantepec was the narrow neck of land, (2) the Land of Nephi was in the highlands of Guatemala, and (3) the impressive ruined city of Kaminaljuyú on the outskirts of Guatemala City was the City of Nephi. Map #6, p. 259 shows the major ruins in Mesoamerica which date to the Nephite time period.

Location of the important city of Zarahemla is dependent on which major river system one considers to be the Sidon River. (Zarahemla is found on the western side of the Sidon, according to Alma 2.) The earliest "limited Tehuantepec" theories emphasized the large River Usumacinta as the possible River Sidon. Most of the explorations up to 1960 had been on that river, and impressive ruins had been found. Many of them, however, have been found to date only as far back as the "Classic" archæological period, or A.D. 300. Serious work on the other possible drainage system that could be the Sidon, the Grijalva, began in about 1960. The Grijalva flows through the heart of the "Central Depression of Chiapas." It has subsequently been established that this area was a hive of activity in Late Preclassic times, that is, from the first few centuries (as early as 600 B.C.) to as late as the Early Classic period when many cities were abandoned. There are estimated to be thousands of settlements which are found within the state of Chiapas, about half of which date to the Late Preclassic period. Map #10, p. 264, shows major ruins discovered in the Central Depression.

Most of the research there was carried out by the BYU New World Archæological Foundation. Concerning this work it has been said,

> . . . the New World Archæological Foundation has already devoted some twenty years to mapping, surveying, and digging in the hitherto little-known regions of Chiapas and the Isthmus of Tehuantepec. Through generous financial support for concentrated methodical excavation and prompt publication of information, the archæological progress has been enormous in this region. To judge from preliminary reports and the number of newly discovered sites, digging here has just begun.   (Weaver, 1972:301)

Much of this work has been literally invaluable, since many of the ruins on the upper river have been submerged by waters from the Angostura dam. Included in the ruins now lost is a site referred to later, which Sorenson has equated with Zarahemla. In the subsequent discussion the Grijalva will be equated with the River Sidon and the Central Depression of Chiapas with the land of Zarahemla.

Through analysis of the geographical criteria in the Book of Mormon, many scholars have arrived at the conclusion that the hill Ramah/Cumorah is somewhere between the Isthmus of Tehuantepec and the northern desert region of Mexico. Ferguson (1947) suggested the Valley of Mexico as a possible location, but among other problems, it appears to be too far from the sea. Some members of the Zarahemla Research Foundation have suggested, after some serious research, that a hill called Rabon near Jalapa de Diaz could be Cumorah. It is located near Tuxtepec on the inland side of the coastal plain by the Papaloapan river. Its location could make some sense provided that the Nephites did not have a rotation of their coordinate system, as discussed previously.

A more probable location, from my perspective, is an isolated mountain peak called the Cerro Vigía at the north-western end of the Tuxtla mountain range. After examination of satellite pictures, visits to the hill and the ancient mounds which surround it, and analysis of the topography and archæology of that immediate area, I have become fairly convinced that it is the correct spot.

In this chapter I will show that the Cerro Vigía ("lookout hill") fits all reasonable interpretations of the Book of Mormon geographical criteria. I will not prove definitively that it is the correct place. That could only be done absolutely by discovery of Mormon's record repository. However, there is strong archæological evidence. Any other candidate would have to pass through the same strainer of criteria to which we will subject the Cerro Vigía. At the present time it does not appear that there is any alternative site which has archæological support to the degree that the Cerro Vigía does.

As we examine the archæological information in this and subsequent chapters, it will be helpful to first consider the broad perspective of Mesoamerican history.

Chart #1

Archæological Sequences in Mesoamerica During Book of Mormon Times

Date	Period	Culture and Remains in Mesoamerica	Book of Mormon
2300 B.C.	EARLY PRECLASSIC	Permanent villages Farming Pottery Puerto Marques, Santa Luisa, El Cuello, and highland Oaxaca villages built	Jaredites built towns in highlands of Moron
1500 B.C.	MIDDLE PRECLASSIC (Olmecs)	Theocratic government Great ceremonial centers at San Lorenzo and La Venta Massive monuments Large trading network Disappearance of Olmecs: 600 B.C.	Great cultural advances at city of Lib Civil wars Destruction about 600 B.C.
600 B.C.	LATE PRECLASSIC	Development of cities Theocratic government Extensive use of platforms pyramids, altars, and incense burners	Arrival of Nephites and Mulekites from Palestine Highly stratified society in Land of Nephi (200 B.C.)
100 B.C.	(Protoclassic Development)	Use of cement, calendar, astronomy Efficient agriculture and crafts Belief in Quetzalcoatl (the feathered serpent)	Organization into states about 100 B.C. Visit of Christ Period of peace
A.D. 300	EARLY CLASSIC	Abandonment of sites in Central Depression of Chiapas Expansion of Teotihuacán and alliance with Kaminaljuyú Dated monuments glorifying rulers in Mayan area	Nephites driven from Zarahemla Nephite destruction Continued wars (400A.D.)
A.D. 450	MIDDLE CLASSIC		

CULTURAL TRADITIONS IN MESOAMERICA

Chart #1 gives an overview of the archæological sequences in Mesoamerica during Book of Mormon times. The terminology of the major periods is quite simple. In essence, the Book of Mormon cultures developed during the different phases of the Preclassic period. In commenting on this chart, it is useful to point out that during the Book of Mormon history there were two cultural traditions which developed. The first lasted from the Jaredite time of Lib (roughly 1500 B.C.) to about 600 B.C., which is the approximate date of the destruction of the Jaredites. This coincides with the "middle Preclassic" culture, the most outstanding part of which was developed by the archæological Olmecs on the Gulf Coast. These people will be discussed in Chapter 6. As required by the Book of Mormon, pottery and other evidences of civilized man go back almost a millennium before that in the period known as the "Early Preclassic."

The Book of Mormon indicates that in the Nephite areas the population was quite limited from 600 B.C. to 100 B.C. That interregnum is also seen in the archæological record. There are only a few large ruins dating to that time period and no great cultural tradition in evidence. This does not mean that there is no evidence for the cultures described in the Book of Mormon during that period, for there was. However, the Book of Mormon does not really require development of a lasting cultural tradition until after the time of Christ. That is precisely the time that the foundations were laid for the subsequent classic Maya and Teotihuacán cultures which began to sweep Mesoamerica and throw it into turmoil towards the end of Book of Mormon history.

The period from 100 B.C. to A.D. 300 is sometimes referred to as the "Protoclassic," though it is usually just considered part of the "Preclassic" period. The Book of Mormon history extends into the "Classic period" for about one hundred years.

To summarize, there were two great cultural traditions which developed in Mesoamerica at times coincident with Book of Mormon requirements. This very important fact will pervade much of the subsequent data that will be presented.

COMPARISON OF MESOAMERICAN MODEL WITH GEOGRAPHIC AND TOPOGRAPHIC CRITERIA

In Chapter 2, thirteen criteria were presented based on topographical and geographical information in the Book of Mormon. They will now be compared with the Cerro Vigía in Veracruz, Mexico. (Refer to Map #4, pp. 256-257.)

ERTS Satellite picture showing the Paploapan lagoon system
(Waters of Riplicancum?) in relationship to the Cerro Vigía
(Hill Ramah/Cumorah).

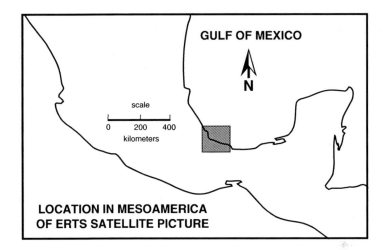

**LOCATION IN MESOAMERICA
OF ERTS SATELLITE PICTURE**

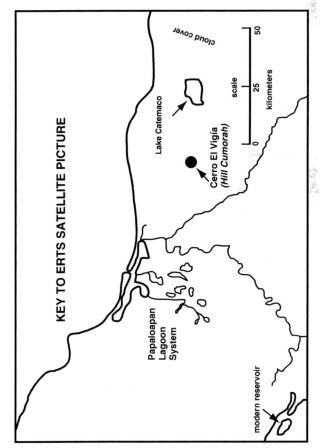

1. Near Eastern Seacoast

The hill is only about 15 kilometers from the coast. The concept of Omer passing by the hill Cumorah and going from "thence eastward to a place which was called Ablom, by the seashore", is very possible in the context of the Book of Mormon coordinate system. The site of Roca Partida on the coast is appropriately situated; an Olmec monument was discovered there and it could be an appropriate place to search for older pottery.

2. Near Narrow Neck of Land

It is just 100 kilometers to Coatzacoalcos, which is at the outlet of the Coatzacoalcos River. That river generally divides the isthmus of Tehuantepec.

3. On a Coastal Plain and Possibly Near Other Mountains and Valleys

From the top of the Cerro Vigía, looking inland, there is an expansive plain. That plain connects with the coast. There are a few minor peaks and valleys between Vigía and the Paploapan basin. Behind Vigía, towards the Gulf of Mexico and stretching down towards Coatzacoalcos, lies the heart of the volcanic Tuxtla mountain chain.

4. One Day's Journey South of a Large Body of Water

About twenty kilometers north (B of M coordinates) of Cerro Vigía is the beginning of the vast expanse of water known as the Papaloapan lagoon system. Large oceangoing vessels are used to fish those waters. The lagoons are the largest body of water in the area, not counting the sea. They form part of the great Papaloapan drainage system which carries enormous quantities of water into the Gulf of Mexico at the port of Alvarado. The accompanying ERTS satellite picture of this region shows this area quite clearly at the time of its minimum extension, the height of the dry season. Even then it is quite impressive. Because of the type of photography used, (lower infra-red) water appears black in the photograph. White clouds are apparent on the right hand side of the picture. Labels have been added for clarity.

Since this area is neither a lake nor a river it is a good candidate for "Ripliancum" which was interpreted as "large, or to exceed all." It is quite possible that there was no word for "lagoon" in the Jaredite language. Recent statistical studies have shown that Joseph Smith's translation was essentially a word-for-word translation, (Larsen 1980:225)[1] which could account for the fairly nebulous reference to this body of water.

5. IN AN AREA OF MANY RIVERS AND WATERS

Map #4 shows that the Tuxtla range is encompassed by two great drainage systems, the Papaloapan, and the Coatzacoalcos. There are minor rivers at the very base of the hill. The general area of the Cerro Vigía was known anciently as "Nonohualco," which means "place where water is everywhere."

6. PRESENCE OF FOUNTAINS

Before my first onsite visit to the hill, the question of "fountains" was considered unresolved. What could Mormon have meant? That question was clearly answered. I discovered that at the base of the Cerro Vigía there are large fountains. At one that is particularly beautiful, "Los Chaneques," a stream of underground water springs forth from the hillside and cascades over a ledge to a tranquil pool below. Fountains such as this are the source of the rivers which encompass the hill. Water from under the earth was considered pure by early Americans, and had a mystique of its own. It is not surprising then, that Mormon should have mentioned fountains which would have been a reliable source of drinking water. Such fountains are used today as the source of drinking water for the city of Santiago Tuxtla.

7. THE ABUNDANCE OF WATER MUST PROVIDE A MILITARY ADVANTAGE

The Cerro Vigía is not only surrounded by fountains and rivers, but water comes from the hill itself, running down in small streams which make the old road up the hill almost impassable. This is typical of the area, which receives from 1.5 to 4.5 meters of rain each year! When Matthew Stirling of the Smithsonian Institution first came to this area to carry out archæological investigations, he was very impressed by this phenomenon. "Down the sides of the peaks race innumerable streams. As they flow through the gullies and narrow valleys that separate the sedimentary ridges, they retain their mountain-stream appearance,

---

1. The same studies have proven that there were twenty-four authors of the Book of Mormon. Study of wordprint patterns shows that none of these many Book of Mormon authors had wordprints resembling those of Joseph Smith, his associates, or people ever claimed to have influenced his writing. This study definitively discredits theories that Joseph Smith, Sidney Rigdon, or Solomon Spaulding was the author of the Book of Mormon.

clear and brisk-flowing, quite unlike the sluggish muddy rivers of the lowlands into which they disembogue." (Stirling, 1943)

The soils are able to handle the large volume of rainfall because they are well drained. This characteristic is a consequence of the periodic outpouring of modest amounts of volcanic ash from some of the volcanoes in the chain which have been active during the last three thousand years. (Stark, 1978)

One question which is often asked is the extent to which the climate has changed during the last few thousand years. According to the prominent Mexican archaeologist Ignacio Bernal, there have been few changes in the climate of the Veracruz area in this period. However, he notes that the swampy areas were larger. "Geographical studies indicate that from the beginning of the first millennium B.C. until the present the habitat of the area has not changed; that is to say, it has had the same climate and bodies of water." (Bernal, 1969)

What does all this information about climate and water have to do with a military advantage? I postulate that the military advantage sought was attraction of people. The battle was basically a numbers game. People could only be attracted to the army if they were fed, and how does one go about providing food for an army of a quarter million people? It should be noted that just prior to the last battle the lack of food was a major consideration. (Moroni 9 & 16) The way Mormon chose to provide food for his people during the four-year gathering period was to choose as the place of his last stand one of the most fertile areas of the Western Hemisphere. Sanders (1953) claims that the area of the Cerro Vigía was "the prize area of the state" of Veracruz where ". . . one of the major economic climaxes of the state was apparently located."

Two crops per year can be grown in the Tuxtla region. Blom (1926) reported that at Piedra Labrada three crops of corn per year are usual. To the staple of corn was added beans, squash, chilies, melons, papaya, and sweet potatoes. They even had a bush with red fruit used for flavoring meats, according to Blom, who was one of the first North Americans to traverse and report on the area.

Cacao was being grown at the time of the Conquest as a "cash" crop and as tribute for the Aztecs. Sterling (1943) reported that they also had tomatoes and xicamas, a root like a turnip. Fishing contributed to the economy and would have provided additional protein for the diet. Traps, spears, and arrows were probably used to catch the fish.

Another source of food would have been wild animals, such as tapirs, jaguars, monkeys, birds, armadillos, rabbits, and wild pigs. Domesticated flocks of turkeys and a species of pig may have been used by the Nephites. It is also possible that the cow-like tapir was domesticated. However, agriculture was undoubtedly the primary source of food, as it had been throughout Nephite history.

It thus seems likely that this area was chosen by Mormon because of its potential for feeding his army, and hopefully adding to the size of that army. He could have done no better than to pick the ecological climax area of Mesoamerica.

8. ESCAPE ROUTE TO THE LAND SOUTHWARD

Those escaping to the "south countries" would have followed the route of Omer, skirting the northern flank of the Tuxtlas and approaching the sea. From there they would have been able to travel down to the isthmus virtually undetected, having a mountain range between them and the Lamanites.

A small band of Conquistadores once followed this coastal route looking for a place for Cortez to land his ship. The route is so difficult that it is largely abandoned. Blom reported, "We were told that here and there pirates had taken shelter and we heard

View of the cloud-shrouded Cerro Vigía as it appears from the side of Tres Zapotes.

stories of political refugees who had taken this route. But otherwise, it had apparently been deserted by everybody for centuries."

9. HILL MUST BE LARGE ENOUGH TO PROVIDE A VIEW OF HUNDREDS OF THOUSANDS OF BODIES

Cerro Vigía is 800 meters high, easily large enough. I questioned whether it might be too high, since the last Nephite battle lasted only one day. However, a Mormon living in the microwave relay station on top of the hill told me that he could make a round trip on foot to Santiago Tuxtla, at the base of the hill, in three hours.

10. HILL MUST BE A SIGNIFICANT LANDMARK

Cerro Vigía is easily distinguishable since it sits on the plain out of the main line of the Tuxtla chain. For whatever it's worth, Friedlander found in 1922 that the Indians considered Cerro Vigía sacred. (Williams, 1955) This may be related to the fact that a number of the Olmec monuments were carved from basalt taken from Cerro Vigía.

This hill also appears to have been used for astronomical sightings. Three ancient towns, Tres Zapotes, Cerro de la Piedra, and Cerro de las Mesas are located along a line which intersects the peak of Cerro Vigía. That line of sight gives the exact position of the winter solstice at sunrise. (Malmstrom, 1978) It now appears that many Mesoamerican centers were located, in part, on the basis of potential for solstitial sightings. These were important for maintenance of the calendar which was used for a guide in the planting of crops.

11. THE HILL SHOULD BE FREE STANDING SO PEOPLE CAN CAMP AROUND IT

Cerro Vigía stands apart from the rest of the Tuxtla Mountain chain, separated from it by the city of Santiago Tuxtla. There is an outcrop, a second much-smaller peak to the north of Vigía. They are connected by a gentle ridge on which people live today. Part of the slopes of the hill are farmed, while the remainder are covered with trees. In the time of Mormon it was probably used more extensively for crop production. It is a simple matter to find evidence of ancient occupation at the hill since ancient mounds literally surround the hill and are clearly visible from the roads.

12. IN TEMPERATE CLIMATE WITH NO COLD OR SNOW

The Tuxtlas are a year-round resort for the Mexican tourists who want to avoid the commercialism of spots frequented by

Americans. Here and throughout Mesoamerica the seasons are determined more by rainfall than by temperature variations, which are slight. The climate is best described as temperate, with cold temperatures only encountered at the highest elevations.

13. IN A VOLCANIC ZONE SUBJECT TO EARTHQUAKES

Mesoamerica has been an area of very heavy volcanic activity. Mexico has about 37 recent volcanoes, twelve currently active. In Central America there are 67 recent volcanoes, 32 presently active. Both Mexico and Central American countries are plagued by earthquakes. The massive 1975 destruction in Guatemala was a vivid reminder that the Spaniards moved the capitol of Guatemala away from Antigua because that city was destroyed so often by earthquakes.

The Tuxtla mountain chain is itself volcanically active. About half of the mountains are inactive, including Cerro Vigía. The active cones include San Martin Tuxtla, San Martin Pajapan, Santa Marta and Pelon. These major volcanoes and their parasites have erupted within the last few thousand years. (Williams, 1955) The most recent eruption was that of San Martin Tuxtla in A.D. 1793. Moziflo reported that ash and dust from that eruption fell as far away as Oaxaca.

It is relevant to consider whether major volcanic eruptions in Mexico can be dated to the time of Christ's crucifixion. Answering that question may be difficult since Drucker (1943) reports that today there are no traces at Tres Zapotes of the 1793 San Martin eruption. Prevailing wind direction at the time of the eruption and depth of the ash layer are important factors. If an ash layer is not too thick, it can be converted by natural processes into a fertile soil within a period of thirty to forty years. Nevertheless, ash layers are sometimes preserved in occupied settlements.

DATING THE ASH LAYER AT TRES ZAPOTES

One of the most significant ash layers found in ruins near the Tuxtlas is at Tres Zapotes. The site is of special significance since it is in the shadow of the Cerro Vigía. The site was explored by Matthew Stirling (1943) and was excavated by Drucker (1943) and Weiant (1943). One of the extraordinary features of the excavations was the discovery of a pronounced ash layer between several cultural strata. The dating of the site has been very uncertain for two reasons. The excavations were carried out a decade before discovery of radiocarbon dating. Furthermore, the principal investigators could not agree on the interpretation of the results. Covarrubias (1957) criticized their work and Coe (1965) ignored their interpretations. Coe used only their raw data and developed a new interpretation consistent with materials from other sites.

The famous monument found at Tres Zapotes had a bar and dot style date pertaining to the so-called "Mayan Long Count" calendar system. Because of the style of carvings on the back of the monument Coe locates it in the cultural horizon below the ash layer. If interpreted according to the Goodwin-Martinez-Thompson (GMT) correlation the date on the stela is 31 B.C.!

From this information we can draw the tentative conclusion that the ash layer could have been laid down in 34 A.D. at the time of destructions spoken of in the Book of Mormon. Hopefully, the new series of excavations at Tres Zapotes will firm up the date of that eruption.

Stela C from Tres Zapotes, Veracruz. It is on display in the National Museum of Anthropology, Mexico City. The upper part of the monument was discovered more recently and is displayed in the town of Tres Zapotes. This monument recorded a date of 31 B.C. and appears to be from the period of cultural development found below the thick layer of volcanic ash that fell on Tres Zapotes. Chase has indicated that the eruption occurred in late spring when prevailing winds would have carried the ash from volcano San Martin over Tres Zapotes.

Small traditional-style pyramid at Cuicuilco which was covered
with lava at about the time of the crucifixion of Jesus Christ.
Cuicuilco is located south of the university of Mexico City.
Note the well-defined staircase leading up the pyramid.

DATING THE VALLEY OF MEXICO ERUPTION

Evidence of volcanic destruction of ancient cities is easily seen
by the tourist visiting Mexico City. On the southern end of the
city are the archæological zones of Copilco and Cuicuilco. At the
former site, a lava flow about six meters high covers the remains
of the village. Cuicuilco was an impressive ceremonial center with
a large circular pyramid and other pyramids of more traditional
form. They were all covered with lava during an eruption of the
volcano Xitle. Archæologists have not agreed upon the date of
that eruption. Corrected radiocarbon dates from carbon found
below the lava give A.D. 60 + 110 years and 70-100 B.C. + 210
years. These dates are consistent with an eruption in A.D. 34.

Warren associates this eruption with an ash layer discovered
in a well-defined stratigraphic sequence at Teotihuacán, located
sixty kilometers from Cuicuilco. According to Millon, (1961) the
department of geology at the University of California, Berkeley,
has determined that the ash layer was not man made. The
deposit varies from eight to sixteen centimeters in thickness. It
was preserved because shortly after falling it was covered with fill.
Of special significance is the fact that the broken pottery in the
fill came only from the Tzacualli phase known as Teotihuacán 1.

Lava flow overlaying the ruins of Copilco. The stone construction of the
ruins comes up to the position indicated by the author's left hand.

A radiocarbon date from a nearby mound with similar pottery gives a corrected date of A.D. 70 ± 90 years. Some of the same pottery style was found just below the lava layer at Cuicuilco (Warren, personal communication). Within the limits of uncertainty of the measurement, this is consistent with an eruption in A.D. 34.

DATING THE EL SALVADOR ERUPTION

At the southern extension of Mesoamerica there is evidence of an even greater volcanic eruption. The volcano Ilopango erupted explosively in El Salvador during the Late Preclassic period. As described by Payson Sheets of the University of Colorado,

> In two separate stages, the volcano Ilopango erupted with such violence that whole forests were uprooted and carbonized in an instant. Trees flew like matchsticks in the fierce, hot wind which caught up immense amounts of ash in its turbulence. By the time the eruption was over, thousands of people were dead and land within a radius of 100 kilometers had been rendered uninhabitable. In the area immediately surrounding the eruption, volcanic materials ejected through the air called "tephra" lay as much as 50 meters deep. The vitality of southeastern Maya highland society had ended.
> (Sheets, 1979a)

There is evidence that due to the poor water retention qualities of the fine white ash which fell, disastrous floods followed the eruption. Though volcanic zones are usually very productive, the type of ash laid down in this case was resistant to the rebuilding processes of nature. As a consequence, it was not until the sixth century A.D. that the area was once more inhabitable.

The dating of that eruption is somewhat speculative. Sheets has suggested a date of A.D. 300, consistent with a theory he is trying to promote. However, his evidence rests primarily on movements of ceramics in a time frame stated as 100 B.C. to A.D. 300. (Sheets, 1979b:552) Sheets, a geologist, discusses the presence of pottery with mammiform supports, found under the Ilopango ash layer, in connection with his theory. He is apparently unaware that such vessels are found in Monte Albán in the 600-200 B.C. time period (M.A.I. phase) (cf. Caso,1967: Figures 138,141, and 182) and in Chiapa de Corzo beginning in 50 B.C. (Chiapa Vl phase). (cf. Warren, 1978) Furthermore, his own corrected radiocarbon date, 20-40 A.D. (Sheets, 1977) from the sub ash layer at Laguna Seca, tends to support a hypothesis that the eruption was earlier than he states. Laguna Seca is just one kilometer from the important Preclassic site of Chalchuapa, El Salvador, which is shown on Maps #6 and #9, pp. 259 and 262.

The evidence I have given for eruptions in the Tuxtlas, the Valley of Mexico, and El Salvador does not prove conclusively that they occurred at the time of the Crucifixion, but within the limits of experimental uncertainty the timing on all three could be compatible with a date of 34 A.D. If there were eruptions of three volcanoes at such widely scattered locations, it is highly probable that there were other eruptions in the same general area which are as yet undiscovered.

Thus far in this chapter it has been shown that the Cerro Vigía meets all of the geographic criteria established for Mormon's Cumorah from the test of the Book of Mormon. This is a necessary but insufficient test, however. We must also satisfy the archæological and cultural criteria described in chapter 3.

COMPARISON OF MESOAMERICAN MODEL WITH CULTURAL TRAITS AND PHYSICAL REMAINS

Fifteen traits and types of archæological information are required for the candidate hill. These are listed in the summary of chapter 3 and will be used below in evaluation of the Mesoamerican model. Modern coordinates will be used in the remainder of this chapter.

1. CITIES IN THE VICINITY OF THE HILL

The Cerro Vigía is surrounded by ruins dating to Jaredite and Nephite times. Covarrubias reported over six hundred archaeological sites in the state of Veracruz, only a few of which have been thoroughly explored. The more ancient ruins are found in southern Veracruz, where the Cerro Vigía is located.

Because of the lack of exploration there are probably many sites as yet undiscovered. Berger, Graham, and Heizer (1967) recommended intensive survey and excavation in the Tuxtla area, feeling that " . . . some very important things were going on in this region just before and just after 1000 B.C." To make the necessary discoveries, they suggested, in a masterpiece of understatement,

> He who fancies himself as a rough and ready archæologist need only secure a permit from INAH, equip himself with a knowledge of Spanish, some high boots for protection against the fer-de-lance, insect repellent, water purifier, dysentery remedies, a four-wheel drive vehicle, plenty of money, considerable patience, and some reserve nerve for unpleasant confrontations, and go into the field and locate a new batch of ten-ton sculptures.

LAGUNA DE LOS CERROS

Fortunately, the tourist is able to see a number of impressive sites without all that fuss. For example, roughly halfway between Cerro Vigía and the Isthmus City of Acayucan there are mounds, apparently dating only to Jaredite times. Over ninety of them have been identified. but little archæological work has been carried out there. The site, Laguna de los Cerros, is visited so seldom that villagers at Corral Nuevo, four kilometers away are mostly unaware of its existence.[2] This site, and many of the others mentioned below, can be located on Map #4, pp. 256-257.

EL MESÓN

In the immediate vicinity of the Cerro Vigía there was a very heavy population in both Jaredite and Nephite times. Stretching along the highway from north of Santiago Tuxtla to the sugar processing town of Lerdo, the road is lined on both sides with mounds covered with sugar cane. Coe notes that you can travel eleven kilometers without ever being out of sight of these mounds. These extensive ruins are called El Mesón. Originally the mounds were likely platforms for perishable wood or "wattle and daub" (reinforced mud) houses. Very little has been done there of a serious archæological nature, but the art and pottery seems to be Preclassic.

Mathew Stirling explored the area between Tres Zapotes and El Mesón, finally concluding that El Mesón was a very important center " . . . in aboriginal times." He also concluded that the area at the base of the mountains was heavily populated in early times, with settlements centering mainly on the streams flowing from the mountains to the rivers. He noted many impressive

---

2. *How to find Laguna de los Cerros:* Proceeding on the Veracruz highway from Acayucan, just before arriving at the town of Corral Nuevo, there is a kilometer 194 sign. Go thirty meters past the sign and turn left onto a dirt road. Follow it for 0.2 kilometers. At a fork in the road, go right and travel parallel to the main highway for about 1.4 kilometers. The road then turns left. Follow it in a westerly direction for another 1.4 kilometers. The road then swings left, heading south. The largest of the pyramids are to the right, about a kilometer further. From the top of one of them a ballcourt can be seen, and scores of low mounds stretch off in a southwesterly direction. The ruins probably date to the Middle Preclassic or late Jaredite period. The few pottery sherds seen on the surface are very badly worn. A few excavations were carried out here by Alfonso Medellin, as well as Francisco Pereau. (1972)

**Stela found and presently located at Tres Zapotes, Veracruz.
It dates to Book of Mormon times and records a ceremony. This
monument and others on display at the village of Tres Zapotes
can be reached from either Lerdo or Santiago Tuxtla.**

mound groups in the vicinity of the base of Vigía which are
unmapped and unexcavated.

Tres Zapotes

Tres Zapotes, on the western side of Cerro Vigía, is one of the
more important archæological sites of Mesoamerica.[3] It has been
dated on the basis of pottery and sculpture which is closely related

---

3. A small museum in Tres Zapotes protects many of the basalt sculptures that
were not taken to the museum in Mexico City. Of particular interest is the recently discovered missing part of Stela C. The other half is in Mexico City. Museum personnel can
give directions to the mound groups. There are about fifty mounds at Tres Zapotes,
mostly constructed of earth. Potsherds and obsidian cover the ground near these
mounds. The village of Tres Zapotes is accessible from both Lerdo and Santiago Tuxtla.

to other sites such as La Venta and Izapa. There were many occupations, beginning during Jaredite times, and extending until after A.D. 1000.

Many monumental sculptures have been found at Tres Zapotes, some of which were carved from stones taken from Cerro Vigía. Some of these are Olmec in style, thus being from the "Middle Preclassic" period which ended in about 600 B.C. However, most of the evidence suggests that the site was primarily "Late Preclassic," or from the Nephite/Mulekite time period. The calendar date of 31 B.C. found there has been mentioned previously. It is suggested that Tres Zapotes was a minor Jaredite village (possibly Ogath), which was built up by the Mulekites and later by the Nephites.

Tres Zapotes was likely on a major trade route, and connections are evident with other important areas of Mesoamerica from Guatemala to the Valley of Mexico.

SITES NEAR TRES ZAPOTES

Bernal reports that within roughly twenty kilometers of Tres Zapotes eight other sites are found. Most of them have mounds, ". . . which indicates a relatively dense population." (Bernal, 1969:45) Some are shown on the accompanying map of the Tuxtla area. Not all, however, date to Nephite or Jaredite times. One interesting discovery by Valenzuela was a ceramic plate with a picture of two warriors on it. One was shown in the act of throwing his atlatl (spear). The site dates to just after the Nephite destruction. (Valenzuela, 1945b:87)

From the Tuxtla mountains came an interesting statuette with a Long Count date of A.D. 162 (GMT), which helps pinpoint the time of cultural development in the area.

While travelling along the road from Santiago Tuxtla to Tres Zapotes, I let my family examine one of the many mounds that are alongside the highway at the base of Cerro Vigía. The mound had been partially destroyed for agricultural purposes, leaving a vertical cut of the mound exposed. We picked out of the dirt a collection of potsherds and obsidian. The sherds were examined by Professor Bruce Warren, who identified some of them as definitely Preclassic. Others were from the Early Classic period, which would correspond to the time of the Nephite destruction. One small sherd had a design on it which looked very similar to a design found at Chiapa de Corzo, pertaining to the Chiapa III phase. That would place that particular sherd in the 650 B.C. to 500 B.C. time frame, excellent correspondence with the time of the last Jaredite battle.

View of El Cerro Vigía, which is believed to be Mormon's Cumorah.

Coe (1965:696) believes that La Mechuda, about twelve kilometers south of Vigía, has materials in the ruins which date to both Middle and Late Preclassic periods. (Jaredite and Nephite times) Several other ruins reported by Stirling have received little attention since. A few kilometers north of Tres Zapotes, there is a mound group by a stream called "la Puente." A ball court was created by these mounds, with a basalt sculpture partially buried in the court. The basalt sculpture suggests appropriate age for Jaredite connections, but a ceramic study would be needed to confirm this conclusion.

Somewhat farther away, but still relevant, is the site of Cerro de las Mesas. Located seventy kilometers west north-west of Tres Zapotes, on the far side of the Papaloapan lagoons, it was not a Jaredite town but was very active in late Nephite times. Coe reports that it had strong afilliations with cultures in Oaxaca and Chiapas, not unexpected in the context of the overall geography. Other neighboring towns north of the Papaloapan were Los Cerros and Nopiloa, which have yielded very interesting ceramic representations of culture as it may have appeared in Nephite times. These artifacts are on display in the museum located at Jalapa, Veracruz.

Many of the townspeople from Santiago Tuxtla have their own small collections of artifacts and figurines. Most of their figurines are very ancient, going back at least to Nephite if not Jaredite times. A representative collection of artifacts has been assembled in the museum at Santiago Tuxtla. The most impressive artifacts are the basalt sculptures, which probably date to Jaredite times. The massive stone head in the central plaza has a much different style than other Olmec sculptures and is thought by Professor Robert Squier to be unfinished.

Professor Valenzuela discovered ancient constructions at the southern edge of the peak.

> We visited the extreme south of the peak of the Hill Vigía, or Tuxtla Hill, which is to the west of (Santiago) Tuxtla. We were able to find in the underbrush prehispanic constructions and stones with human faces represented on them. It is supposed that when research can be carried out in this part of the summit of the hill there will be excellent results.   (Valenzuela,1945b:90)

At the base of Cerro Vigía are seventy large mounds which have yet to be thoroughly studied. That site is called Tatocapan. Another place with large mounds that appear to be Olemec is Tilapan. It is located a few kilometers southeast of Cerro Vigía.

An extensive field survey around the Cerro Vigía was recently completed by Dr. Bruce Warren, Garth Norman and Richard

Hauck. Their objective was to determine whether there was an influx of people in the fourth century, A.D. They examined over fifteen sites, only part of which had been previously recorded. According to Dr. Warren, there indeed was very significant occupation in the fourth century, A.D. in the area surrounding the Cerro Vigía. (Norman and Warren, personal communication)

2. TOWERS OR STEPPED PYRAMIDS FOR RELIGIOUS PURPOSES

The pyramid at La Venta is in the form of a volcano, very similar to the volcanic cones in the Tuxtlas. Entirely manmade, it apparently served as a focal point for the Olmec religion from about 1000 B.C. to 600 B.C. Robert Heizer estimated that about 2000 man years were required to build it. Another Jaredite period pyramid is seen at San José Mogote in Oaxaca.

In the Nephite period there were large pyramids in Guatemala (Kaminaljuyú), the state of Chiapas, Mexico, (Izapa, Chiapa de Corzo, etc.) the state of Oaxaca, (Dainzú) and the valley of Mexico (Cuicuilco, Teotihuacán, Tlapacoya, and Cholula).

3. EFFICIENT AGRICULTURE

At the time of the Conquest of Mexico, "slash and burn" agriculture was widely practiced. This method involved clearing the land and exploiting it for crops for a few years. The ground was abandoned to the tropical rainforest after being depleted of nutrients. Such an approach required constant movement of the farmers. Recently, it has been discovered that more intensive cultivation strategies were practiced, dating back to Book of Mormon times. Matheny (1979) states,

> Cultivation strategies known to have been employed in the Maya area include, among other devices, raised fields and terraces. Water-control techniques, such as canals, wells, reservoirs, and cenotes (deep sinkholes with a pool at the bottom), were also used at many sites. Our preliminary investigations indicate that the ancient Maya of the Chiapas highlands, in southeastern Mexico, employed a variety of strategies in managing water and soil resources which were necessary for the successful establishment of large communities. That communities were sustained by permanent cultivation is suggested by extensive landscaping, which helped to bring much of the environment under control.

Santley (1982) has found strong evidence for intensive Early Preclassic dryland farming in the Tuxtlas.

Work by Flannery in Oaxaca has shown that the people exploited the high water table by digging wells and carrying water to irrigate their crops. As many as ten wells would be located in a one-acre plot. This technological advance allowed such efficient food production that at least half the population was able to turn to craft manufacture and mining. (Flannery, 1967) Three crops per year are possible using intensive irrigation. In the very dry highland Tehuacan valley, large dams have been found which date to as early as 1600 B.C. (MacNeish, 1972) The use of canal systems for irrigation can be firmly dated to at least 400 B.C. in Oaxaca, with some village runoff canals going back to 1000 B.C. (Flannery, 1976)

In a very contrasting environment, the low-lying Coatzacoalcos river basin, there is annual flooding which deposits mud and silt, similar to the effects of the Nile in Egypt. Two corn crops can be grown each year, one after the rainy season and one after the floods. (Meyer, 1978) At San Lorenzo, reservoirs were filled through special troughs from nearby river waters.

Corn, beans, and squash were the standard fare in Mesoamerica, providing a reasonably nutritious diet. It was supplemented, of course, but that was the foundation. Field corn (strictly, maize) was the staple which made Mesoamerican civilization possible. It could be stored for a long time before removal of the kernels and conversion to flour for tortillas. It is one of those remarkable overlooked facts in the Book of Mormon that corn was apparently the principal crop. In the history of Zeniff's colony in the land of Nephi tribute was paid to the Lamanites. Corn was mentioned first. (Mosiah 7:22) It was the first crop mentioned that they planted (Mosiah 9:9), and the only crop mentioned when they were attacked. (Mosiah 9:14)

An Olmec iron mirror with a concave center. It is of a type worn by the Olmec rulers, (see Photo 6-8) as depicted in a number of their monuments. This mirror was fashioned by hand, and may have required hundreds of hours of labor.

4. METALLURGY

The antiquity of use of ancient metals in Mesoamerica is placed at 1500 B.C. This is based on language studies called glottochronology (Campbell and Kaufman, 1976). They found that the word for metal was in use in the Mixe-Zoque language at that time. This was the time of development of the Olmec culture. According to Coe, excavator of the first Olmec city, seven iron beads were found at San Lorenzo in association with the large Olmec heads. They could be dated no later than 100 B.C. Ferreira (1976) reported the discovery of a large number of Preclassic period iron beads at Amatal, Chiapas. An unusual feature was holes drilled in both ends. If iron was used for luxury purposes, it would be strange if the thought might not have occurred to use metal for weapons as well.

One source of iron was in the Oaxaca Valley iron mines. Small mirrors were manufactured in workshops at San José Mogote from about 1000-850 B.C. The metal that they used was magnetite, a form of iron. Olemecs also made concave iron mirrors, illustrated on the preceding page. they obviously had th necessary technology to do this. Monuments of the Olemec rulers often show the iron mirror on their chests.

In Nephite time the presence of iron is found at Kaminaljuyú, Guatemala. This may have been the earliest Nephite city. Several conical lumps of iron oxide were found during excavation in a tomb within Mound E-lll-3 (Shook, 1952).

One of the most fascinating uses of metal in early times was conversion of cinnabar (Mercuric sulfide) into elemental mercury. Mercury has been found at an underwater site in Lake Amatitlan where it was placed as an offering. It has also been found in a tomb at Kaminaljuyú (Kidder, 1946:144). A discussion of finds of other metals in Mesoamerica is given by Sorenson (1976b).

5. FORMAL POLITICAL STATES

Wherever we find construction of massive public works projects such as temples, pyramids, and tombs of considerable extravagance, we can be quite certain that there were formal political states in operation. There had to be in order to organize and marshall the human resources needed to bring such projects to fruition. Mesoamerica offers the best examples of organized political states in America during Jaredite and Nephite times.

The Olmec centers of San Lorenzo and La Venta, with their monumental sculptures, are the best examples from Jaredite times. During Nephite times the centers of Kaminaljuyú, Izapa, Chiapa de Corzo, Monte Albán, Dainzú, Santa Rosa, and Teotihuacán are just a few examples. More will be said concerning this in later chapters.

6. ORGANIZED RELIGION

No one seriously questions the fact that organized religion was a very important cultural and historical factor in Mesoamerica from the very earliest times. From the jaguar cult of the Olmecs to the construction of the pyramid of Quetzalcoatl with its serpent heads at Teotihuacán, religion was extremely important in Mesoamerica. This is documented in the accounts of ancient Mesoamerican history, such as the writings of Ixtlilxóchitl.

Sejourne (1962) states quite emphatically that if we don't try to understand the fragments of historical truth underlaying the myths of god figures such as Quetzalcoatl, we will remain forever in ignorance of the political life in ancient Mexico. She has shown that some of the concepts taught by the life god Quetzalcoatl include the union of fire and water, spiritual rebirth, and striving for celestial status through inner growth. (1956) It has also been shown that the symbol identifying anthropomorphic representations of Quetzalcoatl, the shell, represented spiritual rebirth. (Palmer, 1967). Other authors who tried to understand the complex theology which came down to the time of the Conquest include Alfonso Caso (1953), Jose Franchi, (1957) and Miguel León-Portilla. (1962)

The development of a complex theology does not develop without the support of priests, a church, and other trappings of religion.

7. IDOLATRY AT CERTAIN TIMES

From archæology we have been able to learn quite specifically what types of idols were worshiped in Lamanite-Nephite times and even in Jaredite times. The reason is that many of the idols were made in either stone or ceramic, and have survived. The jaguar or were-jaguar was apparently worshiped during Jaredite times. In Guatemala, probably the heartland of the Lamanites, there were a number of different idols including the toad or frog. This may be due to the fact that their variety produced hallucinations when eaten. In the highlands of Oaxaca the bat god was worshiped.

The area where we should see the fewest idols is in the land of Zarahemla, since the Nephite prophets constantly warned against idolatry. One area with large populations in Nephite times but very little in the way of monuments is the Central Depression of Chiapas, which may be the land of Zarahemla.

8. CRAFT SPECIALIZATION

Thanks to agricultural advances and organization of political states, craft specialists were in demand. Their prime market, of course, was supplying luxury goods to the rulers.

Probably the earliest city where craft specialization has been documented was San José Mogote. There were workshops for manufacture of pottery. Some people mined or worked iron into luxury items and possibly tools. Jade and shell were imported and worked into delicate and beautiful pieces of jewelry for export.

Other professions which can be archæologically documented developed in Jaredite and Nephite times. These include spinners, weavers, architects, rock quarriers, sculptors, transportation experts, paper makers, artists, and workers of obsidian. In Teotihuacán alone, over five hundred craft workshops have been found.

9. TRADE

Long-distance trade developed in Mesoamerica at least by 1500 B.C. and was an important factor thereafter. The Olmecs developed a far flung trading network to bring in a flow of luxury goods. It now appears that they even imported obsidian from the highlands of Guatemala. Archæologists use the presence of traded objects as evidence of movement of peoples in ancient times. I will spare the reader the details since they could occupy volumes.

10. WRITING

Tremendous progress was made during the 1980's in understanding the meaning of all the Mayan hieroglyphics. This can best be seen in the book destined to be a true classic, *Forest of Kings*, Linda Schele being the primary contributor. It shows how the glyphs give the history of the rise and fall of the different city-states, and also how they support the ruling lineage's divine rights to kingship. The "Black Altar" at Kaminaljuyú shows the beginnings of Mayan hieroglyphics and we look forward to its interpretation. The monument dates to the time of King Noah in the Book of Mosiah.

The Zapotecs may have had the earliest writing system of which we have evidence. It appeared about 600 B.C. in Oaxaca. There are many hieroglyphics on the Monte Albán monuments

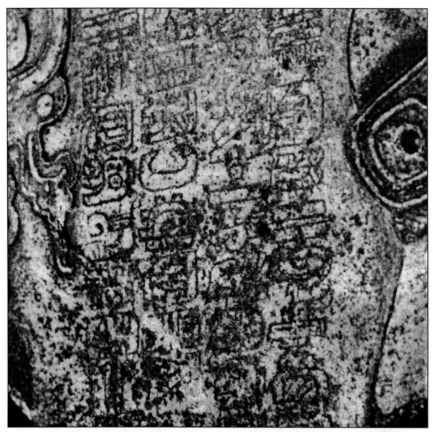

A portion of the "Black Altar" found at Kaminaljuyú, Guatemala, pertaining to the two-hundred-year period "Miraflores" preceding the coming of Christ. These untranslated glyphs from Stela 10 are either late Olmec or early Mayan.

which carry themes of war and peace. At the ruins of El Mirador, demonstrably dated to Nephite times, the remains of an ancient codex was found interred. It has not been separated into individual pages, but probably contained some form of writing.

Secondary evidence suggests strongly the use of writing on paper in early times. The archæologist Norman Hammond concluded that the presence of bark beaters in the Late Preclassic time period " . . . suggests the making of writing surfaces and hence the use of writing to record sacred or secular matters" (*Origins of Maya Civilization*, 63). For the last part of the Nephite time period, Bernal (1974:253) infers the presence of writing at Teotihuacán even though few confirming hieroglyphics have been found there.

Scripts are found on cylinder seals as well as monuments. Such seals, which are similar to those in use in Mesopotamia, have been found in a number of places in Mesoamerica, including the Cerro Vigía. Tim Tucker found a cache of them in a stone box in a temple complex at Chiapa de Corzo, while working for the NWAF. Probably the most significant cylinder seal discovered in Mexico was found at Tlatilco. The stamp impression appears to give a definite linear script; there is not a single pictograph on it. (Ricks, 1969; Kelly, 1966)

The presence of writing can also be inferred from secondary information. For example, astronomical knowledge exhibited in Mesoamerica must have required maintenance of detailed records for centuries.

Coe (1962) believes that by the time of the Classic period (A.D. 300-A.D. 900), literacy was Pan Mexican, with a few isolated areas excepted. "Although no books have survived into our day, we have every reason to believe that most people possessed them."

Circular stone instrument believed to be a weapon with a hand grip in the middle. It is about 20 centimeters in diameter.

Two stone instruments believed to be weapons, or axe heads, found in the museum at Santiago Tuxtla, which is at the base of the Cerro Vigía.

11. WEAPONRY IN IMMEDIATE VICINITY OF HILL

The museum in Santiago Tuxtla, at the base of the Cerro Vigía, has on display only a few artifacts from the vicinity of the hill. However, the director was kind enough to allow us to inspect and photograph artifacts brought in by townspeople which are stored in large boxes at the museum. Not only are there arrowheads and spear points, but also a variety of axe heads and other fearsome stone weapons. One, since placed on display, is shaped like a large donut with a hand grip in the middle. Hopefully, future investigations will provide weaponry from known locations and time periods. One farmer living on the southern slope of the hill showed me a stone axe head found on his property.

Nephite swords were probably not of the stainless steel variety often pictured. Rather, they were more likely pieces of hardwood edged with obsidian, a volcanic glass. The wood could not survive in that climate down to the present time from A.D. 400, but the obsidian would. We have found obsidian blades at open mounds on the base of the hill. The presence of obsidian is not a distinguishing feature, however, because it is found in abundance at most Preclassic archæological sites.

12. ASTRONOMY, AND 13. CALENDAR

Observation of the heavenly bodies was intimately tied to development of an accurate calendar. So accurate were the observations recorded that the Maya possessed a calendar superior to that of the Europeans who came to "civilize" them. According to Aveni (1979), the periods of Venus were represented with such high accuracy in the Dresden Codex that the error in the predicted Venus period was just four hours in one millennium.

Ancient historical accounts place intense interest in astronomy sometime before Christ. The earliest records were interwoven by an eighteenth-century Spanish/Mexican scholar, Mariano Veytia. He reported concerning the early inhabitants of Mexico:

> Experience had taught them through the years that there was a connection between the invariant order and regulated movement of the stars, and the climate, variety of the seasons and productivity of the earth. Therefore, they began to dedicate themselves to observation of the stars, and especially the sun and the moon, whose magnitude made it easier for them to follow its movements. This does not mean that until that time they were so stupid that they were ignorant of the movements of the heavenly bodies and their effect upon the seasons, but at that time there began to be some men who distinguished themselves. They were thoughtful and attentive to the study of the heavenly bodies, and dedicated themselves to measurement of the annual movements which they computed. (Veytia, 1836:31)

Veytia suggests that they followed a lunar calendar for some time while they were making those measurements. Finally, the astronomers all got together in a place called Huehuetlapallan to ". . . correct the calendar and reform the computation system. They knew that the system they had been following was erroneous." (p. 32)

Malmstrom (1978) theorizes that the Mayan long count was established at Izapa in 235 B.C. Whether or not he is correct as to both the date and place is not quite as important as recognition that there was very sophisticated knowledge of the true length of the solar year, derived from astronomical measurements, sometime before Christ. In accordance with the ancient writings, archæologists now believe that solstitial sightings using the sun were most important in these advances. For example, at Izapa the monuments are aligned with a pyramid and the top of Volcano Tajumulco in such a manner as to give an accurate sighting of the summer sunrise solstice.

The manner in which the Mayan long count was constructed resulted in a great, great cycle of 25,626 years. Astronomer Robert Bass, in an unpublished paper, pointed to the coincidence of that computation with the precession of the equinox that has a cycle of 25,695 years. If they were aware of the precession of the equinox, it could only have been due to maintenance of accurate written records for many generations.

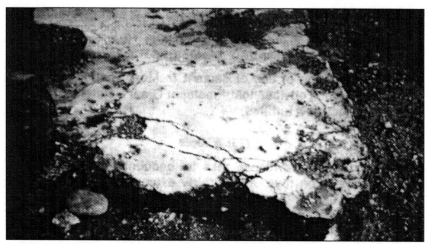

Cement used to surface the temple at Chiapa de Corzo now known as Mound 1. A picture of that temple is shown in Chapter 7.

14. CEMENT

The use of cement and concrete spread throughout Mesoamerica in a time span from at least as early as 100 B.C. through A.D. 400. The tourist sees it in great abundance at Teotihuacán. At Kaminaljuyú the concrete mix was similar. Tiny pieces of volcanic stone, 0.5 to 2 millimeters in diameter, were mixed with clay and lime. After drying, a very smooth and durable surface is formed. An early manifestation of the use of cement is at Chiapa de Corzo, where it was used to surface the temple known as Mound 1. This can also be seen at Monte Albán.

The knowledge of this use of cement in Mesoamerica has not been around for many decades. In 1929, Heber J. Grant, a former president of The Church of Jesus Christ of Latter-day Saints, made the following statement in general conference:

> . . . I have often said, and desire to repeat here that when I was a young unmarried man, another young man who had received a doctor's degree ridiculed me for believing in the Book of Mormon. He said he could point out two lies in that book. One was that the people had built their homes out of cement and that they were very skillful in the use of cement. He said there had never been found and never would be found a house built of cement by the ancient inhabitants of this country, because the people in that early age knew nothing about cement. He said that should be enough to make one

disbelieve the book. l said: "That does not affect my faith one particle. l read the Book of Mormon prayerfully and supplicated God for a testimony in my heart and soul of the divinity of it, and I have accepted it and believe it with all my heart." I also said to him, "If my children do not find cement houses, I expect that my grandchildren will." He said, "Well, what is the good of talking with a fool like that?" (April 1929 C.R. p.128 ff)

The documentation of use of cement in Mesoamerica is now so overwhelming and obvious that President Grant's statement stands out as prophecy now fulfilled.

15. WHEELS

The only direct evidence thus far encountered for wheels in Mesoamerica is on toys. About thirty examples of wheeled toys have been found, the earliest of which were discovered at Tres Zapotes by Matthew Stirling. For a more complete discussion, the reader is referred to Cheesman. (1974) So far there is no solid evidence for practical application of the wheel, but its use might be inferred from the movement of twenty-ton monuments, in Olmec times, over very large distances. At least part of the distance was overland. If the wheels in general use at that time were wooden, which is most likely, we would not expect to find evidence of them today because of the poor preservation factor caused by the high humidity of Mesoamerican lowlands.

Wheeled toy found in Veracruz.
On display at museum of Jalapa, Veracruz.

SUMMARY

1. The Cerro Vigía ("lookout hill") is proposed as the location of Mormon's Cumorah, site of the last Jaredite and Nephite battles. It stands out from the Tuxtla mountain chain in southern Veracruz.

2. All geographic criteria are met remarkably well by this location.

3. All archæological criteria are met by this location.

4. The military advantage sought by Mormon was production of food, in what is one of the best-watered and most fertile areas of the New World.

5. There is evidence that at least three volcanos erupted in Mesoamerica at about the time of the Savior's crucifixion.

6. Important archæological ruins dating to both Jaredite and Nephite times surround the Cerro Vigía.

7. Weaponry has been found around the hill and there are ancient constructions on top of it.

8. Though the Cerro Vigía passes all the criteria set down in the pages of the Book of Mormon, that does not necessarily prove that the correct hill has been identified. Any proposed alternative must, however, be subjected to the same stringent tests and pass them all.

6

THE TIMES OF THE JAREDITES

> *And they were exceedingly industrious, and they did buy and sell and traffic one with another . . . And they did work all manner of fine work . . . And they did work all manner of work of exceedingly curious workmanship.*
>
> *Ether 10:22-28*

Olmec head found at San Lorenzo and now on display at museum in Jalapa, Veracruz.

In about 1860, a laborer working in a sugar cane field on the ranch called Hueapan discovered on the surface of the ground something that had the appearance of an inverted iron kettle. The owner of the hacienda ordered it excavated. What they discovered was an enormous granite head, two meters in height. The location of this find was near the town of Tres Zapotes, just west of the Cerro Vigía. Reports of the discovery were obscure until the pioneering expedition of Matthew Stirling in 1938.

Stirling not only uncovered a number of monuments, but with support from the Smithsonian Institution and the National Geographic Society he began archæological studies of the group of great earthen mounds which comprised the remains of an ancient city. In the course of the diggings the expedition uncovered the famous Stela C of Tres Zapotes, now believed to give the date of 31 B.C.

What was the connection of these ruins with Book of Mormon peoples? If Cerro Vigía was Mormon's Cumorah, there must have been some direct connection, but what was it? These questions are not too different from the questions and arguments which swept the archæological community in the 1940's and early 1950's.

The name of the people who built Tres Zapotes and related sites is unknown. Unfortunately, a name was chosen which would both stick like glue and cause confusion; "Olmec." The name was picked on the assumption that these were the Olmecs spoken of in the ancient chronicle accounts as the Ulmeca-Xicallanca. We shall speak of those people in the next chapter, distinguishing the earlier people of Tres Zapotes as the archæological Olmec. In this chapter we shall refer only to the latter.

The second problem in identification of these people relative to the Book of Mormon was chronology. Though Mexican archæologists and Matthew Stirling believed that the Olmec civilization was older than the Maya (A.D. 300-900), their opinion was subordinated to that of the "establishment" which held that the Olmec couldn't possibly be older than the Maya. The Mexican theorists were vindicated in 1957 when a series of radiocarbon dates from charcoal and wood found at La Venta showed that the Olmec civilization flourished from the late second millennium B.C. to the middle of the first millennium B.C. The Olmecs had apparently developed the first great civilization and cultural tradition in the New World.

Could the Olmecs have been Jaredites? I am not alone in believing that the latter half of Jaredite history is closely related to that of the Olmecs. Now in order to understand why that claim is made, it will be necessary for the reader to examine with me two areas of importance: the chronology and geography of the Jaredites. After establishing that foundation, I will try to give an understandable summary of the culture history of the Jaredites down to the time of their destruction. The close match between the archæological record and the Book of Ether account will reinforce what has been said concerning the logical setting of the Cerro Vigía for the last Jaredite battles. The archæological record also helps to flesh out many details which are omitted in the Book of Ether, and to develop a mental picture of what their culture may have been like.

THE JAREDITES IN TIME AND SPACE

The chronological development of the Jaredite civilization is vitally important to our attempts to correlate it with archæology. Because of the absence of absolute dates in the Book of Ether, a number of assumptions and approximations have been made. The logic behind those assumptions can be found in the Appendix. Overall, I place the Jaredite culture between 2700 B.C. and 600 B.C. Chart #2, p. 128, shows the division of time in an arbitrary but consistent manner throughout the generations of the Jaredites. Two lost generations are assumed between Riplakish and Morianton, where there is no indication in the text that a father-son relationship existed, and where a "space of many years" is mentioned. (Ether 10:9) Throughout this chapter frequent reference will be made to the chronology chart. The dates listed should be considered subject to an error of from 50 years in the time of Ether to as much as 150 years during some of the intermediate generations.

Map #3, p. 255, shows the land of Moron in the valley of Oaxaca. Moron was important to the Jaredites from the very beginning down to the time of the final destruction. The other area of importance is the isthmus area and southern Veracruz, which we will look to beginning in the time of Lib, about 1500 B.C. The other areas of Mesoamerica are not referred to directly, except in connection with trade where wider contacts might be inferred. Therefore, they must have been peripheral to the main focus of Jaredite life. Map #7, p. 260, shows the relative location of these areas and indicates the location of important ruins from the 2300-600 B.C. time period.

It should be emphasized that there were more lineages than just the Jaredites. There were the descendants of the brother of Jared, and perhaps other offshoots. There may have even been other peoples who arrived on the scene and made their mark. These lineages, possibly even different races, competed with each other for power continually. That was, in the end, the path to destruction.

Famous Olmec sculpture known as the "wrestler."
Found at Santa Maria on the Uspanapa River in the Isthmus of
Tehuantepec. This statue quite likely represents one of the
races of people competing during Jaredite times.

Chart #2
Jaredite Chronology

B.C. Dates	Generation (mid life age)	Event or Cultural Feature
2700	**Jared**	Departure from Mesopotamia and over-water journey.
2630	**Orihah**	Establishment of Moron in highlands.
2560	**Kib**	
2500	**Shule**	Knowledge of "steel."
2430	**Omer**	Short-lived settlement on east coast near Ramah. Moron population reduced to 30 by wars.
2370	**Emer**	Domesticated animals including elephants and horses.
2290	**Coriantum**	Cities built.
2230	**Com**	
2160	**Heth**	Destruction of most people by drought and famine; poisonous serpents.
2090	**Shez**	
2020	**Riplakish**	Society organized, many cities, grain, domesticated animals, precious metal working.
1820	**Morianton**	
1750	**Kim**	In captivity.
1680	**Levi**	In captivity.
1620	**Corom**	
1550	**Kish**	
1480	**Lib**	City built by narrow neck of land, development of a great new culture.
1410	**Hearthom**	In captivity.
1350	**Heth**	In captivity.
1280	**Aaron**	In captivity.
1210	**Amnigaddah**	In captivity.
1140	**Coriantum**	In captivity.
1070	**Com**	Civil war and division of kingdom; secret combinations.
1010	**Shiblom**	Wars, famine, pestilence.
940	**Seth**	In captivity.
870	**Ahah**	Obtained the kingdom and caused much wickedness.
800	**Ethem**	
740	**Moron**	Civil war.
670	**Coriantor**	
600	**Ether**	Final civil war destruction of Jaredites. Coriantumr and Ether survive. Ether completes his history of the Jaredites.

THE STRUGGLE FOR SURVIVAL (2700 B.C.-2000 B.C.)

The Jaredites came from the great tower commonly known as "Babel" where there was a confusion of tongues and the people dispersed throughout the world. Arguments can be made for travel to America either across the Pacific in an easterly direction, or across the Mediterranean and the Atlantic in a westerly direction. Archæological sites consistent with a trans-Atlantic crossing in 2700 B.C. are El Cuello on the coast of Yucatan or Santa Luisa in Veracruz. It makes little difference to our archæological interpretation of Jaredite history which ocean was crossed, since the first mentioned settlement was Moron, in the highlands of Oaxaca. That area could have been approached either from the Pacific or the Atlantic.

Unfortunately, a period of about 700 years passed before the Jaredites were able to even begin to establish a civilized nation. It was about four hundred years before any cities were mentioned. Subsequent to that, in about 2160 B.C., the population was decimated by drought and serpents.

The problem was that the Jaredite leaders were power-hungry tyrants. In one account Jared, the son of King Omer, rebelled against his father and brought him into captivity. In a counterrevolution, Jared's warriors were killed and he capitulated. He then schemed to obtain the kingdom by trading his daughter to another schemer named Akish. The price was the head of Jared's father. King Omer learned of the plan and fled. After Jared took the throne he was the one to lose his head, because Akish killed his own father-in-law. Later, jealous of a son, Akish starved him to death. His other sons rebelled against him, and the resulting war reduced the population in that part of the land to a total of thirty people.

The archæological record indicates that prior to 2000 B.C. there were a few sites in Oaxaca exhibiting evidence of sedentary populations which did not have the use of pottery, or other trades. For example, the site of Zazanu in Oaxaca dates to about 2400 B.C. and was preceramic. Radiocarbon dates reported by Bernal (1965) have been corrected, giving 2340 and 2440 B.C., plus or minus about two hundred years.

Overall, the archæological record and the data in the Book of Ether are both sketchy for this earliest period. However, there is congruence in the general picture of a people who are struggling, trying to develop their agricultural technology in order to break loose from the total preoccupation with finding food. The greatest advances during this period were the domestication of corn, a hardy hybrid, as well as varieties of beans and squash.

Early Formative Village Life (2000 B.C.-1500 B.C.)

Archæologists apply the term "early preclassic" to this period of time, which in some accounts goes back as far as 2300 B.C. It applies to those areas where settled villages and evidences of pottery are found. These villages are found in the Tehuacan valley, the valley of Mexico (El Arbolillo, Zacatenco, Tlatilco), on the coast near Acapulco, and near Oaxaca City.

A distinguishing feature of this early time period is an abundance of figurines of nude women with very exaggerated hips. Some are depicted wearing short skirts. This cultural style carries on down to at least 1000 B.C. One feature of society at this time was the development of harems. We read that "Riplakish did not do that which was right in the sight of the Lord, for he did have many wives and concubines . . ." (Ether 10:5)

In my chronology of the Book of Ether the beginning of the Early Preclassic period corresponds with the time of Riplakish. He apparently created a certain amount of social organization, for ". . . he did lay that upon men's shoulders which was grievous to be borne; yea he did tax them with heavy taxes; and with the taxes he did build many spacious buildings." He also built a throne, and many prisons. Those who would not be subject to the taxes, or those who could not pay the taxes, were cast into prison ". . . and he did cause that they should labor continually for their support . . ." The prisoners provided the fine workmanship and refined gold.

Several generations later, at the time of Morianton, there were "many cities." Evidently the social organization developed by Morianton, perhaps coupled with improvements in agriculture, bore fruit. He was able to build up many cities, "and the people became exceeding rich under his reign, both in buildings, and in gold and silver, and in raising grain, and in flocks, and herds . . ." (Ether 10:12)

We are told only of the lineage of Jared in identifiable terms. If they were in Oaxaca, perhaps the descendants of the brother of Jared were in the valley of Mexico. Descendants of the friends of Jared may by that time have been in other Mesoamerican settings or in remote spots that would have no further direct contact with the "Jaredites."

THE GREAT LEAP FORWARD (1500 B.C.-1000 B.C.)
HIGHLANDS AREA

In about 1500 B.C. a number of important ceremonial centers sprang to life. One which represented a continuation of occupation from 2000 B.C. was San Jose Mogote, near Etla (north of Oaxaca City). Typical of the public buildings erected was Structure 6, which measured 4.4 x 5.4 meters. It had a solid foundation upon which was built walls with pine interiors. The walls and floor were daubed with clay and then stuccoed with white lime plaster. This town ("city" in Jaredite terminology) developed into a ceremonial center covering over twenty acres.

Stone construction at the top of a large mound at San Jose Mogote. The enclosed area protects a monument which has early calendar inscriptions. There is a possibility that this was the city of Moron.

Contributing to the economic base of the town was development of advanced irrigation techniques. (Flannery, 1967) Canals (now fossilized) and ancient wells have been found. A consequence of the introduction of irrigation was that half the population was able to turn to craft manufacture. Some of the objects discovered in the excavations at San José Mogote can be seen in a tiny museum in the village. These include big-hip figurines, delicately-worked shell ornaments, worked jade, and even worked iron. There were a score of iron mines in the valley which were exploited. The workers somehow extracted the iron in chunks and polished it with whetstones, a sample of which can be seen there. Pieces of iron mirrors and chunks of the magnetite ore can also be seen in the museum. It is clear that the workshops were part of a trading network that developed, but where were the elite that demanded such luxury goods?

DEVELOPMENT IN THE ISTHMUS

The answer to that question is to found on the Gulf Coast of Mexico in the region of the isthmus of Tehuantepec shown on Map #7, p. 260. There were earlier occupations, but sometime after 1500 B.C. San Lorenzo was constructed as a full-blown Olmec city. Dates by Coe and Diehl (1980) were corrected based on the article by Damon, et al (1974). Phase A dates run from 1422 B.C. to 1266 B.C. and phase B dates run from 1266 B.C. to 1130 B.C. The adjacent sites of Tenochtitlan and Potrero Nuevo were supporting sites to San Lorenzo. It was the first capital of Olmec culture.

Great amounts of physical labor were expended in construction of this city. Their water system had large artificial ponds with clay bottoms to prevent water loss. These were connected to the entire site by a series of covered troughs so everyone could have access to the water. The population was about 1000. This became the center of a large and far-flung trading empire. It brought jade, obsidian, iron, and probably some perishable items. The most conspicuous consumption related to sixty-five large stone monuments found there. There are massive stone heads weighing up to eighteen tons that appear to have represented the different rulers. There were also large altars and other images that appear to have represented the rulers. They were transported all the way from the Tuxtla mountains, probably using water transportation in part. The land journeys may have been accomplished using ropes and rollers.

CITY OF LIB

Reference to Book of Mormon chronology shows that the important "San Lorenzo" phases at that site may have begun during the time of Lib. See also Norman's work on the subject ("San Lorenzo as the Jaredite city of Lib," SEHA Newsletter, #153, June 1983). Perhaps the explanation Coe seeks could be found in examination of the generations just preceding Lib. About two

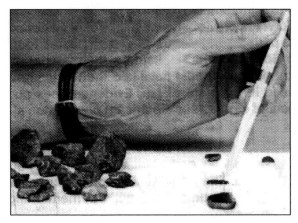

Chunks of magnetite ore and remnants of very smooth iron mirrors which were found by the University of Michigan in excavations of workshops at San Jose Mogote. They are three thousand years old.

Photographer Dan Bates stands atop a partially uncovered Olmec head at the site of San Lorenzo.

hundred years previously, king Levi ended a period of civil wars and began a period of righteousness which lasted four or five generations. The Book of Ether is silent on the material progress made during that time, but it must have laid the foundation for the great advance made in the time of Lib. Evidence does suggest several hundred years of earlier, less significant occupation at San Lorenzo.

There has been a tendency for hard lines to be drawn between those who believe that culture developed in America independent of outside influence and those who believe it was mostly due to diffusion from the Old World. The Book of Mormon describes a magnificent cultural advance in the time of Lib without mentioning any outside influence whatsoever.

During the time of Lib the area described by Moroni as southward from the isthmus (eastward in modern coordinates) was opened up to development, beginning with hunting. At that time the Jaredites ". . . built a great city by the narrow neck of land, by the place where the sea divides the land." (Ether 10:20) The location of San Lorenzo in the heart of the isthmus of Tehuantepec just where the river Chiquito and the river Coatzacoalcos create an island (see Alma 3:3 for use of "sea" to refer to a river) could not have fit better the Book of Mormon description of the location of the city of Lib.

Not only do the location and timing of Lib's city fit San Lorenzo, but there is also the description of development of a great culture at that time.

> And they were exceedingly industrious, and they did buy and sell and traffic one with another, that they might get gain. And they did work in all manner of ore, and they did make gold, and silver, and iron, and brass, and all manner of metals; and they did dig it out of the earth; wherefore they did cast up mighty heaps of earth to get ore, of gold and of silver and of iron, and of copper. And they did work all manner of fine work. And they did have silks, and fine-twined linen; and they did work all manner of cloth, that they might clothe themselves from their nakedness. And they did make all manner of tools to till the earth, both to plow and to sow, to reap and to hoe, and also to thrash. And they did make all manner of tools with which they did work their beasts. And they did make all manner of weapons of war. And they did work all manner of work of exceedingly curious workmanship. And never could be a people more blessed than were they, and more prospered by the hand of the Lord. And they were in a land that was choice above all lands, for the Lord had spoken it.   (Ether 10:22-28)

**Olmec were-jaguar. On display at Parque La Venta
in Villahermosa, Mexico.**

ARCHÆOLOGICAL VERIFICATION FOR THE CULTURE OF LIB

Items from the preceding list which have been archæologically verified include

1. *traffic in goods*—the flavor of Olmec culture is seen
throughout much of Mesoamerica, principally along trade
routes, and especially those routes which led to sources of serpentine and jade. Important stopovers on the northern trade
route included Chalcatzingo in Morelos, Las Bocas in Puebla,
Tlatilco and Tlapacoya in the valley of Mexico. Along the Pacific
coast from Laguna Zope in the isthmus of Tehuantepec, the
Olmec established way stations down as far as El Salvador and
Costa Rica. Bernal (1969:87) believes that for the most part the

Olmec imported the raw materials and worked them at home, exporting a certain number of them. Bernal's hypothesis may be modified somewhere due to the discovery of workshops at San José Mogote in Oaxaca which must have exported finished goods directly to the Olmecs.

2. ***working in ore***—thus far we have evidence only for iron.

3. ***all manner of fine work***—amply evidenced by the expertly designed and polished serpentine and jade figurines which have been found.

4. ***weapons of war***—war-like themes are seen in rock carvings at Chalcatzingo. Bernal is convinced that the Olmecs maintained their empire with armies. (Bernal, 1969:88) Obsidian-edged swords, knives, and lances are shown on the monuments. Altar 4 at La Venta shows a captive bound with a rope, and scenes of war are shown.

5. ***cloth and clothing***—no cloth has survived from the period, and many of the figurines show men wearing only loincloths and the women wearing only short skirts. If that was the tradition, then the period of righteousness at the time of Lib may have been a time for more modesty as noted by this phrase ". . . that they might clothe themselves from their nakedness." Deep within a cave near Acapulco has been found the only surviving Olmec painting. Nearly a mile from the entrance to the cave of Juxtlahuaca there is a painting of a king wearing a feathered headdress and an orange and red striped tunic. A man kneeling in front of him, who is bearded, wears a colored hat. A word for "spinning thread" is found in the earliest Olmec language, Mixe-Zoque, by Campbell and Kaufman (1976). They take it as evidence for for use of textiles as early as 1500 B.C.

6. ***all manner of work of exceedingly curious workmanship***— this phrase is probably more true for the art produced during the Olmec period than during any other period of Mesoamerican history. Long after the Olmecs themselves had been destroyed, attempts were made to copy the style. Particularly noteworthy are the jaguar characteristics infused into otherwise normal representations of humans, such as having the mouths turned down at the corners. Clefts in the heads and elongated heads were also characteristic. The great heads and other monuments created after the time of Lib were likely seen by Moroni, and may have contributed to his commentary. I have already noted the large stone head found on the Cerro Vigía and the Olmec monuments at Tres Zapotes which were probably seen by Moroni.

Typical Olmec statue. Note the cross below the chin, the notch in the middle of the cap, and the facial features which resemble those of a jaguar. From the National Museum of Anthropology, Mexico City.

OTHER JAREDITE CITIES

There were other great cities built during this time period around the isthmus of Tehuantepec and the land southward. Laguna Zop, located on the Pacific side of the isthmus, just a kilometer from Juchitan, was a very important regional trading center covering one-hundred acres. Going back perhaps as far as 1700 B.C., it developed ties with the Olmec heartland, with Oaxaca, with the Central Depression of Chiapas where Chiapa de Corzo was getting started, and along the Pacific coast towards Guatemala. The Olmec art style was simply superimposed there on existing art forms. Obsidian found at Laguna Zope came from El Chayal, near Guatemala City. (Zeitlin, 1978)

Within the Olmec heartland, several other cities were started before 1000 B.C. These include Laguna de Los Cerros, which in terms of population was probably the largest and may have been one of the named Jaredite cities. La Venta was the greatest of the ceremonial centers. It was built along a ridge in a symmetric manner, centering about courts and a volcano-shaped pyramid.

**Monument of seated Olmec ruler on display in the
National Museum of Anthropology, Mexico City.
Note the pendant hung from the neck, believed to be a representation
of the concave iron mirrors worn by the rulers. The head and arms were
knocked off deliberately, probably in a civil war.**

THE CIVIL WAR

The first phase of Olmec culture came to an end with a civil war centering about San Lorenzo. It was followed by a precipitous decline in the influence of San Lorenzo and the ascendency of La Venta. Coe placed this destruction at about 900 B.C., which must be moved back about two hundred years due to the recalibration of radiocarbon dates and the dendrochronological correction factor. The latest of the series of radiocarbon dates from the San Lorenzo phase (pre civil war phase) of San Lorenzo is 1110-1140 B.C.

An unfortunate consequence of the civil war was destruction of the monuments at San Lorenzo. Heads were knocked off the smaller monuments, and most were buried deep in the earth. It took a magnetometer survey of the site to discover their location. Coe speculates concerning their purposeful destruction as follows: (1968:86)

> The amount of pent-up hatred and fury represented by this enormous act of destruction must have been awesome indeed. These monuments are very large, and basalt is a very hard stone. Wherever possible, heads were smashed from bodies, "altars" were smashed to pieces and strange dimpled depressions and slots were cut into Colossal Heads. There are no signs that wedges or the fire and water treatment were used to break up the larger stones; rather, I suspect that they built huge tripods over monuments, hoisted other monuments over these, and let them drop from great heights. Why was this done? Because the Olmec monuments must have stood for the class of leaders that held the tributary populace in such a firm grip, forcing from them incredible expenditures of labor. These stones must have been the symbols of all that had held them in thrall, and they destroyed these symbols with as much fervor as the Hungarian revolutionaries toppled the giant statue of Stalin in Budapest in 1956.

Let us now question how these data and interpretations from archæology relate to the Book of Mormon.

We learn from the Book of Ether that soon after the cultural advances had been made, the king was dethroned and there was a slave state established. We do not know what lineage was responsible. Were these a lineage that came with Jared, or were they new arrivals from the Old World? That cannot be answered now, and the Book of Mormon doesn't even hint. What we are told is that the slave state carried on through the generations of Hearthom, Heth, Aaron, Amnigaddah, and Coriantum. These truly Jaredite slaves could have been the manpower used by the rulers of San Lorenzo to create the giant stone heads and other monuments.

In our chronology, the time of a great civil war was in the generation of Com, which falls in about 1070 B.C. The rebellion was led by Com in attempting to gain freedom from servitude.

> And it came to pass that Com drew away the half of the kingdom. And he reigned over the half of the kingdom forty and two years; and he went to battle against the king, Amgid, and they fought for the space of many years, during which time Com gained power over Amgid, and obtained power over the remainder of the kingdom.   (Ether 11:32)

Statue of a crouching man found at San Lorenzo.
The head was deliberately knocked off, probably during the destruction
which accompanied a civil war at San Lorenzo. It appears that
the statue may have originally had wooden arms that pivoted.

DEGENERACY AND DESTRUCTION
(1000 B.C. TO 600 B.C.)

The Book of Mormon paints the last four hundred years of Jaredite history as having reeked with degeneracy. There was another civil war in which the unrighteous took the upper hand, just a generation after Com. The prophets were put to death. In the next generation the reins of power shifted again and Seth was in captivity. His son Ahah regained the kingdom. "He did do all manner of iniquity in his days, by which he did cause the shedding of much blood . . . ." The subsequent king, Ethem, (about

800 B.C.) "also did do that which was wicked in his days." Furthermore we read, "Ethem did execute judgment in wickedness all his days." His son Moron succeeded him on the throne and "did that which was wicked before the Lord." Not only the kings but also the people rejected the prophets. ". . . the people hardened their hearts, and would not hearken unto their words; and the prophets mourned and withdrew from among the people."

In the days of Moron, just two generations before the final Jaredite war, there were two civil wars. The first was a battle between the bad and the worse. (11:14-15) In the second, a descendant of the brother of Jared, obviously a competing lineage, took over the kingdom. Right down to the end, the people failed to repent. ". . . There were none of the fair sons and daughters upon the face of the whole earth who repented of their sins." (Ether 13:17) Other than these spiritually-motivated judgments, there is nothing said concerning the culture during this period of time.

JAREDITE DESTRUCTION DESCRIBED BY THE BOOK OF MORMON

The last king was Coriantumr. He is often called the last Jaredite king, but it appears that he was in fact a descendant of the brother of Jared. (See 11:17-23, 12:1.) He was told by Ether, a prophet descended from Jared, that his entire household (lineage) would be destroyed if they did not repent. He was also told that he alone would survive to see other people take over the land. This prophecy was literally fulfilled, as a terribly bitter civil war that went on for years eventually resulted in the deaths of all but Coriantumr. The geographical references pertaining to that last battle have been discussed previously. It will suffice to say that there is no indication that they left their heartland. The Cerro Vigía was very much part of that Olmec heartland and could very well have been the hill called "Ramah" by the Jaredites where so many people were killed. Altogether, something on the order of three million people were reported killed in these battles. This must have completely depleted the heartland of the Jaredites of population, bringing their culture pretty much to an end.

The Book of Mormon does not say that everyone on the continent was destroyed, only the lineage of Coriantumr. It is reasonable to assume that elsewhere in Mesoamerica there were people who had no interest in fighting in somebody else's war. They could be expected to carry on with a few of the crumbs from the table of Jaredite culture.

OLMEC LIFE

The center of Olmec power shifted from San Lorenzo to La Venta, located close to the Gulf of Mexico and just a couple of miles east of the River Tonalá. There is now evidence that it had many supporting sites along several rivers that used to run close to it. Some of those sites had luxury goods while others did not. That would be indicative of some lineages serving in slavery for long periods. The most impressive pyramid of its time was built here. It was shaped like a volcano, apparently imitating the form of many volcanic peaks in the Tuxtla Mountains.

Most of the monuments from La Venta have been moved to La Venta Park in Villahermosa. Entering that park is to enter into an ancient world with much grandeur and awe that those monuments inspired. Yet, most of the materials for these monuments had to be brought some 100 kilometers from the Tuxtla Mountains. The monuments exemplify rulers, animals and events in formats that are extraordinary.

The Olmecs probably had writing. An example of a late form appears on a stela down in Guatemala that is dated to 148 B.C. It is still undeciphered. The early leaders may have had charge of astronomical observations so they could regulate the planting of crops. They had many tools with which they could carve the monuments, work their animals and harvest crops. Many benefits came from the social organization of the Olmecs. Towards the end of 1000 B.C. to 600 B.C. life in La Venta, richly-stocked tombs constructed of enormous basalt columns were constructed for protection. Perhaps the leaders became enamored with power and riches. For whatever reason, the Olmec civilization suddenly died in about 600 B.C. "By that time," says Bernal, "the city was at its zenith and, like ripe fruit, ready to fall." (Bernal, 1969:111)

THE MYSTERY OF THE DISAPPEARANCE OF THE OLMECS

Michael Coe summarized what archæologists know about the demise of the Olmecs when he said,

> Then La Venta comes to an end. The cause and nature of its fate is lost in mystery, a mystery that we shall also see at the great Olmec center of San Lorenzo. All construction comes to a halt, no more tombs are built and stocked, no more offerings are made beneath its multi-colored floors. Its ruler and people are gone, and year after year the nortes come howling in from the coast, shrouding the ruins of La Venta in drift sands. Olmec civilization had died.   (Coe,1968)

Central pyramid at La Venta, constructed one millennium before Christ by the Olmecs. It is over thirty meters high and gives a commanding view of the countryside. It is shaped like one of the volcanoes in the Tuxtla Mountains. Basalt columns in the foreground were hewn anciently and transported perhaps a hundred kilometers to La Venta.

Fables were invented to explain the destruction of these people. As the legend goes, there was a terrible calamity, with hurricanes so strong they knocked over the trees. The only ones to survive were those who hid in caves. Veytia says, "In this calamity the greater part of the giants who had inhabited the land of Anahuac perished. The only ones to escape had gone inland, and lived along the banks of the river Atoyac, between the city of Tlaxcala and the city of Puebla." (Veytia, 1836:27-28) Though his dating must be viewed with some caution, his date of 601 B.C. for this destruction is certainly interesting.

Archæology bears record that life continued on after the destruction of the Olmecs. The satellite areas such as the Pacific coast and the valley of Mexico continued on, as did life in the newly formed centre of Monte Albán in Oaxaca. Traces of the old art style continued on, being called "Olmecoid." Particularly

**Stone monument on display at La Democracia, Guatemala.
It was likely carved by remnants of the Jaredites who may
have been subjugated by the Lamanites.**

interesting is the adaptation of the stone-head idea on the Pacific coast of Guatemala. At sites such as Monte Alto and Bilbao there were large boulders turned into images of very rotund men. Bernal places these sites at about 500 B.C., based on radiocarbon dates.

I speculate that the Lamanites subjugated some of these indigenous people when they separated from the Nephites. This gave them a power base and sufficient manpower for their many wars with the Nephites.

SUMMARY

1. The history of the Jaredites in the Book of Ether runs from about 2700 B.C. to 600 B.C.

2. Until about 2000 B.C. there was a struggle for survival. Archæological sites dating to that time indicate an unsophisticated population.

3. From 2000 B.C. to 1500 B.C. the Jaredites made significant cultural advances and built many towns. Their highland capital of Moron was likely in the valley of Oaxaca. Archæologists call this period the "Early Preclassic" because there was pottery, farming, and settled villages.

4. Olmec culture developed in the isthmus of Tehuantepec at San Lorenzo, beginning in 1500 B.C. There was massive social organization and creation of enormous basalt monuments hauled long distances. The location, timing, and nature of this city coincides with the Book of Mormon description of the city of Lib.

5. The timing of the civil war which destroyed San Lorenzo coincides with a civil war in the time of Com. It resulted from a revolt of those who had been enslaved.

6. The decadence of the remaining years of the Jaredites can be seen in the monumental works of stone at sites such as La Venta. Exploitation of the masses was required to create the monumental, jaguar-centered culture of the archæological Olmecs.

7. The Olmecs disappeared at the same time as the Jaredites were destroyed, in about 600 B.C.

8. A location of the last battle at the Cerro Vigía, which is within the Olmec heartland, is completely consistent with the theory that the Jaredites and related lineages are connected to the Olmecs.

9. There is evidence for survivors of the last battle, particularly from places remote from the last battleground.

7

THE MULEKITES— FROM CUMORAH TO ZARAHEMLA

> *. . . and the land north was called Mulek, which was after the son of Zedekiah; for the Lord did bring Mulek into the land north . . . it being the place of their first landing. And they came from there up into the south wilderness.*
>
> *Helaman 6:10, Alma 22:30-31*

The Book of Mormon was not written as a comprehensive history, but rather as the record of the people of Nephi. It is, therefore, only from occasional glimpses that we catch the impact upon the Nephites of their contemporaries. The story of Mormon's Cumorah would not be complete without bringing into focus the Mulekites, a major group of people who bridged the historical gap between destruction of the Jaredites and the rise of Nephite culture. The context of the Mulekite contact with Jaredite culture is useful in further substantiating a Gulf Coast location for Mormon's Cumorah. We will go beyond that encounter, however, and follow the Mulekites as they developed their culture in the land of Zarahemla and branched out into other areas.

WHO WERE THE MULEKITES?

The account by Mormon speaks of the "people of Zarahemla," a group found by the Nephites in about 250 B.C. The Nephites encountered them after leaving their mountain-valley home of the Land of Nephi to avoid persecution by the Lamanites. The people serving King Zarahemla were more numerous than the Nephites. (Omni 13-22; Mosiah 25:2) Zarahemla was a descendant of Mulek, the only son of King Zedekiah to survive the Babylonian destruction of Jerusalem. (Helaman 8:21) The word "Mulekites" is not found in the Book of Mormon. However, it is an apt designation for not only those under the leadership of Zarahemla, but also others in the original migration whose descendants went to other areas of Mesoamerica. A FARMS publication (*Insights*, June 1984) gives interesting evidence that the name "Mulek" could mean "son of the King" in Hebrew.

MIGRATION FROM JERUSALEM

The Mulekite migration to the New World appears to have been between the destruction of Jerusalem, 587 B.C., and the overthrow of Babylon in 539 B.C. This I adduce from the phrase "driven out," used in the following account:

> And now we know that Jerusalem was destroyed according to the words of Jeremiah . . . And now will you dispute that Jerusalem was destroyed? Will ye say that the sons of Zedekiah [king of Judah] were not slain, all except it were Mulek? Yea, and do ye not behold that the seed of Zedekiah are with us, and they were driven out of the land of Jerusalem? (Helaman 8:20-21)

The idea that they may have been led by men of God is conveyed by this statement:

> Mosiah discovered that the people of Zarahemla came out from Jerusalem at the time that Zedekiah, king of Judah, was carried away captive into Babylon. And they journeyed in the wilderness, and were brought by the hand of the Lord across the great waters, into the land where Mosiah discovered them. (Omni 15-16)

There are two indicators that the Mulekites crossed the Atlantic Ocean rather than the Pacific Ocean. First, the people of Mulek encountered the sole survivor of the Jaredite battle which occurred at the hill Ramah, known to be located near the eastern sea. We can only guess that he had not crossed from one side of the land to the other. Second, the city of Mulek was on the eastern seacoast (Alma 51:26), in Book of Mormon coordinates.

The Phoenician Connection

It is likely that the migration would have been made with assistance from the Phoenicians. Ross T. Christensen (1972) has shown that the Phoenicians were allies of the Jews at that time. They also had the sailing expertise, having circumnavigated Africa in 600 B.C. There is also a hint in the Book of Mormon; the only named river was called "Sidon," which was the name of the principal metropolis of Phoenicia.

Most evidence for Phoenician influences in America is quite indirect, involving comparisons of traits or trait complexes. Such studies began around the turn of the century when a leading Americanist, Zelia Nuttall, documented a number of parallels between Phoenician and Mesoamerican culture. (Nuttall, 1901) Her work was largely ignored, but others have tried the same approach, such as Constance Irwin. (1963) Thomas Stuart Ferguson (1957) drew parallels from the cultures of a broad area of the Middle East with Mesoamerican culture. The most impressive comparisons of trait complexes were compiled by Sorenson. (1971) Some skeptics such as Nigel Davies (1979) ignore such serious efforts and dismiss the work of others as meaningless. I suspect that in the final analysis, cultural traits that are shared by isolated cultures will be considered by the skeptics as evidence that ancient migrations could have taken place, not that they actually did.

We do not have to prove a major Phoenician influence in America because the Book of Mormon does not require it. Indeed, the language of the Mulekites, or possibly multiple languages of the Mulekites if we include the Phoenicians, changed radically in the three or four hundred years preceding their encounter with the Nephites. (Omni 17) This suggests significant influence by natives who spoke the ancient tongues, and who may have superimposed native cultural tradition on the newcomers.

The Coriantumr Encounter

The discovery of Coriantumr, the last king of one of the warring Jaredite factions, was an event which tied the Jaredite history chronologically and geographically to other Book of Mormon events. Soon after the Nephites and Mulekites peaceably combined, a stela was brought to King Mosiah.

> And it came to pass in the days of Mosiah there was a large stone brought unto him with engravings on it; and he did interpret the engravings by the gift and power of God. And they gave an account

of one Coriantumr, and the slain of his people. And Coriantumr was discovered by the people of Zarahemla; and he dwelt with them for the space of nine moons. It also spake a few words concerning his fathers. And his first parents came out from the tower, at the time the Lord confounded the language of the people; and the severity of the Lord fell upon them according to his judgments, which are just; and their bones lay scattered in the land northward. (Omni 20-21)

THE STELAE COMPLEX

Large stone monuments with engravings (stelae) are found by the hundreds in the Mayan area from A.D. 300 to 900. New discoveries have pushed the stelae complex much farther back in time. One monument at Abaj Takalik on the Pacific Coast of Guatemala is dated at A.D. 126. (GMT correlation) Another damaged inscription yields a date somewhere between the third and first centuries B.C. Inscribed monuments centuries older have been discovered in Guatemala and Oaxaca. That, of course, is entirely consistent with the timing of Mosiah's interpretation of a stela in about 250 B.C. The stela brought to Mosiah may have been considerably older for him to have needed special translating powers, and for the oral tradition surrounding the inscription to have been lost. Perhaps it was carved early in the Mulekite period in Phoenician characters. The stela may have been transported a considerable distance to Zarahemla. This is not unthinkable; a seven-ton stela found at Abaj Takalik is believed to have been transported there some three hundred kilometers from its point of origin in the Isthmus of Tehuantepec!

TWO MULEKITE LANDINGS

We are told that the Mulekites landed in more than one place. Their first landing was north of the narrow neck, and by implication their second was south of it (all in Book of Mormon coordinates).

And it [Bountiful] bordered upon the land which they called Desolation, it being so far northward that it came into the land which had been peopled and been destroyed, of whose bones we have spoken, which was discovered by the people of Zarahemla, it being the place of their first landing. And they came from there up into the south wilderness. Thus the land on the northward was called Desolation, and the land on the southward was called Bountiful . . . ." (Alma 22:30-31)

Another verse emphasizes this fact that the Mulekites first landed north of the isthmus:

Now the land south was called Lehi and the land north was called Mulek, which was after the son of Zedekiah; for the Lord did bring Mulek into the land north and Lehi into the land south. (Helaman 6:10)

From these passages it has been supposed, and I believe correctly, that the Mulekites encountered Coriantumr and the remains of the Jaredites shortly after their first landing north of the isthmus. The nearness of their "first landing" to Ramah and the time lapse before they found Coriantumr is not spelled out. I have assumed that Coriantumr did not travel far, due to his battle wounds, and that his eventual death could have been a consequence of that battle or possibly old age. I have also guessed that the Mulekites found Coriantumr within a few years of landing in the land northward. The uncertainty in dating this encounter is transparent. However, I shall be bold and place the encounter between 530 and 575 B.C., with the Jaredite battle sometime between 550 and 600 B.C.

I suggest that the Mulekites landed somewhere between the Tuxtlas on the south and Tampico on the north. Some of the groups, perhaps not all, traveled towards the isthmus and came upon Coriantumr and evidence of the Jaredite battle. Thereafter they moved on, possibly by boat, until they came to the area of La Venta. They established a settlement there, and then migrated up the Grijalva River to the area which would become known as Zarahemla. These movements are illustrated on Map #8, p. 261.

OTHER DOCUMENTS AND THE MULEKITE MIGRATION

Ancient chronicle accounts and a tapestry painted shortly after the Conquest appear to be intertwined with the Mulekite migration. Both the Nephite and Mulekite migrations had root in the destruction of Jerusalem. Leaving Jerusalem, both groups were led across the ocean by inspired leaders. In the New World, leadership was passed on to the succeeding generations. The whole epic left such a lasting impression that centuries later the Nephites and Lamanites were still arguing over who had wronged whom during their migration. (e.g. Alma 20:13 and Mosiah 10:12-16)

A PATTERN FOR ANCIENT RECORDS

Mullen (1974) has emphasized the importance of ancient native records in preserving the history of these origins. He said that the writers of the Mesoamerican chronicles considered it necessary ". . . at all costs to preserve an account of sacred origins, and the tellers held to their instinct that the sacred had been declared at the times of catastrophe." Distinguishing between the ancient and more recent is a problem in these accounts because important events were expected to be repeated periodically. (Weaver, 1972:109)

Mullen, a professor of classics, identifies a three-part structure in ancient records which applies both to the Old Testament and to the Mesoamerican chronicle accounts. He says that it consists of:
1. destructive acts of the gods which ended one world age and initiated the next;
2. wanderings of the people at the time of transition under the guidance of heroic leaders who interpreted the god's will;
3. termination of the wanderings with the passing on of leadership by these heroes to the first generation of rulers in the newly-occupied land. Once this structure was established, it became the basis for every subsequent telling of the history of the people; and if later migrations occurred and later kingships were founded they were inevitably accommodated to the earlier ones of the sacred era, and finally identified with them.

This recurring pattern has been specifically noted among the Zapotecs (Flannery et al, 1976) and among the Maya (Thompson, 1956:148 and Roys, 1967:183-185).

THE TAPESTRY OF JUCUTÁCATO

A fascinating Mexican tapestry is available for study which not only fits that ancient pattern, but which might be an important connection with the Mulekite migration. The tapestry of Jucutácato was painted in western Mexico by a Tarascan Indian shortly after the Spanish Conquest. It was probably drawn in accordance with ancient oral traditions, supplemented by pictographic writings.[1]

The tapestry shows nine men emerging from a cave and receiving a special ball suspended from three chains. The men cross a body of water mounted on nine turtles. The drawings then indicate a migration across Mexico, led by a man with a colored cloak who controls the special ball. The migration ends in Michoacán (western Mexico) where they find a "tree of life." There they worship, build, and make metal plates. This is probably the point of departure for the next generation, which separates and goes in different directions. Some look for mines while others establish themselves in Patzcuaro, Michoacán, as shown in the middle of the tapestry. (León, 1903)

---

1. The tapestry was discovered by Nicolas León, in 1877, at the First Exposition of Michoacán. It came from an Indian woman who was chieftan of the village of Jicalan. It is a coarse weave of cotton fiber, measuring 2.63 meters by 2.03 meters. The text was written with European letters in the Nahuatl language. The badly deteriorated original is at the Sociedad Mexicana de Geografia y Estadistica, Mexico City. A copy hangs in the Museo Nacional de Antropologia, Western Mexico room.

Tapestry of Jucutácato. Photograph of a copy on display in the Western Mexico room of the National Museum of Anthropology, Mexico City.

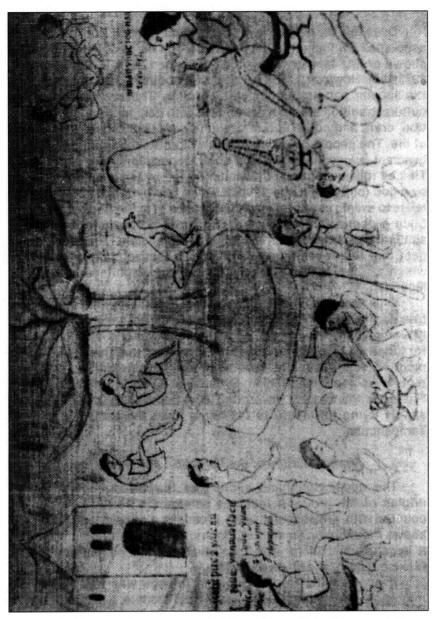

Tree of Life scene from Tapestry of Jucutácato. Note the men at the bottom fabricating some type of metal plates. Note also the bird by the tree and the special ball suspended from three chains and located in front of the seated leader on the right. Orange flames appear above the branches of the tree, possibly indicating European influence.

The Tree of Life Scene

Does this tapestry have anything to do with the Book of Mormon accounts? On the surface it does not. The cross-country migration shown on the tapestry likely took place in 1272 A.D. (Chimalpahín, 1975:169) However, the tree of life symbolism (see page 153) fits the ancient pattern suggested by Mullen. The culmination of the cultural tradition seems to be shown, with demonstration of instruction, craft, and construction capability, all tied to belief in the tree of life. The people go off in different directions from the tree of life quadrant, suggesting a passing on of leadership to new generations. This all follows a period of wandering led by leaders accompanied by a god (bird) and a special ball. Does this pattern of presentation relate to events as ancient as those spoken of in the Book of Mormon? Such a connection cannot now be proven, but there are enough similarities to make such a connection plausible. Therefore, I suggest that this tapestry may represent a reenactment of traditions which sprang from the amalgamation of Nephite and Mulekite legends.

One factor which suggests the ancient connection is the tree of life scene itself, which represents an ancient city called "Tamoanchan." It was known as the cultural and spiritual center for tribes in Mesoamerica, but was so ancient that there is no agreement on where it might have been located.[2] (Henning, 1912) The tapestry is depicting Xicalan, Michoacán as if it were Tamoanchan. Professor Plancarte y Navarette (1934) believed that the artist was simply trying to impute to his home town the ancient honors of Tamoanchan.

Representation of the Migration Across the Sea

The upper right-hand section of the tapestry presents the origins of the group. It includes emergence from a cave, an encounter with a messenger who presents a special ball, a man is shown mounted on an animal, men riding on nine turtles landing by a large aquatic plant, and then they begin their journey across Mexico. This is shown on page 155.

It appears that more than one lineage was involved in the migration. There were the nine principal leaders, a group of others walking below, and eight heads. The meaning of the various

---

2. The best clue comes from J. Eric Thompson (1960), who points out that the word comes from Chiapas. We shall see later on that such an identification is consistent with a location proposed for the land of Zarahemla.

heads and types of people is not clear, but may convey the idea of multiple lineages.

The first quadrant from the tapestry of Jucutácato depicts the leader of the group emerging from a cave and receiving a special ball suspended from a chain. It also depicts an over-water crossing on nine turtles which likely represent boats.

THE CAVE AND THE EAST SEA

The Nahuatl text describes the cave. Professor Corona Nuñez interprets the text as follows: ". . . the cave is the tipped over vessel made of green stone where man was molded from ashes . . ." He suggests that it is a geographical location on the other side of the sea or a mythological place. The famous anthropologist Edward Seler indicated that this green stone is the east sea. (Seler, 1908) These interpretations are consistent with a hypothesis that the tapestry depicts ancient cultural origins and a migration across the Atlantic Ocean (east sea).

LANDING IN A PLACE OF MANY WATERS

The group is referred to on the tapestry by the name "Chalchiuihtlahpazco." According to Moreno (1948) these were the Nonoalcans, whom I associate with the Mulekites in at least a traditional sense. The identification of the group as Nonoalcans is reinforced by the name of the place where the group first settled which is called "Nunuualco."[3] The word Nonoalco (or Nonohualca) means "place where there is water everywhere." This is most significant in light of Mormon's statement that Cumorah was located in a "land of many waters." Several archæologists identify the landing place as the shores of Veracruz. (Jimenez Moreno, 1948)

CROSSING IN NINE BOATS?

Corona Nuñez says that "The nine men on turtles can signify tribal heads who are coming in boats which are represented by turtles." (see also Rock, 1960) As early-Americanist Plancarte y Navarette (1934) states: "In the legends it says that the first settlers, Nonoalcans, arrived riding on turtles, using their shells as boats." Without more information it would be premature to suggest that there were in fact nine ships being suggested by this representation.

EVIDENCE FOR A SACRED BALL: A LIAHONA TRADITION?

A most significant event depicted in the first quadrant is presentation to the group leader of a ball suspended from a chain. According to Professor Corona Nuñez (in a personal communication) the bird just above them represents a god, so its inclusion emphasizes the religious importance of the event. This special

---

3. A printed reproduction by the Sociedad Mexicana de Geografia y Estadstica gives the reading "Nimualco." The original is now too deteriorated to tell which is correct.

ball had an important role in the migration to the tree of life. Some archæologists have called it an incense burner, but it does not appear to be open at the top.

The concept of a sacred ball was not unique to the Tarascan Indians. The Guatemalan Quiche and Cakchiquel histories mention a sacred ball or rock in connection with their legends of migration across the sea.

The Quiché-Maya people left two histories, written in their own language but with the European alphabet, shortly after the conquest of Guatemala in 1524 A.D. The English translations of the titles are *Title of the Lords of Totonicapan* and *Popol Vuh, the Sacred Book of the Quiché Maya*. The two histories are complementary. The Totonicapan version tells of four great leaders bringing their people from the other side of the sea, from Pa-Tulán, Pa-Civán. The leader chosen was Balam-Quitzé. Before leaving he was given a present by the god Nacxit. It was called the Girón Gagal. Taking it with him, by miraculous means Balam-Quitzé was able to lead his people across the sea. The Girón-Gagal, or sacred bundle, was a symbol of the power and the majesty of the Quichés. (Recinos, 1950:216)

This sacred relic was kept completely wrapped up in memory of the four men who led their ancestors across the sea. "They had been here a long time before they died, being very old. They were called the chiefs and sacrificers." (Recinos, 1952:140)

The Cakchiquels also had a sacred object called the "rock of obsidian," which was associated with their legendary migration across the sea. Their legend states:

> Go my sons and daughters these will be your obligations and the work which we give you to do. Thus speaks the rock of obsidian. Go where you see mountains and valleys. Oh my sons there your countenances will become happy. These are the presents which I will give you your riches and dominion over all.   (Recinos 1950:52)

These legends and the tapestry representation of a special ball associated with migration across the sea may have a common origin. During the migration of the Nephites, the leader Lehi was given a very curious instrument:

> And it came to pass that as my father arose in the morning to his great astonishment he beheld upon the ground a round ball of curious workmanship; and it was of fine brass. And within the ball were two spindles; and the one pointed the way whither we should go into the wilderness.   (1 Nephi 16:10)

This object, called the "Liahona," was taken by the Nephites when they fled from the Lamanites. (2 Nephi 5:12) It was kept as a sacred relic, and Alma made special mention of it when he gave the records to his son, Helaman. (Alma 37:38-45)

I have suggested a relationship between the migration shown in the tapestry and the migration of the Mulekites. They may also have had a Liahona. However, with the intermeshing of the Mulekites with the Nephites, it is more likely that the migration tradition and especially the sacred-ball tradition comes from a synthesis of different historical traditions.

On the first quadrant of the tapestry we thus encounter an event of religious import which seems to relate to the ancient traditions of a sacred ball, and the Book of Mormon compass or "Liahona" tradition. It is followed by an over-water crossing, again in the Book of Mormon tradition. Other documents must be examined, however, to tie this tapestry to the Mulekites.

CHRONICLE ACCOUNTS OF THE MIGRATION

The conquistadores and priests who followed them destroyed a large portion of the native documents which were preserved in painted books. Those books, known as codexes, were made either from deerskin or a paper made from the inner bark of special trees. Some of these documents contained maps and had hieroglyphics giving place names and dates. Unfortunately, some of the ancient documents were destroyed by the Aztecs themselves during a previous period when they were rewriting history to suit their own political ambitions. Documents which did survive these two great acts of destruction fell prey to all kinds of political intrigue. It is likely that a library assembled by Lorenzo Boturini in about 1740 was more complete than the total catalog of documents now available to scholars.

Supplementing the native records were oral traditions. In fact, the codexes served as a mnemonic device to help preserve those oral traditions. Natives such as Chimalpahín and Ixtlilxóchitl, and priests such as Bernardino Sahagun and Juan Torquemada tried to interview the natives having the greatest knowledge of those legends. The records which they compiled in both the Nahuatl and Spanish languages are now known as the "chronicles." (Palmer, 1976)

MIGRATION OF NONOHUALCANS FROM THE "PLACE OF THE RED"

An A.D. 1620 account by Chimalpahín discusses the "second settlers" in the land. Chimalpahín's account mentions the "beginnings, origin, and method of immigration" of the Nonohualcas.

He states that they were of "extremely ancient lineage." This account reads: "When the nonohualcas tlacochcalcas left the country of Tlapallan, they crossed the great sea, the ocean, and came bringing with them marine shells and turtle shells as musical instruments. They landed at the mouth of a very large river." The word "Tlapallan" means "place of the red." Chimalpahín equated it with the "Red Sea." (Chimalpahín, 1975)

Associated with these people was a language change in ancient times. This data provided by Chimalpahín relates to one of the few details we have about the Mulekites. When encountered by the Nephites a few centuries after the migration, they no longer spoke Hebrew. (Omni 17-18)

AN OVER-WATER MIGRATION LED BY PRIESTS

A most detailed and important account of the ancient origins of the Gulf Coast peoples is recorded by Bernardino de Sahagun (my translation):

Here is the story that the old men used to tell:
In a certain time which nobody can count anymore,
Which nobody can remember anymore . . .
Those who came here to plant, our grandparents,
It is said of them that they arrived and came . . .

By water in their boats they did come, in many groups,
And they arrived at the water's edge, on the north coast,
And where they left their boats is called Panutla,
It means, "over where one crosses over the water."

Right away they followed along the coast of the sea
And they went looking for mountains,
Some for white mountains and the smoking mountains.
They arrived at Quauhtemalla following the seashore.

Furthermore, they did not go on their own whim
But their priests led them
And their god showed them the way.

Afterwards they came,
They arrived there,
In the place called Tamoanchan
Which means "we are looking for our home"
In the place called Tamoanchan
They were in authority for a long time.

Sahagún, Codex Matritense

The Mexican anthropologist León-Portilla believes that this tradition refers to the most ancient cultural origins of Mexico, and that the migration occurred in the middle of the first millennium, B.C. (León-Portilla, 1964) Michael Coe also ascribes authenticity to this account and suggests that it is ancient enough to connect with the archæological Olmecs. (Coe,1968:118)

There has been some uncertainty concerning the location of landing. Hunter and Ferguson (1950) believed that the landing place was a spot known as Panuco in the state of Veracruz near Tampico, and thus about 600 kilometers northwest of the isthmus of Tehuantepec. Panuco had ruins going back to the sixteenth century B.C., though it was located on the northernmost fringe of the Mesoamerican cultural area.

An alternative interpretation for the location of Panuco is given by the astute eighteenth-century historian, Mariano Veytia. He placed "Panuco" in the heart of Veracruz at "nineteen degrees latitude." (Veytia, 1836:151) That would be either at the present city of Veracruz or south of there at the port of Alvarado. These latter possibilities are more consistent with the tapestry of Jucutácato. Both the Panuco and Alvarado alternatives are shown on Map #8, p. 261.

After the landing, Sahagun points out that the group went southward along the seashore. The "white mountains" may have been snow-covered peaks, like Orizaba, spotted by exploring parties going inland. The smoking mountains were likely the volcanicly active Tuxtla mountains.

This account is consistent with our knowledge of the Mulekites for the following reasons:

1. The landing was on the Gulf Coast.
2. The apparent antiquity matches that of the Mulekite landing.
3. There was southward travel from an area north of the isthmus to an area south of the isthmus.
4. They passed right by the area of the Tuxtlas where the Jaredites were destroyed and where they could have found Coriantumr.

The description of having been led by their god, and of having an association with the tree-of-life city, Tamoanchan, is entirely consistent with an origin in Jerusalem. This account is also consistent with the record of Chimalpahín, which provides a link via the name of the Nonohualcans to the tapestry of Jucutácato.

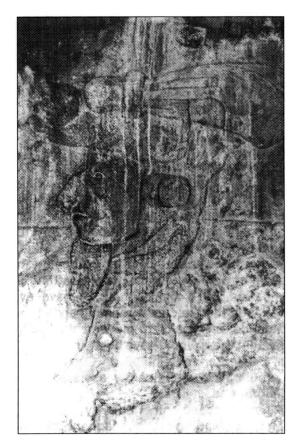

**Man with large hat, long nose, and beard, from monument at La Venta.
Possibly King Mulek.**

SECOND LANDING: LA VENTA

The Book of Mormon speaks of a "first landing" in the land northward. From that it could be inferred that there was a subsequent landing south of the isthmus, which served as an embarcation point for exploration and colonization of the land southward. La Venta, located near the coast, may have been a Mulekite settlement in that early time period. Ultimately, they colonized the area known as Zarahemla and identified here as Chiapas.

After drift sands covered La Venta in about 600 B.C., a new people moved in and established a culture somewhat inferior, at least in terms of monumental sculpture. Nevertheless, there are several monuments which have been erected that show very clearly a transition to serpent worship from the old jaguar worship of the Olmecs. They also show bearded men, an anomaly in Mesoamerica. We do not have definitive proof that these monuments are from the time period of the Mulekites. However, the best current estimates are that they date to 400-550 B.C.

It does seem reasonable to conclude that the changes in occupation at La Venta are consistent with the Jaredite destruction and subsequent resettlement by Mulekites.

MIGRATION TO CHIAPAS

There is very strong archæological evidence for a migration from the area of Tres Zapotes (Cumorah region) to Chiapa de Corzo. Sometime during the Chiapa III period (650-500 B.C.) some very unique pottery appeared in Chiapa de Corzo. This style (Tapilula unslipped) not only appeared to resemble pottery from Southern Veracruz, but analysis of its composition proved that it was made from the same clay beds as Tres Zapotes pottery. At the same time, there is evidence of a new group of people settling in the Central Depression. (Warren, 1978:45-47) Thus, we have evidence for a movement in exactly the direction proposed and at the time period expected. Evidence on obsidian movements during preclassic times indicates that there would have been known trails connecting Tres Zapotes, La Venta, and Chiapa de Corzo in 600 B.C. These connections would have significantly assisted the Mulekites in making their migrations.

None of these archæological data by themselves prove that there was a Mulekite landing and subsequent migration. However, there is enough scattered evidence to make the whole Mulekite history plausible, particularly since it finds corroboration in the chronicle accounts.

SETTLEMENT OF THE LAND OF ZARAHEMLA

It is most likely that the Mulekites split into different groups and migrated to different areas within Mesoamerica, such as Oaxaca, before Zarahemla's group went up to the land of Zarahemla. I have used the word "up" advisedly since that word was also used to describe the location of Zarahemla relative to the coast. (Alma 22:31) Zarahemla was also "down" from the land of Nephi, but it was surrounded by mountains, infested in sundry times by the Gadianton robbers. The Central Depression of Chiapas, shown on Map #10, p. 264, fits all these criteria. This map, adapted from a map prepared by the New World Archæological Foundation (Lowe, 1959), has been oriented in line

Professor Bruce Warren inspects a monument exhibited in La Venta Park, Villahermosa. It shows a man with a headdress, apparently bearded. There are elements of serpent symbolism in this monument, which differs in style from the other La Venta monuments.

with the Nephite directional system. It is obvious that the course of the river tends to reinforce the directional system of the Nephites.

There is another qualitative factor which reinforces the theory that the Central Depression of Chiapas was the Land of Zarahemla. In about 17 B.C. there was a great drought in the land of Zarahemla, which caused a famine. "For the earth was smitten that it was dry, and did not yield forth grain in the season of grain; and the whole earth was smitten . . ." (Helaman 11:6) Where would this be possible in such a wet area as Mesoamerica? The Central Depression is the best possibility.

> It is true that climatically the Central Depression is one of the drier regions of tropical America as a result of the rain-shadow effect of mountain ranges which surround it on all sides. The dry season is extended, and vegetation distant from surface water is generally poor, with level lands supporting tall forest confined to low areas near the major rivers. Also, as is generally true of drier regions, rainfall is spotty and irregular from year to year and droughts are frequent in particular areas of the valley . . . irregularity of precipitation is apparently the chief liability of Central Chiapas as an occupation area.   (Lowe 1959:#2:2)

The Central Depression is separated from the Pacific Coast by the Cuchumatanes mountains, as illustrated on Map #3, p. 255. During the early part of the Nephite-Lamanite conflicts, the Lamanites had control over the narrow coastal plain on the Pacific side of those mountains. This explains Mormon's statement that the Lamanites dwelt "on the west of the land of Zarahemla, in the borders by the seashore . . ." (Alma 22:28)

At this point the reader is advised to carefully study Alma 22:27-34, which gives the overall plan of the geography, and compare it against the maps which have been prepared. That passage will be better understood if it is noted that these statements were written from the standpoint of someone in the land of Nephi. Thus, the "borders of the wilderness which was on the north by the land of Zarahemla" would actually be south for someone situated in Zarahemla.

THE CITY OF ZARAHEMLA

The place which came to be known as the city of Zarahemla was founded by the Mulekites. (Omni 13-19) There are two large sites along the Grijalva's western bank which have the possibility of being the ancient city of Zarahemla. These are Santa Cruz, and farther upstream, Santa Rosa. Santa Rosa is the leading candidate at this time. It was the largest site on the upper Grijalva, and was surrounded by smaller sites of comparable

(Late Preclassic) age. Radiocarbon dates from Santa Rosa are 270-390 B.C. ± 90, and A.D. 10 ± 90 years.

The excavator, Agustin Delgado, describes Santa Rosa in the following general terms:

> There is considerable conjecture as to the ancient role played by Santa Rosa and similar sites—were they cities or sacred precincts? Basically, it appears that Santa Rosa was a large habitation, as well as ceremonial center, poor in objects of high artistic quality, but relatively rich with respect to the more prosaic architecture and ceramics. It is one of several partially excavated Mesoamerican archæological sites that appear to have had a climactic development in the Early Protoclassic period . . .   (Delgado, 1965, #17, 3)

The period of greatest activity in Santa Rosa was 100 B.C. to A.D. 200, precisely the period anticipated based on the Book of Mormon account. We know that Zarahemla was burned in A.D. 34. (3 Nephi 9:3) There were a number of different ash layers in the mounds, but insufficient radiocarbon determinations to tell which one could have been at 34 A.D.

The rather large mounds at Santa Rosa had different functions. Mound A, for example, with a height of eleven meters, was probably one of the substructures for temples. There were also quadrangular platforms which "probably bore the state residences of the important officials or/and were the locale for the more public ceremonies . . ." (Delgado, 1965:36)

Santa Rosa was not the type of city portrayed as Zarahemla by modern artists. However, it does seem to fulfill most of the criteria required for it in the Book of Mormon. It is fortunate that the site was studied by the NWAF prior to its flooding by waters from the Angostura Canyon Dam.

CHIAPA DE CORZO

The only ruins in the Central Depression of Chiapas which have been the object of restoration work are at Chiapa de Corzo. A fair amount of information will be given about the ruins, not only because they can be visited by tourists, but also because the site was very important in ancient times. Extensive excavations by the New World Archæological Foundation have revealed that the site was occupied continuously from 1500 B.C. to the present. The chronology of Chiapa de Corzo has taken on special significance in helping to date and interrelate archæological data throughout Mesoamerica.

What Book of Mormon significance did Chiapa de Corzo have, if any? It was likely one of the cities referred to as being in the "more capital parts of the land" which lay northward from

Zarahemla. (Helaman 1:27) Directionally, it could fit with the descriptions of the city of "Sidom." Sidom was apparently a city with a preexisting religious structure that had sanctuaries and an "altar." (Alma 16:17) As an hypothesis, I suggest that Chiapa de Corzo was initially settled by Jaredites, was occupied by the Mulekites who moved in from the Gulf Coast, and was later influenced by Nephites. It was abandoned during the last Nephite wars with the Lamanites. The subsequent data presented will give some substantiation for these postulates.

CHRONOLOGY OF CHIAPA DE CORZO

The first three phases occurred during Jaredite times. During the Chiapa IV phase (500-300 B.C.), platforms and pyramids were built, using lime plaster over compacted earth fill. There was a modest amount of contact with Monte Albán. Nearly all of the large sites developing in the Central Depression at that time had similar pottery, suggesting to me that there was fairly complete Mulekite domination of the area. According to the Book of Mormon, the Nephites did not migrate into Zarahemla during this period.

The Chiapa V phase (300 B.C.-50 B.C.) saw the introduction of cut-stone construction. Writings have been found on pottery vessels. In total numbers of supporting centers, the emphasis during this period shifted to Santa Rosa. This would be expected if Santa Rosa were Zarahemla. A related site, La Perseverancia, was built on the Pacific coastal plain at this time. That may have been an attempt to control Lamanites in that area. It is during this period that influences from Kaminaljuyú are observed, as would be expected from migration of the Nephites into this area in about 250 B.C.

The Chiapa VI phase (50 B.C.-A.D. 100) fits into the time period when the Nephites started extending their control over the "land northward." It was a period of intense activity, with migrations and trade (Helaman 6:6-10) being carried on. This corresponds to the observations at Chiapa de Corzo, where substantial long-distance trade connections have been archæologically established. This was the climax phase of the city, which grew to a size of 1½ kilometers by 2 kilometers, with a population of about 7,000. (Warren, 1978) There were some thirty enlargements made on Mound 1 (probably a temple) during this phase. The earliest discovered Long-Count calendar date was found in this phase and gives a date of December 8, 36 B.C. (Julian).

During Chiapa VII (A.D. 100-250) and VIII (A.D. 250-400), the site continued to flourish, but is was abandoned at the end of this time, coincident with destruction of the Nephites at Cumorah.

Mound 1 at Chiapa de Corzo, dating from 600 B.C. to A.D. 100 Photo
taken during the process of reconstruction by the New World
Archæological Foundation. This was once an ancient temple structure
with columns and rooms. It was constructed in various stages from
stone and cement. Photo courtesy of Dr. Bruce Warren.

Possible Mulekite Migrations to Oaxaca

In Chapter 5, it was shown that Oaxaca may have figured prominently in Jaredite history. Since that area is archæologically very important, we must consider its role in the period between the Jaredite and Nephite destructions.

There was a change in highland Oaxaca cultural patterns and settlements in about 600 B.C.-500 B.C. From then until about 200-1 B.C. there was a new cultural stage known as Monte Albán 1, which is seen in about 84 known sites in the valley of Oaxaca. That culture had a decided Olmec flavor but was not strictly Olmec. Some archæologists use the word "Olmecoid." I speculate that there was a massing in Oaxaca of survivors from the Jaredite holocaust. There may also have been some Mulekite contacts.

Ruins in Oaxaca

The most impressive ruin dating from this period is Monte Albán, near Oaxaca City. Constructed on a series of hilltops some 400 meters above the surrounding plain, Monte Albán has a central courtyard which is 300 meters by 100 meters. As a point of reference, six football fields could fit into the plaza. Most of the buildings seen today were built after A.D. 450. However, the plaza itself appears to have been created in about the fifth century B.C. (Treat, 1979)

During the Monte Albán I period, a well-defined pattern of idolatry developed centering on the bat god. It was elaborated in subsequent centuries. Other sites from that period which can be seen today, though only the later periods are restored, are Yagul and Mitla. The impressive site of Dainzú also dates back into the first phase of Monte Albán. There are two humanized jaguars, shown on bas relief carvings at the base of a large temple, which are suggestive of Olmecoid influence.

Incense Burners

One of the interesting cultural manifestations of the Monte Albán I phase is the use of a number of forms of incense burners. This phenomenon is seen at the same time in Chiapa de Corzo. Incense burners may have been introduced into both places by the Mulekites. Incense burners were used in Israel among the Jews. The practice of burning incense was instituted during the Exodus as part of the law of Moses. (Exodus 30) The large number of incense burners found gives an interesting connection to Palestine. (Ferguson, 1958:87)

Ruins of Dainzú, located between Oaxaca City and Mitla. This Impressive
Late Preclassic period temple was decorated with dozens of bas reliefs,
many of which related to the ritual ballgame played in Mesoamerica.

Collector Howard Leigh of Mitla, Oaxaca, holding a
four-horned incense burner found in Oaxaca. It may relate
to observance of the Law of Moses in Ancient Mexico.

Migration from Chiapas

The second cultural phase at Monte Albán is distinguished by entry of a new people who came in from "Chiapas or Guatemala." (Bernal, 1965:800) These people were a ruling class who came to dominate Monte Albán and other ceremonial centers, but not the rural areas. According to Bernal,

> Study of the list of traits tends to show that the bearers of Period II culture (at least at Monte Albán) were an aristocracy of rulers or priests who imposed their own ideas but did not constitute a majority capable of obliterating the old culture, which survived among the bulk of the population.

The beginning date for Monte Albán II is important, but is the subject of some controversy. A commonly-accepted dividing point is 200 B.C. However, while Blanton used the date, he indicated that he was more comfortable with a later date. The problem is that the chronology is not as firmly established at Monte Albán as it is at Chiapa de Corzo, and the radiocarbon dates have been somewhat contradictory. An authoritative synthesis of Mesoamerican chronologies resulted in the conclusion that Monte Albán II began near 1 B.C., but possibly sooner. (Tolstoy, 1978:267)

The significance to the Book of Mormon is that in 55 B.C. the Nephites began a number of migrations to the "land northward." These migrations are discussed in more detail in the next chapter. They coincide with introduction of Monte Albán II if the latter part of the 200 B.C.-1 B.C. time span is accepted. If the earlier (200 B.C.) time frame is used, then the bearers of the new culture were probably Mulekites from Chiapa de Corzo. In this latter case the movement was not described directly in the Book of Mormon.

Presently, more work is needed by the specialists to make a firm choice on the date of the migration into Monte Albán. The Book of Mormon makes clear that 50 B.C. is the latest possible time that can be considered. On Map #8, p. 261, a movement is indicated which would have been consistent with either time frame.

For a long time it was thought that Monte Albán had a peaceful existence. That picture is now reversed. Some three hundred carvings of nude men called "danzantes" are now believed to represent captives and conquests. Monte Albán itself was created as a military capital to tie together the three branches of Oaxaca valley into a cohesive unit. It apparently exercised a hegemony over surrounding areas, and the display of the danzantes was a crass act of military propaganda. Blanton (1978) has even found evidence of fortifications at Monte Albán. They helped control access to the central plaza.

Unfortunately, the Book of Mormon does not give enough information about the Land Northward to permit a name identification of Monte Albán, or to even decide how it fit into the scheme of the last battles. What is beyond dispute is that it was an important autonomous city during Mulekite and Nephite times.

Pottery showing a human face from the valley of Oaxaca, from the collection of Howard Leigh, Mitla. The style suggests a Monte Albán II time period (1-200 A.D.). (See for example Bernal, 1969:165, Fig. 31.)

Mound J at Monte Albán, constructed in the Monte Albán II phase when new people came in from the south. The south platform shown behind Mound J was also constructed during that phase. There are passageways within mound J which have inverted V-shaped arches.

Bas reliefs of two captives, commonly called "danzantes."
They are on Mound J, which dates to Monte Albán II, a period in which Nephites may have exercised control in the valley of Oaxaca.
It is now believed that the carvings were for propaganda purposes, and that Monte Albán was a military capital.

SUMMARY

1. The Mulekites were a group which fled from Jerusalem in the sixth century B.C. and crossed the Atlantic. They may have been assisted by Phoenicians.

2. They landed on the Gulf Coast of Mexico, somewhere between Tampico on the north and the Tuxtlas on the south.

3. The Mulekites encountered Coriantumr, the last Jaredite king. The location of Ramah-Cumorah south of Veracruz makes this most probable.

4. The tapestry of Jucutácato and chronicle accounts by Sahagun and Chimalpahín seem to mirror the Mulekite migrations across the eastern sea.

5. Evidence for a sacred ball or a "Liahona" tradition is found on the tapestry and in Guatemalan traditions of ancient date.

6. Archæological evidence for the Mulekite intrusion into Mesoamerica includes taller skeletons, monuments showing bearded men, and incense burners. Other authors have identified many cultural-trait similarities with the Near East.

7. The Mulekites went up to an area they called Zarahemla. Evidence is presented which indicates that the area in question was the Central Depression of Chiapas. Hundreds of ruins dating to the Mulekite-Nephite period have been found in that area. Archæological data prove that in the sixth century B.C. there was movement from the area identified as Cumorah to Chiapa de Corzo.

8. Archæological data make plausible an identification of the ruins of Santa Rosa as Zarahemla.

9. Chiapa de Corzo was an important city which may have been settled by the Mulekites.

10. Phase II at the military capital of Monte Albán saw the introduction of new leadership and culture from Chiapas. Present estimates for the beginning date are 200 B.C. to 1 B.C. These new leaders were Mulekites if the 200 B.C. date is supported. If the phase begins as late as 50 B.C., it coincides with Nephite migrations documented in the Book of Mormon.

8

THE NEPHITES—FROM KAMINALJUYÚ TO TEOTIHUACÁN: SETTING THE STAGE FOR THE NEPHITE EXTERMINATION

> *And now behold, saith the Lord, concerning the people of the Nephites: If they will not repent, and observe to do my will, I will utterly destroy them, saith the Lord, because of their unbelief notwithstanding the many mighty works which I have done among them; and as surely as the Lord liveth shall these things be . . .*
>
> *Helaman 15:17*

The seeds of a tradition of hatred, which resulted in destruction of the Nephites, were sown before Nephi and his family even reached the New World. In the book of First Nephi we read of a number of very serious encounters which Nephi had with his brothers. He eventually had his way in each one of them. He in effect ruled over them. At the death of Lehi, his family was no longer able to coexist. Therefore, Nephi led those who would follow him from the place of their landing to a highland valley, a journey of "many days." (2 Nephi 5:7) Nephi took with him all of the sacred relics which had been acquired as part of their epic exodus from Jerusalem. These included the plates of brass, the "ball or compass, which was prepared for my father by the hand of the Lord . . ." (2 Nephi 5:12), and the sword of Laban.

The Nephites placed great value upon those sacred relics, and the entire thirty-seventh chapter of Alma is a speech by Alma to his son Helaman on the importance of those things. In fact, the definition of a Nephite was one who believed in the brass plates and other records which were kept by the Nephites.

> And it came to pass that whosoever would not believe in the tradition of the Lamanites, but believed those records which were brought out of the land of Jerusalem, and also in the tradition of their fathers, which were correct, who believed in the commandments of God and kept them, were called the Nephites, or the people of Nephi, from that time forth . . . (Alma 3:11)

The Lamanites had their own traditions, chief of which was that the Nephites had stolen from them their possessions, meaning specifically the sacred relics and the plates of brass. (Mosiah 10:12-16) Almost five centuries after the separation of the Nephites and Lamanites, elements of that tradition were evident in a lecture that the king of the Lamanites gave to Ammon, a missionary from the Nephites. He called Ammon the son of a liar, meaning Nephi. "Behold, he [Nephi] robbed our fathers, and now his children are also come amongst us that they may, by their cunning and their lyings deceive us, that they again may rob us of our property." (Alma 20:13)

In this chapter we shall follow a few of the significant threads of Nephite/Lamanite history from the time of the initial separation to the time of the last battle at Cumorah. These threads will take us from the great city of Kaminaljuyú on the south, to Teotihuacán on the north. Those two cities will figure prominently in the discussion of the setting of the last battle, given in Chapter 9. A few important ruins and some significant topography in between will be discussed to help put some physical meaning into the account, particularly with respect to the major movements of people. It would be impossible in a single chapter to cover either the archæology of this period, known as the Late Preclassic, or to attempt to analyze the entire Nephite geography in any detail. What I would like to attempt is a description of a few of those things with which I have personal acquaintance, some of which can be easily visited by the tourist to Mexico and Guatemala.

The City of Nephi: Kaminaljuyú

During Late Preclassic times there were occupations in many places in Guatemala and Mexico. The most important Guatemalan center of the highlands was near Guatemala City, Kaminaljuyú. Many other smaller ruins which dot the valley of Guatemala and other areas of the highlands date to the Late Preclassic/Protoclassic period (600 B.C. to A.D. 300). They are shown on Map #9, pp. 262-263. Data for placement of these sites came from Smith (1955), Shook and Ptoskouriakoff (1956), Shook (1957 and 1965), Longyear (1965), and miscellaneous sources including private communication with Edwin Shook. The map is known to be incomplete, but gives a fair representation of settlement patterns during the period of interest.

The valley of Guatemala City is a most favorable spot. With an elevation of over 1500 meters it is cooler and more pleasant than the tepid coast. The soil is rich from volcanic dust, there is adequate rainfall for several crops a year, and the area boasts mineral and plant resources. There is small game in the forests, and the nearby spot of El Chayal was a source of obsidian which could have been used for fashioning of weaponry.

For many years it has been thought by Mormon archæologists that Kaminaljuyú was a good candidate for the City of Nephi. Fortunately, a vast amount of research has been done on that site by the Carnegie Institution of Washington and by Pennsylvania State University. Documentation of much of that work has just been published.

Archæological Investigations

Kaminaljuyú covers about five square kilometers, though most of that area has now fallen prey to subdivisions of the present city of Guatemala. There were over two hundred mounds, which served as foundations for temples, palaces, and other important structures. Some of them were as much as twenty meters high. Throughout the valley of Guatemala there have been discovered six hundred archæological sites which range in size from small farming hamlets to substantial civic centers. In examination of this large amount of ancient material Pennsylvania State used sampling techniques. The idea is not unlike that of opinion polls, where only a small percentage of a representative group of people are asked their opinion. In a like manner, the university sank 550 test trenches and examined the data which came from each of them. From those they made approximations of the population levels at different times during the history of the area.

In developing the chronology of events, they made calibrations of the rate of obsidian hydration in the valley. They then used that to calibrate 3000 measurements of hydration layer thickness made on obsidian taken from different strata in the test trenches. These data were supplemented with nineteen radiocarbon dates. Their chronology uses the same type of dendro-corrected radiocarbon dates I have been using throughout. (Michels, 1973) The absolute dates collected were related to the two million artifacts they collected and information on architecture and archæological phases.

SUMMARY OF THE CULTURAL PHASES

The phases defined for the site, based on all that information, are as follows:

Dates	Penn State Designation	Traditional Designation
2500-100 B.C.	Early Formative	Arevalo
1000-500 B.C.	Middle Formative	Las Charcas
500-200 B.C.	Late Formative	Providencia
200-1 B.C.	Early Terminal Formative	Verbena-Arenal ⎫ Miraflores
A.D. 1-200	Late Terminal Formative	Santa Clara ⎭
A.D. 200-400	Early Classic	Aurora
A.D. 400-700	Middle Classic	Esperanza-Amatle

The reader does not have to memorize these designations but they could be of use during followup study.

EARLY NEPHITE PERIOD

Up until the Late Formative period there were no mound constructions at Kaminaljuyú and culture was on a fairly low level. Some time in the sixth century a big change occurred. Large mounds were built and monumental architecture was created. All mounds were built with the same construction technique. To prevent the mounded volcanic sand from slipping, retaining walls were built around the base of each mound. During this period, leading up to 200 B.C., the population climbed to an estimated 2,600. (Michels, 1979a:290)

This Late Formative Phase could easily be related to the period of Nephite construction in the City of Nephi. In roughly 570 B.C. there were a number of families which left their coastal settlement and traveled in the wilderness for the space of many days. (2 Nephi 5:7) The families involved were those of Nephi, Sam, Jacob, Joseph, and Zoram. Nephi's sisters also went but they may not have been counted as a separate lineage. In any event, it is interesting to note that there were five principal

**One of the mounds in the center of Kaminaljuyú, with suburbs
of Guatemala City surrounding it. The people at the left give
comparative indication of the large size of these mounds. The city was
begun about the time that the Nephites arrived in the New World.
Its greatest physical and cultural growth began in 200 A.D., coinciding
with the time of kings Zeniff, Noah, and Limhi.**

mound groups established at Kaminaljuyú. The orientation of each was north-north-east, possibly setting a pattern for other Late Preclassic sites that would be built in Chiapas, Mexico.

It is not difficult to reconcile the presence of other people previously living at the site. Nephi would have simply taught them and organized them. This would explain how in short order he was able to teach them how to build buildings, including an elaborate temple. That could have been difficult if he was just counting on the children from a few families. He says ". . . we began to prosper exceedingly, and to multiply in the land." (2 Nephi 5:13) Perhaps part of that multiplication was by conversion rather than reproduction.

The Nephites had a reign of kings, each calling himself Nephi. (Jacob 1:11) Lineages were seen as being most important. The high conical mounds constructed during this period have been explained by Michels in a manner consistent with what we know about the Nephite hierarchy. (Michels 1979b:141) "We may hypothesize therefore, that a high conical mound is a ceremonial monument to the memory of the ruling lineage of a given subchieftan moiety." Maintenance of this worship of reverencing of important ancestors thus helped to enhance the position of the person currently in the leadership role.

Migration to Zarahemla

In about 400 B.C. the Nephites were firmly in control of the Land of Nephi, which probably embraced the Valley of Guatemala at that time. However, after 300 B.C. the Lamanites gained more power and the Nephite position became precarious. In roughly 250-230 B.C. their king (Mosiah I) led part of the people down to the land of Zarahemla, hoping to avoid further bloodshed. Only those went who ". . . would hearken unto the voice of the Lord." (Omni 12) Thus, we can surmise that the elite of the Nephites left, but that their city was not deserted.

As an interesting aside, Kaufman (1976) describes a linguistic influence in the eastern Central Depression of Chiapas which he believes came in about 300 B.C. He describes the influence as coming from "refugees from Kaminaljuyú," precisely what the Book of Mormon would lead us to expect.

Revival of the City of Nephi by Nephites

In 200-170 B.C. there was a migration back to the City of Nephi. A "considerable number" of people apparently preferred the climate of the Guatemalan highlands. The Lamanites yielded up the city of "Lehi-Nephi" (presumably the same place as the City of Nephi).

The Nephites set to work in a vigorous building campaign, and they began to multiply and prosper. They had one battle (Mosiah 10:18) in which they killed 3,043 Lamanites while losing 279 themselves. The Pennsylvania State population estimate at this time was 3,000 for the city and 3,000 for the environs. That seems reasonable, given the Book of Mormon descriptions.

The Great Building Program

During the next generation taxation was introduced by King Noah. This permitted the construction of many elegant, finely ornamented, and spacious buildings. (Mosiah 11:8) A palace, a temple, and a tower near the temple were all constructed. A priestly caste was developed which lived off the work of the common people.

Altogether, this phase lasted only about eighty years, at which time a large number of this group returned to Zarahemla. Nevertheless, their cultural impact must have been substantial.

Michels describes the development at this time of ". . . truly spectacular ceremonial precincts" which were erected for the "subchieftans." Within the city itself a very high percentage of the households were found to be "elite," or well-off. In the rural areas the households were non-elite. This suggests considerable social stratification. In addition to differences in household goods, the better households were built on platforms, while the more modest households were just built on the valley floor. Weaver (1972:83) suggests that at this time the glory and luxury at Kaminaljuyú meant that the power and prestige was in the hands of an elite few. It was tied into a formalization and patterning of the religion.

The largest mound at the site, E-III-3, was built during this phase. It is actually composed of a number of structures superimposed on each other. Each one served in its time as the foundation for a temple. Shook (1952) estimates that 120,000 tons of adobe were used in the construction. To that was added so many pottery sherds that they were the equivalent of (by the author's estimate) a half million complete vessels!

MONUMENTS IN THE TIME OF KING NOAH

There is ample archæological evidence of the idolatry of King Noah's people during the so-called "Miraflores period." It led eventually to the burning at the stake of Abinadi and in the following year of King Noah. It was a significant event mentioned at other times in the Book of Mormon. The Black Stela, shown in part on page 117, has a date in three different calendar systems, Kaminaljuyú, Olmec, and Teotihuacán. That date is November 10, 147 B.C. (Edmonson, 1988:25) An event is depicted in which an important person. probably King Noah, is dying in flames. the Book of Mormon gives the date of Abinadi's death as "about 148 B.C." The time is correct, the place is apparently correct, and the event appears to be the one spoken of in the Book of Mormon. the stela also shows the ascension to the throne by King Limhi.

CITY OF NEPHI AS LAMANITE CAPITAL

When the Nephites fled the city in about 122 B.C., the city was not deserted. Rather, it was converted into the Lamanite capital. Trade developed with the Nephites in about 80-90 B.C. (Alma 23:18), as a consequence of Ammon's missionary efforts. The city was abandoned again due to religious persecution in about 74 B.C. However, it was still the capital of the Lamanites two years later. (Alma 47:20) It would thus appear that while the leaders came and went, the common people continued to maintain the traditions and customs.

It was probably at about this time that the builders of one of the enlargements to the pyramid known as E-III-3 dug a hole into the existing pyramid. It was rectangular shaped, with the corners braced by wooden upright beams. The tomb received a person covered with red paint who was lowered on a litter. Both adults and children were sacrificed, and then over three hundred very fine objects were placed in the tomb to accompany the dead in the afterlife.

Though it is strictly speculation, there might be a connection between this burial and one of the interesting stories in the Book of Mormon. Through treachery, a Nephite deserter named Amalickiah schemed to gain power over the Lamanites. He had the Lamanite king slain and blamed it onto the king's servants who fled. He pretended to have loved the king, and thus won the favor of the queen. "And it came to pass that Amalickiah sought the favor of the queen, and took her unto him to wife; and thus by his fraud, and by the assistance of his cunning servants, he obtained the kingdom." (Alma 47:35) Now if Amalickiah were trying to impress the queen with his great love for the dead king, arranging for a spectacular funeral would have been one of the best ploys. It should again be noted that this funeral event is not mentioned in the Book of Mormon.

Subsequent to this story there is no further mention of the City of Nephi in the Book of Mormon. Indeed, within a geographical context there is no further mention of any specific Lamanite city from that point in time on. However, it is significant to note that the City of Nephi was not listed (3 Nephi 8 & 9) among the cities destroyed in 34 A.D.

Archæologically speaking, Kaminaljuyú continued to grow. Its urban population climbed to 4,500 and the rural population in its vicinity climbed to 5,700. However, the quality of goods produced deteriorated significantly. (Shook, 1967:99)

TRAVEL FROM THE LAND OF NEPHI TO ZARAHEMLA

If the City of Zarahemla was at Santa Rosa and the City of Nephi was at Kaminaljuyú, then are these two sites the proper distance from each other? There was frequent communication after 100 B.C., with missionaries and armies going back and forth. Such communication has been verified archæologically. For instance, I have in my photo collection pictures of two very unique pots, one from Kaminaljuyú, and the other almost identical pot from La Libertad in the Central Depression. (see Map #6, p. 259.)

The distance between them is established by the story of the group led by Alma. They were congregating near the "Waters of Mormon" in the borders of the land. This was likely between the Valley of Guatemala and Lake Atitlan. When they fled from the king they traveled eight days into the wilderness. (Mosiah 23:3) "And they came to a land, yea, even a very beautiful and pleasant land, a land of pure water. And they pitched their tents, and began to till the ground, and began to build buildings; yea they were industrious, and did labor exceedingly." (Mosiah 23:4) They eventually built a city, which they called the city of Helam. (23:20)

THE CITY OF HELAM

An excellent candidate has been found for the City of Helam. Today there is a road which may follow the same path taken by the people of Alma. It goes from Lake Atitlan through Chichicastenango, Santa Cruz del Quiché, and Sacapulas, heading north alongside a very dry river valley. Another valley heads off in a westerly direction from that point, going towards the Central Depression of Chiapas. Again, the road is extremely dry until one arrives at a pretty green valley in which is located the present town of Aguacatan. Though the roads are poor, Aguacatan is well worth seeing. There is a native market which must be reminiscent of markets held several thousand years ago. Standing out in the fields, in very marked contrast to the fertile black soil, are large mounds. Large pottery sherds line the stone fences, as the sherds are more of an obstacle to cultivation than stones.

After careful examination of many of these pottery pieces, Dr. Bruce Warren concluded that they dated to the Late Preclasssic period, probably around 100 B.C. (It should be noted that Dr. Warren is one of the best-qualified experts to make such a judgment.) Ceramics have also been reported at that site, called Chalchitan, dating to the Classic and Postclassic periods. (Smith, 1955:11)

Of additional consequence in identification of Chalchitan as Helam is the fact that within a few hundred meters of the ruined pyramids, the River San Juan gushes out of the side of the mountain. It is beautiful clear water, which reminded us of Alma's phrase that it was "a land of pure water."

The valley is remote, so Alma probably thought his people would be safe there. However, they were in fact discovered and enslaved. With the help of God they finally were able to flee, and their trip to Zarahemla took *twelve days.* Thus, from the waters of Mormon, on the borders of the land of Nephi, it is a total of twenty days for a group of people with their animals to travel to the city of Zarahemla. (Mosiah 24:25)

Chalchitán (possible City of Helam). Reconstruction drawing by
artist/archaeologist Tatiana Proskouriakoff. Reproduced from Smith
(1955), with permission of Ms. Proskouriakoff and the Peabody Museum.

John Lloyd Stephens made a trip which traversed similar territory and in a similar amount of time. The first part of his journey took him from Guatemala City to Quetzaltenango. (see Map
#2, p. 254.) Excluding side trips to see volcanoes and ruins, that
took five to six days by mule. The second part of the journey took

him on an eight-day trip through Huehuetenango, across the Guatemala border by the head of the Grijalva River, and on to Comitan, Chiapas. (See Map #10, p. 264.) That took eight arduous days by mule. It is probably only about two more days' journey from there to Santa Rosa, the proposed location for Zarahemla. Altogether he probably took twelve days to cover the same ground covered by the people of Alma in twenty days. He had the advantage of mules and a more direct route.

THE HEAD OF THE RIVER SIDON

The description given by Stephens of his descent into the area believed to be the "head of the River Sidon" is most revealing. It will be recalled that this is the area which is proximate to the strip of wilderness that separates the Land of Nephi from the Land of Zarahemla. (Alma 22:27) Part way down the mountainside, descending into the area of the headwaters of the Grijalva, the adventurers ". . . dismounted, slipped the bridles off our mules, and seated ourselves to wait for our Indians, looking down into the deep imbosomed valley, and back at the great range of Cordilleras, crowned by the Sierra Madre, seeming a barrier fit to separate worlds." In fact, this probably was the physical boundary between the land claimed by the Nephites and the land claimed by the Lamanites.

Stephens shortly reached the River Dolores which was one meter deep. Half an hour later his party arrived at the River Lagartero, ". . . the boundary line between Guatimala (sic) and Mexico, a scene of wild and surpassing beauty . . . ." At this point he was within a few kilometers of the springs which give rise to the River Lagartero, as well as the junction of the various branches which come together to form the River Grijalva.

I concur with Stephens' description of the area. It is indeed a place of spectacular beauty where the water takes on deep shades of green and blue. With a backdrop of the mountains, a climate suitable for raising virtually every crop imaginable, and plenty of water, it must have been a wonderful place to live in ancient times.

MANTI: LA LIBERTAD

The largest ruins in the area are called "La Libertad," and are located between several branches of the headwaters. They were inhabited as early as 600 B.C. (Chiapa III time period) Ceramic affiliations continued to be with the Central Depression of Chiapas, but in the period from 300 B.C. to 50 B.C. there were other influences. Just as would be expected based on Book of

Mormon descriptions of movements between Nephi and Zarahemla, there are also cultural affiliations with Kaminaljuyú. (Warren, 1978:57)

La Libertad was abandoned during the Chiapa VI Phase, sometime between 50 B.C. and 100 A.D. All indications point to La Libertad having been the city of Manti, which was located at the head of the River Sidon. (Alma 16:6-7; 43:22-54; 58) It was the scene of a number of battles between the Nephites and Lamanites, all of which make sense in the geographical setting of the ruins of La Libertad. In fact, a Lamanite retreat *towards* Nephite territory of Manti can be explained by the fact that the Lamanites were trapped in a box canyon at the base of the divide, by forces of Moroni and Lehi. The fact that Manti is never mentioned subsequent to the battles in 62 B.C. is completely consistent with the archæological record.

Although the site is only seven kilometers from the Pan American Highway, it is unfortunately very difficult to reach. An unusual feature of the mounds themselves is the large amount of obsidian and pottery exposed on the surface. While the town was functioning, the people must have been particularly active. Perhaps it was abandoned because it was in such a vulnerable position, being right on the frontier.

MIGRATIONS TO THE LAND NORTHWARD

In the course of a single generation the Nephites changed the Land Northward from a place of potential refuge into an extension of their homeland. This was likely due to population pressures in the land of Zarahemla.

CONTAINMENT OF MIGRATION

The first recorded Nephite attempt to migrate to the land northward was in 67 B.C. Border disputes, probably due to shortage of agricultural land, led to a decision by one group to move into the land northward.

> Therefore, Morianton put it into their hearts that they should flee to the land which was northward, which was covered with large bodies of water, and take possession of the land which was northward. And behold, they would have carried this plan into effect, (which would have been a cause to be lamented) . . .   (Alma 50:29-30)

The strategic importance of that move is not explained, nor is the reason why the Nephites forcibly prevented the migration.

The next few years were years of internal and external dissensions. General Moroni, architect of the Nephite strategy for containment of the Lamanites, retired after bringing about significant victories for the Nephites. It may have been coincidence, but the very year after general Moroni died, the first major Nephite migration took place into the land northward. Perhaps it was his personal influence that held down desires to take large numbers of people northward.

MAJOR MIGRATIONS

The year of the first major migration was 55 B.C. ". . . there was a large company of men, even to the amount of five thousand and four hundred men, with their wives and their children, departed out of the land of Zarahemla into the land which was northward." Much shipbuilding and migration by ship is mentioned also. "Corianton had gone forth to the land northward in a ship, to carry forth provisions unto the people who had gone forth into that land." (Alma 63:4-10) Many others migrated at about the same time. (63:9)

Several years later, the Lamanites made a desperate attempt to cut through the heart of Zarahemla and Bountiful that they might obtain "the north parts of the land." (Helaman 1:23) They were routed in the attempt.

A great many Nephites migrated to the land northward in 46 B.C.

> And they did travel to an exceeding great distance, insomuch that they came to large bodies of water and many rivers. Yea, and even they did spread forth into all parts of the land, into whatever parts it had not been rendered desolate and without timber, because of the many inhabitants who had before inherited the land.   (Helaman 3:4-5)

One possibility for the area settled at that time would be the Gulf Coast plain of Veracruz. The "previous inhabitants" referred to may have been Mulekites. At this time we read of the construction of cities, buildings made of cement, temples, sanctuaries, etc., but are also told that we are being given less than a hundredth part of the history of that time.

The shipping of timber at this time is an interesting sidelight to the history. "And it came to pass as timber was exceeding scarce in the land northward, they did send forth much by the way of shipping." (Helaman 3:10) If the wood was being shipped to southern Veracruz, it may have come from along the coast of Tabasco, otherwise known as the Chontalpa region. That region served as an important source of building wood just after the Spanish conquest of the area. Sisson reported, "Logwood became an important natural resource, attracting English logwood cutters and pirates."

In about 28 B.C. a large number of Lamanites were allowed to migrate into the land northward. A "free market" developed between the Nephites and Lamanites, resulting in development of a prosperous trade. However, in spite of the preaching of great prophets, secret societies were formed and idol worship grew.

Finally, just a few years before the destructions at the time of the Crucifixion, there was a rebellion and the people of Jacob fled to the "northernmost part of the land." There, they reasoned, they could build up a kingdom which would someday be more powerful than all the Nephites and Lamanites. (3 Nephi 7:12)

A substantial amount of archæological and historical corroboration of these migrations is available. In the previous chapter there was a discussion concerning the important ruins of Monte Albán. The influx of a ruling class from Chiapas or Guatemala began a new cultural phase sometime during the first two centuries B.C. More archæological work will be required before we know the date of that influx with enough accuracy to assign it securely to the Nephite migrations just mentioned.

HISTORICAL VERIFICATION OF MIGRATION IN SHIPS

The Indian historian, Ixtlilxóchitl (1952, Vol. I, pp. 19, 470, Vol. II, p. 22) has recorded a significant migration from the "east" (modern coordinates) into the Book of Mormon land northward. The one fixed date associated with that migration, according to the eighteenth century historian Veytia, is 55 B.C., exactly the same year recorded for the beginning of Nephite movements into the land northward. A significant corroboration of the use of ships at this time is included in the account. It appears that the immigrants encountered and eventually murdered some culturally backward remnants of the Jaredite civilization. My translation of Ixtlilxóchitl's account is as follows:

> Those who possessed this new world in the third age were the Ulmecas and Xicallancas. It appears from their histories that they came in ships or boats from the East to the land of Potonchan. From there they began to settle along the banks of the Atoyac river which passes between the city of Puebla and the city of Cholula. They found there some of the giants who had escaped the calamity and destruction of the second age. They were robust and so confident of their strength that they completely dominated the new settlers. The giants had them as oppressed as if they were slaves. For this reason the heads and principal leaders of the Ulmecas and Xicallancas sought some means of liberating themselves from this slavery. They thus formally invited the giants to a great feast. After feeding them and getting them inebriated, they used the weapons of the giants to kill them. With this act the new settlers were free and exempt from the plague. They went on to build up their dominion and command.

Though none of this information about the encounter with the "giants" is in the Book of Mormon, it is not inconsistent and may have happened. It is interesting to note that the Book of Mormon states that the Jaredites were "large and mighty men as to the strength of men." (Ether 15:26)

SETTLEMENT OF VALLEY OF MEXICO

The chronicle accounts indicate that the building of the pyramids at Cholula and Teotihuacán goes back in time to the migrations of the Ulmeca and Xicallanca. The pyramid at Cholula was in fact begun around that time, though the much larger construction partly visible today was built after Book of Mormon times. Places which were probably thriving at about the birth of Christ included a number of towns along the shores of Lake Texcoco, anciently located where Mexico City now sits.

The most impressive of those towns was Cuicuilco, which can be seen today just south of the University of Mexico City. There is a large round pyramid and other smaller pyramids which were covered by a volcano. (In Chapter 5 the eruption of the volcano Xitle was tentatively placed at the time of the Crucifixion.) Radiocarbon dates from Cuicuilco range from 400 B.C. to the time of Christ.

At the northern end of Lake Texcoco the place now known as "the pyramids" of "Teotihuacán" received its first major settlement between 100 B.C. and A.D. 1. The population influx was estimated at 5,000 to 10,000. (Millon, 1973) These numbers are consistent with the size of the group previously referred to which had 5,400 families and which went northward in 55 B.C. Whether or not that specific group was the one that settled Teotihuacán is not so important as recognition that the size and timing of the migration is consistent with the archæology of Teotihuacán. There may also have been some settlement of Teotihuacán by people from other parts of the Valley of Mexico.

In the preceding statements it has been inferred that the "Ulmeca-Xicallanca" of the chronicles were among the original settlers of Teotihuacán. This hypothesis, arrived at largely through cross-correlation with the Book of Mormon, finds support in other studies. R.E.L. Chadwick (1966) has made a fairly definitive study advancing the same hypothesis. He concluded that the "Olmeca-Xicallanca" participated in Teotihuacán culture from A.D. 1 until destruction of the city. His hypothesis was centered around development of the "Thin-Orange" type of pottery at Teotihuacán, and connections with other areas such as the southern part of Puebla. He notes that these people may have been composed of different ethnic groups, a point entirely consistent with the Book of Mormon account.

In the first major period at Teotihuacán the buildings were in small groups, suggesting to Bernal (1974) and Millon that the city was made up of a number of unified tribes. There was no "state" at that time. We are reminded of the Book of Mormon description of the state of government in the decades between the birth and death of Christ. There was no central government but rather organization was on a tribal basis. (3 Nephi 7:1-4)

THE CENTURIES AFTER CHRIST IN THE LAND NORTHWARD

During the two-hundred-year period of peace which followed the visit of Christ to America we would expect great progress to have been made. The Book of Mormon does speak of it, but only in general terms. The entire period is summarized by Mormon in two pages. He says that cities were renewed, and the people were "blessed and prospered." He reported that they had become rich, and had "spread upon all the face of the land." (4 Nephi 23) During that time there was a rebuilding period going on throughout Mesoamerica which set the stage for entrance of the "Classic" period in Mesoamerica. Indeed, we must look to archæology to fill in some of the detail omitted by Mormon.

DEVELOPMENT OF TEOTIHUACÁN

It appears that there was very early planning of the ceremonial center of Teotihuacán. A careful mapping project by the University of Rochester has revealed that within the central core of Teotihuacán the streets were laid out in accordance with a master plan. Central to that was the great avenue now called the "Avenue of the Dead." Along that corridor two dozen temple complexes were built before A.D. 150.

Teotihuacán was positioned where there were adequate water supplies. They built an advanced irrigation system fed by springs and canals. Another key to the city's location was availability of obsidian. Some of the Olmec obsidian came from the Teotihuacán valley (based on activated neutron analysis of trace elements). On the eastern edge of the valley there is a very rich deposit of black obsidian wedged between layers of red ash and lava. This volcanic glass was the source of razor-sharp blades that were as important in the economy of Mesoamerica as steel is to our modern economy. Within the city there were over five hundred craft workshops, the majority of which were obsidian workshops. Visitors to the city can easily encounter obsidian flakes by walking over unexcavated mounds.

View of the "Avenue of the Dead" from the "Pyramid of the Moon."
The "Pyramid of the Sun,"built in about A.D. 150, is on the left-hand
side. Radiocarbon dates indicate that this part of Teotihuacán was built
beginning in the first century A.D. and was abandoned around A.D. 400,
time of the Nephite destruction. (Photo courtesy Raymond
Treat and the Zarahemla Research Foundation.)

Probably the real key to the ultimate prosperity of Teotihuacán was its development as a religious center. During the first 150 years after Christ it grew rapidly, as news spread of the large temple city. The pilgrims and migrants eventually swelled the population to 30,000.

The city was grand in both plan and scale. Even today a visitor to Teotihuacán cannot help but be almost overwhelmed by the massiveness, the symmetry, and the monumentality of the work of that time. What cannot now be fully appreciated is the fact that the city was a blaze of color. There were murals everywhere. At the end of each fifty-two year calendar cycle all the murals were painted over, giving each generation the opportunity to participate in the creation of this religious center.

Pilgrims were well-received. Structures now believed to have been the ancient equivalent of hotels have been discovered. They were well-constructed permanent buildings set on foundations of moisture-resistant concrete composed of crushed volcanic rock mixed with lime and earth. (Meyer,1978)

By contrast with the openness of the public areas, private dwellings were on a more intimate scale. They were fairly large windowless compounds arranged around an open patio, Mediterranean style. Instead of doors there were curtains which gave privacy. Millon reports concerning their amenities that,

> Each patio had its own drainage system. Each admitted light and air to the surrounding apartments; each made it possible for the inhabitants to be out-of-doors yet alone. It may be that this architectural style contributed to Teotihuacán's permanence as a focus for urban life for more than five hundred years.

THE RELIGION OF TEOTIHUACÁN

I theorize that the Christianity brought to the New World by Christ was taught at Teotihuacán. Furthermore, if the Nephites had temple ceremonies not recorded in the Book of Mormon, Teotihuacán was the most likely place for them to have been practiced. Perhaps 4 Nephi 27 refers to temple recommends.

THE QUETZALCOATL LEGEND

Books have been written by Mormons and non-Mormons alike suggesting the possibility that the serpent god Quetzalcoatl was Jesus Christ. Indeed, there are three references in the Book of Mormon which suggest the use of the serpent symbol for Christ. (1 Nephi 17:41; 2 Nephi 25-20; Helaman 8:13-15) Thus, the worship of a white, bearded god dating back to the first century A.D. and known as Quetzalcoatl (the plumed serpent) should be no surprise. The similarities between the doctrine of Quetzalcoatl and that of Jesus Christ led many of the early Spanish priests who read the ancient accounts to conclude that Quetzalcoatl must have been an early apostle.

Unfortunately, the traditions and legends of the ancient life god have become closely intertwined with those legends surrounding the life of Ce Acatl Topíltzin Quetzalcoatl. He was the tenth century king of Tula who abandoned the city with a retinue of followers and traveled to the Gulf Coast, promising to return. It is now believed that he continued on to the Yucatan where he took over such cities as Chichen Itzá.

Bearded life god Quetzalcoatl, identified by serpent glyph to his right.
This drawing was found on a pottery vessel in the Zacuala Palace
at Teotihuacán. It dates to the second or third century A.D.
(adapted from Sejourné, 1962:42)

Ce Acatl Topíltzin Qetzalcoatl, king of Tula and the tenth-century
cultural hero. (Adapted from Seiourne, 1962:43)

Traditions of Quetzalcoatl at Teotihuacán all antedate that very real cultural hero, and therefore must relate to the life god, whom we believe was Jesus Christ. The very famous temple of Quetzalcoatl, built between A.D. 150 and 400, is the most visual expression of the worship of Quetzalcoatl. It is covered with serpent heads arranged symmetrically.

The flaming serpent, Quetzalcoatl, from the third century temple erected in his honor at Teotihuacán. The flaming serpent may be a representation of Jesus Christ, in conformity with Book of Mormon references to the flaming serpent as a symbol of Christ.
(2 Nephi 25:20; Helaman 8:13-15)

REPRESENTATIONS OF SPIRITUAL REBIRTH

Accompanying the serpent heads on the temple of Quetzalcoatl are an abundance of shell symbols. They are usually associated with Quetzalcoatl as representations of spiritual rebirth. (Palmer, 1967) In anthropomorphic representations, a cross cut of a sea shell is shown on the chest of Quetzalcoatl. In one representation from the Maya codex Dresden a full-grown person emerges from a shell underwater. A god is seated on top of the water holding a serpent. These and other representations of old men emerging from shells suggest concepts of spirituality and baptism. (Sejourné, 1956, 1962)

**Bas Relief of Quetzalcoatl found at Teayo, Veracruz.
Note the quetzal feathers on the headdress and the cross cut
of a large seashell on his chest. Adapted from Saenz (1962).**

Bernardino de Sahagun recorded several instances of baptisms carried on by believers in Quetzalcoatl, shortly after the Conquest of Mexico. In one instance the baptizer said, ". . . now he lives again and is born again, once more he is purified and cleansed." (Sahagun, 1956, 11, 207) In another account the priest is quoted as saying,

> When thou wast created and sent here, thy father and mother Quetzalcoatl made thee like a precious stone . . . but by thine own will and choosing thou didst become soiled . . . and now thou hast confessed . . . thou hast uncovered and made manifest all thy sins to our Lord who shelters and purifies all sinners; and take not this as mockery, for in truth thou hast entered the fountain of mercy, which is like the clearest water. With it our Lord God . . . washes away the dirt from the soul . . . Now thou art born anew, now dost thou begin to live; and even now our Lord God gives thee light and a new sun . . .   (Sejourne, 1956:56, quoting Sahagun)

The similarities between this quotation and Christianity are indeed striking!

Possible symbolism of spiritual rebirth, from the Maya Codex Dresden.
The man emerging from the seashell is underwater.
He is worshipping a god seated on the water and holding a serpent.

Council In Heaven

Within the context of traditions that have come down to the present day concerning the religion of Teotihuacán, there are many other elements which reflect basic truths taught by Joseph Smith.

From the codex Matritense comes this tradition concerning Teotihuacán,

> When it was still night
> When day was not yet
> When there still was no light
> They united
> The gods were convened there
> In Teotihuacán
>
> They talked amongst themselves
> "Come here oh gods!
> Who will take upon himself?
> Who will see to it
> That there are days,
> That there will be light?"

The description of the creation which this legend goes on to present is most significant. In this great council, called to decide who would be the creator, two gods offered to create light for the world by throwing themselves into the fire and being transformed into the sun. The first god was arrogant, but ". . . When the moment of sacrifice arrived, the arrogant god who was the first, tried four times but he didn't have the courage to do it. Thus he lost his chance to be converted into the sun." Then it was the turn of the humble god. "He closed his eyes and threw himself into the fire until it consumed him, his destiny being to be transformed into the sun of this, the fifth age." (León-Portilla, 1964:23)

To Joseph Smith it was revealed that there was a great council in heaven prior to organization of this world. There were two plans presented. The first was by Satan, who arrogantly desired all the glory and whose plan of compulsion would not have required him to sacrifice himself. The other plan was that of Jesus Christ, whose proposal of free agency for man would require him to ultimately make an atoning sacrifice. He humbly proposed that all the glory for this effort would go to his father. (Moses 4:1-4)

ATTAINMENT OF EXALTATION

The very word "Teotihuacán" means "City of the gods." Sejourne (1956, p. 136) made a fascinating statement concerning its meaning:

> Far from implying any gross polytheistic belief, the term Teotihuacán evokes the idea of human divinity and shows that the city of the gods was the very place where the serpent learned miraculously to fly; that is, where the individual, through inner growth, attained to the category of a celestial being.

A doctrine is suggested here that is unfamiliar to most of the Christian world today, but which is entirely consistent with the writings of the apostle Paul in the Holy Bible:

> The Spirit itself beareth witness with our spirit that we are the children of God; And if children, then heirs; heirs of God and joint-heirs with Christ; if so be that we suffer with him, that we may be also glorified together. For I reckon that the sufferings of this present time are not worthy to be compared with the glory which shall be revealed in us.   (Romans 8:16-18)

This doctrine is mentioned by the apostle John, as well. "He that overcometh shall inherit all things; and I will be his God, and he shall be my son." (Revelation 21:7)

The discovery of a city with great temples where man learned how to "overcome" and gain exaltation should not be surprising. The development of the city occurred exactly when the Book of Mormon says there was great righteousness and peace. The Book of Mormon does not describe this doctrine directly, though there are allusions to it. This is not surprising since we are told by Mormon,

> And now there cannot be written in this book a hundredth part of the things which Jesus did truly teach unto the people . . . And when they shall have received this, which is expedient that they should have first, to try their faith, and if it shall so be that they shall believe these things then shall the greater things be made manifest unto them.   (3 Nephi 26:7-11)

Perhaps the motivations for construction of the "pyramid of the sun"[1] were similar to those of the Mormons in Nauvoo who sacrificed greatly to build a great temple where they could receive the "endowment" of keys, signs, and knowledge necessary to gain exaltation. As was the case in Nauvoo, the great pyramid in Teotihuacán required a great deal of organization of manpower.

Pyramid of the Sun at Teotihuacán, constructed during the first two centuries after Christ. A holy temple probably once crowned the pyramid, serving as a focal point for pilgrimages from faraway places In Mexico.

---

1. The identification with the sun was a later development probably bearing no relationship to its true purpose.

Over a million cubic meters of earth fill the interior of the pyramid, which is 222 by 225 meters at its base and 63 meters high. Its purpose was quite unlike the pyramids of Egypt, however. The whole idea was to elevate a temple above the mundane swarms of humanity. Long-since destroyed, that ancient temple was undoubtedly the most sacred spot in the city and the place where the most sacred ceremonies would be performed. Evidence now indicates that the pyramid and temple were constructed around A.D. 150 (Millon, 1961b) to A.D. 200. We may never know whether the pyramid of the sun and related structures along the Avenue of the Dead were part of the true worship of Christ or were the beginning stages of apostasy. According to the great Mesoamerican archæologist, Ignacio Bernal, Teotihuancán suffered two collapses. the first collapse is indicated by a virtual end of building activity and an end to the functions of the Ceremonial Precinct in about A.D. 300. That was followed by the final collapse 350-450 years later (Bernal, 1965:2:27-35). The first decline was probably due to the apostasy, with the city turning from a ceremonial center into a trading center. Trade of a vast amount of goods became the hallmark of Teotihuancán society.

SUMMARY

1. The seeds of the ultimate Nephite destruction by the Lamanites were laid in the conflict between Nephi and his brothers during the migration to America.

2. There are a large number of ruins in the highlands of Guatemala and the Central Depression of Chiapas, Mexico, which are old enough to be related to the Nephite-Lamanite cities.

3. The Valley of Guatemala was likely the early Land of Nephi, and the ruins of Kaminaljuyú are quite likely the ruins of the City of Nephi.

    a. Monumental architecture appeared coincident with the arrival of Nephi in the sixth century B.C. There were five architectural groupings. These may correspond to the number of lineages represented. A reign of kings, begun by the Nephites, finds archæological support.

    b. A linguistic influence entering Chiapas in the third century B.C. may be related to desertion of the Land of Nephi by a body of Nephites in about 250 B.C.

c. The return to Nephi of Zeniff's group in 200 B.C. fits exactly with archæological evidence of a spectacular building program begun at Kaminaljuyú in 200 B.C. Taxation, elaborate temples, and idolatry, all associated with the reign of King Noah, are all verifiable in the data from extensive investigations of the site of Kaminaljuyú.

d. There is evidence at Kaminaljuyú of trade with the Central Depression of Chiapas, which may coincide with trade established between Nephites and Lamanites at about the time of Ammon's missionary work.

4. There is evidence that the ruins of Chalchitan could be the City of Helam.

5. The "head of the River Sidon" was probably the headwaters of the Grijalva River, and the ruins of La Libertad were probably those of the Nephite City of Manti.

6. Nephites began migrating to the Land Northward in 55 B.C., the same year that, according to the chronicle accounts, the "Ulmeca and Xicallanca" peoples made a boat trip and subsequently settled in the area near Cholula.

7. The settlement of Teotihuacán occurred at about the time the Nephite migrations began. Nephites may have been among the first settlers of that great city.

8. Teotihuacán developed into a great temple city during the first two centuries A.D.

9. Worship of the serpent god, Quetzalcoatl, was probably related to worship of Jesus Christ. There are three references in the Book of Mormon to use of the serpent as a symbol for Christ.

10. Among the doctrines taught at Teotihuacán, we find evidence of belief in a preexistence, a council in heaven, the need for a god to sacrifice himself for the world, belief in spiritual rebirth, and the potential of man to become exalted.

11. The great "Pyramid of the Sun" was once the base for a temple. Built in the century after the appearance of Jesus Christ, it may have been used as a center for true worship of Him.

9

A Historical Setting for the Nephite Destruction at Cumorah

> . . . *The land was filled with robbers and with Lamanites . . . and every soul was filled with terror because of the greatness of their numbers . . . they did fall upon my people with the sword and with the bow, and with the arrow, and with the ax, and with all manner of weapons of war.*
> Mormon 2:8, 6:7-10

To what do we attribute the fratricidal war which resulted in extermination of the Nephites? Was it strictly hate, was it racial distinctions, or was it strictly a religious war? These may have been very important factors, but I will suggest in this chapter that there were geopolitical factors at work also. What was the role of the great city of Teotihuacán? That question must be addressed when considering the Nephite destruction. Why were the Nephites allowed four years to prepare for the battle? What was the impact of the Nephite destruction on the subsequent developments in Mesoamerica?

These are all very difficult questions. Some good answers are now available for some of them, but for others we will be left to choose between a number of options, some or all of which may prove to be wrong. I shall try to provide some of the relevant data so that the reader can reach his own conclusions.

THE GREAT APOSTASY: A.D. 200 TO A.D. 300

About A.D. 200, a great change began to sweep Mesoamerica as the people turned away from their egalitarian (all things in common) type of existence and began to develop a class structure. Mormon reports that the search for worldly things such as costly apparel was at the heart of this change. (4 Nephi 24) Historically, those who reject the laws of god have built up their own churches preaching doctrines that justify their actions. This was certainly the case in Mormon's time.

Mormon laments, "And they began to be divided into classes; and they began to build up churches unto themselves to get gain, and began to deny the true church of Christ." Ten years later, Mormon reported that many churches had been built up which claimed to be the church of Christ, but which denied important parts of his doctrine. In other words, they were clearly apostate. Mormon goes on to describe practices which appear to have a direct connection with Teotihuacán, as will be explained later. He says that the churches, ". . . did receive all manner of wickedness, and did administer that which was sacred unto him to whom it had been forbidden because of unworthiness." This sounds as though Mormon is trying to say that the sacred rites were still being used by the apostate churches, and were being sold instead of being used righteously.

Mormon goes on to say,

> And this church did multiply exceedingly because of iniquity, and because of the power of Satan who did get hold upon their hearts . . . . the people did harden their hearts, for they were led by many priests and false prophets to build up many churches, and to do all manner of iniquity. (4 Nephi 28, 34)

By A.D. 242, the situation was even worse. The people had once more separated into traditional factions of Lamanites, Nephites, etc. "And the more wicked part of the people did wax strong, and became exceedingly more numerous than were the people of God. And they did still continue to build up churches unto themselves, and adorn them with all manner of precious things."

Secret combinations spread throughout the land, possibly in response to the need for long-distance traders. Just after mentioning the robbers Mormon says, "And gold and silver did they lay up in store in abundance, and did traffic all manner of traffic." This, he notes, was the situation in A.D. 300. It is probably not coincidental that the archæologists now consider the Classic Period to have begun in A.D. 300, the point in time at which long-

An artist's conception of Teotihuacán as it looked about A.D. 400.
The pyramid at the far left is now called the Pyramid of the Moon.
The artist has depicted fires on the corners of the Pyramid of the Sun,
which may or may not have been there anciently.
Note the regular arrangement of the streets which were laid
out in a well-ordered grid pattern around the main avenue.

distance trade from centers like Teotihuacán began to be felt throughout Mesoamerica.

Role of Teotihuacán in the Great Apostasy

The impressive nature of Teotihuacán does not have to be described, as many of the readers will have visited there or seen pictures of the site. What is of key concern here is the time that various portions of the central city were completed. A large number of radiocarbon dates have been taken at Teotihuacán. The following dates have been found for carbon samples from the Street of the Dead and the Plaza of the Moon: A.D. 70, 160, 160, 177, 207, 207, 207, 260, 320, 400. (All dates have been corrected using the best radiocarbon half life and the dendrochronology recalibration.) The uncertainty in these dates is plus or minus 90 years. Radiocarbon dates from the Zacuala palace are A.D. 290-320 and A.D. 360-380. Many dates are within the time frame spoken of by Mormon as the period of apostasy, with great churches being built up. Could Teotihuacán have been a center for such apostasy?

Millon suggests that the culmination of Teotihuacán culture may have been between A.D. 150 and 300. (Millon, 1973:60) The dates thus far obtained indicate that the Avenue of the Dead may have been abandoned by A.D. 400, coincident with the Nephite destruction. However, the city continued to expand its residential zones and became a potent political and economic force in Mesoamerica in the period from A.D. 400 to 650, when it was abandoned.

It is thought that the temple of Quetzalcoatl was built about A.D. 200, and the "Adosada" which eventually interred it was built about A.D. 350. These were in a very large quadrangle which may have become the center of the city in later times. Also during that A.D. 200-350 period, the Temple of the Moon, with its splendid architecture, was completed. The population grew to some 100,000 inhabitants, and Teotihuacán dominated the nearby Puebla valley and the city of Cholula.

During the period after A.D. 200, a highly-stratified society developed. There were many specialized groups such as artisans of different types. Though there is little archæological evidence for it, Bernal speculates that there must have been a sizeable military group in Teotihuacán. There was a great diversity in types of housing, ranging from very humble dwellings to magnificent palaces built for the priests.

The priestly class was at the pinnacle of Teotihuacán society. They lived in sumptuous mansions beside the temples which they attended. Probably expert in writing, matters of the calendar, mathematics, and astronomy, they were called on to regulate both the affairs of state and the planting of crops. The gods, images, temples, and priests proliferated in Teotihuacán as institutionalized religion became big business, the main drawing card of the city. "It is believed that religion was the most powerful attraction, which from the beginning brought people to Teotihuacán. It contributed more than any other reason to its development." (Bernal, 1974:245)

The large number of temples dating to the period of the great apostasy after 200 A.D., plus the development of a highly classed society, all fit into the Book of Mormon description. This may have indeed been a center for the apostate sects which gave out sacred information to the unworthy and which adorned their temples with all manner of precious things.

It is interesting to note that during this period, Monte Albán had some contact with Teotihuacán but maintained a strict independence from it. This would be consistent with the diversity of sects, some of which had an apostate form of Christian worship and some of which were anti-Christ. Marcus (1980) presents documentary evidence, from Monte Albán inscriptions, of treaties between the two centers.

THE GRAND STRATEGY

The bearers of the first great cultural tradition in America, the archæological Olmecs (Jaredites) had built their empire around the isthmus of Tehuantepec. By controlling the isthmus they were able to move their armies and traders in both directions. It was impossible to develop a Mesoamerican empire without controlling the isthmus and the trade routes that ran through it. By A.D. 300 the influence of Teotihuacán was beginning to be felt on the other side of the isthmus in Kaminaljuyú.

Could an informal alliance have struck between the two powerful cities? If so, the only thing preventing a consummation of that marriage would have been the presence of the hated "Nephites" who controlled areas on both sides of the isthmus. The Book of Mormon evidence suggests that while military pressure came from the Land Southward, they may also have had non-cooperative

Teotihuacános fighting them as well. Note that Mormon (2:8) said that ". . . the land was filled with robbers and with Lamanites." After the last battle Moroni declared (Mormon 8:9) that ". . . there are none save it be the Lamanites and robbers that do exist upon the face of the land."

Bernal (1965:2:27-35) has indicated that Teotihuacán suffered a complete lack of building plus abandonment of its ceremonial centers in the fourth century A.D. The city grew thereafter, but was increasingly commodity rather than religiously oriented. the traders from Teotihuancán, possibly also referred to as "robbers," would have been the people most likely to benefit from an unencumbered passage through the isthmus down to the City of Nephi at Kaminaljuyú. These might have been descendants of the apostles spoken of in the book of 4 Nephi.

THE WAR OF DESTRUCTION

The Classic period of Mesoamerican development is generally considered to have begun in about A.D. 300. This coincides with the beginning of the last series of battles between the Lamanites and the Nephites. The war started "in the borders of Zarahemla, by the waters of Sidon" (Mormon 1:10), in about A.D. 322. It was only a few years until the Nephites were so outnumbered that they abandoned the land of Zarahemla and fortified against the Lamanites in the narrow neck of land region.

ABANDONMENT OF THE LAND OF ZARAHEMLA

This abandonment of the land of Zarahemla, with an influx of Lamanite armies displacing the Nephites, makes sense in the context of what is known about the Chiapas Highlands and the Central Depression of Chiapas. In the highlands (the area between San Cristobal de las Casas and Comitan shown on Map #10, p. 264), there was an abrupt change in ceramics at about this time. Further, the old sites were abandoned and new villages were built on the more-easily-defensible hilltops. (Culbert, 1962:161) Down in the depression by the Grijalva river there was a serious disruption at the same time, according to Culbert.

Lowe (1959:45) noted that in spite of intensive searches, not a single site with Early Classic occupation could be found in the region between the River Concordia and the River San Miguel. That would have been the very heart of Zarahemla. Subsequent extensive excavations at Santa Rosa have revealed some Early

Classic remains, but they were scarce. This suggests a much-reduced population. (Delgado,1965:81)

_ The traditional border between the Nephites and Lamanites ran along a frontier very close to the present border between Guatemala and the state of Chiapas, Mexico. On the Guatemala side of the border there are a number of large archæological sites. So far as can be determined, they were all abandoned at the beginning of the Classic period. There are no Early Classic remains that Shook (1965:185) was able to discover. He reports that Coe likewise was unable to find Early Classic materials at the more thoroughly excavated site of La Victoria. Lowe reported (1977:243) that Izapa was abandoned at the same time.

By the end of the Chiapa IX phase, which ended in A.D. 400, major cities along the route to the coast were abandoned. Ocozocoatla and Vista Hermosa were not occupied any longer. Even the large city of Chiapa de Corzo was left practically uninhabited. (Warren,1978) The site of Mirador was not abandoned, but in about A.D. 400 it came under strong influence from Teotihuacán.

The pattern seems to be quite clear. Throughout the Central Depression and surrounding Nephite territory, the archæologists have found evidence of a revolution which caused the abandonment of cities and migrations of the people. These events occurred between A.D. 300-400, which was the very period when the Nephites were being attacked and were struggling for survival.

Narrow Neck of Land Battles

The Book of Mormon says that the first retreat from Zarahemla was toward the Pacific coast. "And we marched forth and came to the land of Joshua, which was in the borders west by the seashore. (Mormon 2:6) The land of Joshua could have been somewhere in the vicinity of the Preclassic ruins of Tiltepec, shown on Map #4, pp. 256-257. (A description of Tiltepec, a site bisected by the highway between Arriaga and Tonola, is given by Navar-rete,1959:2.)

It is not clear on which side of the isthmus the further battles took place. Arguments made for the final narrow neck battles at the cities of Teancum and Desolation having been on the Pacific side of the isthmus were given in Chapter 2.

An interesting candidate for the city of Desolation is Laguna Zope, a large area of ruins surrounding the city of Juchitan.[1] Associated sites are La Lagunita and Ladrillera. Some mounds at Laguna Zope are about eight meters high. Abundant figurines have been discovered, which relate Laguna Zope to Olmec sites during the late Jaredite period. Different types of figurines from a later period ". . . may represent warriors carrying shields and atlatls or spearthrowers." (Delgado 1965: #18, 7)

The ruins at Laguna Zope were abandoned at the end of the Preclassic period. (Zeitlin, 1979) This again would be consistent with the Nephite retreat. This city was in a key position. Archæologically it has been determined that it was a port of trade in the isthmus for a two-thousand-year period. Though this site was abandoned, the isthmus continued to be important, as its control was part of the master strategy for development of a Mesoamerican empire.

BATTLES NORTH OF THE ISTHMUS

The account in Moroni 9 reflects the complexity of the battle situation after the Nephites were finally forced out of their strongholds in the narrow neck. There were a number of armies, none really responding to Mormon's commands. (Moroni 9:18) They were scattered, they abandoned women and children to be sacrificed to idols of the Lamanites, and they were evidently just as depraved as the Lamanites, if not more so.

It does not appear to have been Mormon's objective to save his people from destruction. He gave them what appeared to be the best obtainable advantage (Mormon 6:4), but was resigned to their destruction.

> . . . they are without principle, and past feeling; and their wickedness doth exceed that of the Lamanites . . . and I pray unto God that he will spare thy life, to witness the return of his people unto him, or their utter destruction; for I know that they must perish except they repent and return unto him. And if they perish it will be like unto the Jaredites, because of the wilfulness of their hearts, seeking for blood and revenge.   (Moroni 9:20-23)

There is insufficient information given by Mormon to assess which of the cities north of the isthmus were affected by the last Nephite battles. I believe it is quite certain that if Teotihuacán was

---

1. Laguna Zope is about one kilometer from Juchitan, to the west of the barrio of Chiguigo. It straddles the Pan American highway.

Warrior dressed In armor found at Nopiloa Veracruz. It is on display at
the museum of Jalapa. The style suggests a period subsequent to the
Nephite destruction. However, it is interesting in its depiction of the
extent of the use of armor. It is reminiscent of the statement
concerning Nephite armor: . . . Moroni had prepared his people with
breast-plates and with arm shields yea and also shields to defend their
heads and also they were dressed with thick clothing . . . (Alma 43:19)

involved, it was in the role of purging Nephites from its society. Monte Albán is in an intermediate position and was more exposed. Further information would be needed to determine whether Monte Albán was the "tower of Sherrizah" (Moroni 9:7) or some other area, perhaps completely outside the realm of battle.

It may be surprising that the Nephites were allowed four years in which to gather to battle. However, that appears to have been traditional for wars designed for total destruction. That was the situation in the final Jaredite battle, and Ixtlilxóchitl records a like battle situation in A.D. 998. Rivals of Topíltzin, the king of Tula, challenged him to battle. He requested and received a *ten year* period in which to prepare for battle. Ixtlilxóchitl (Vol. 1, p. 52) says, "It was a law among them that they give warning some years before the battle so that both sides could be prepared . . . . They did this until the time that the Spaniards came to this country." In preparation for the battle they gathered men out of all the surrounding cities and provinces. They made weapons, and the women brought the food. In the great battle that followed even women bore arms, and were killed along with their children. Though probably exaggerated, Ixtlilxóchitl's estimate of the dead was 3.2 million on the side of Topíltzin and 2.4 million on the side of the rival kings. There are remarkable similarities here to the battle of the Nephites and Lamanites which had occurred six centuries earlier.

THE BATTLE AT CUMORAH

The last battle began and ended in one day on the slopes of the Hill Cumorah. The Nephites had an army of a quarter million; we are not told whether that included women[2] and children. It is quite likely that the women and older children fought alongside the men. However, they may have faced an army of at least a million Lamanites. They were grossly outnumbered so the war ended quickly. Mormon's description of that day is most vivid:

> And it came to pass that my people, with their wives and their children, did now behold the armies of the Lamanites marching towards them; and with that awful fear of death which fills the breasts of all the wicked, did they await to receive them. And it came to pass that they came to battle against us, and every soul was filled with terror because of the greatness of their numbers. And it came to pass that they did fall upon my people with the sword, and with the bow, and

---

2. Peterson (1954) presents evidence for women warriors in ancient Veracruz.

with the arrow, and with the ax, and with all manner of weapons of war. And it came to pass that my men were hewn down . . . and I fell wounded in their midst. (Mormon 6:7-10)

Only twenty-four of the warriors escaped, but there were probably large numbers of dissenters who also survived. Eventually, Mormon was captured and killed. The lone righteous survivor was Moroni.

Moroni did not describe his wanderings, but used the scant amount of space left on the plates to discuss items of religious importance. As previously noted, nowhere does he say where he buried the plates. However, we know that it was in a hill in upstate New York where, as an angel, he later showed them to Joseph Smith. If we consider the hill in Mexico where the Nephites were destroyed as Mormon's Cumorah, then the hill in New York could well be considered Moroni's Cumorah.

THE AFTERMATH OF THE BATTLE

In Chapter 5, we examined the evidence for settlements around the Cerro Vigía prior to the Nephite battle. There is also evidence of Lamanite ruins which date to the period just after the Nephite destruction. Practically on the slopes of the hill, in a place called Tatocapan, evidence was found of a settlement which dates to the time of the Classic Maya, with polychrome pottery and many figurines. Altogether, there are about sixty earthen mounds at Tatocapan. (Valenzuela, 1945) If there is an archæological term which would best fit the Lamanites at that point in time, it would be "Classic Maya" or "Early Classic Maya."

We also find the construction of settlements in about A.D. 400 at San Andres Tuxtla and at Matacapan (midway between San Andres and Catemaco). Those settlements were decidedly satellites of Teotihuacán.

Coe states (1965:704), "Nowhere on the Gulf coast is Teotihuacán influence so apparent as at this site in the Tuxtla Mountains. The one structure that was completely cleared is in the purest Teotihuacán style . . ." Coe believed that Matacapan was an important way station in the route carved out between Teotihuacán and Kaminaljuyú. At Tres Zapotes the population thinned out at this time, but the style became clearly Teotihuacánoid.

According to the archæologists, there was a drastic change in Kaminaljuyú in A.D. 400 (Weaver, 1972) It was occasioned by

Talud-Tablero style of architecture at Teotihuacán.

arrival of Teotihuacános from central Mexico. There is still debate over whether or not this was an intrusion that was welcomed or was forced. What is beyond debate is the extent of Teotihuacán influence over the site. The architecture of Teotihuacán was incorporated wholesale in some areas of the site. Even the concrete used to surface the new structures was made in the same way as at Teotihuacán. (Sanders, 1977) It is also apparent that the Teotihuacános exercised religious influence over Kaminaljuyú.

These archæological facts are consistent with a theory that there was a deal struck between Kaminaljuyú and Teotihuacán. After Kaminaljuyú filled its part of the agreement by destroying the Nephites, Teotihuacán derived the greatest benefit. If we equate the Mayas of Kaminaljuyú with the Lamanites, and the traders from Teotihuacán with the "robbers," it is easy to understand the following statement by Moroni. Referring to a time about A.D. 400 he said, "for there are none save it be the Lamanites and robbers that do exist upon the face of the land." (Mormon 8:9)

In A.D. 400, Teotihuacán assumed a role as a preeminent trade center in Mesoamerica. Its influence at Kaminaljuyú helped control trade of cacao and cotton, and also augmented its

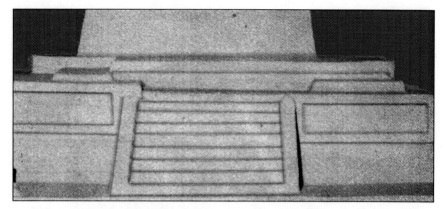

Model of the architecture employed at Kaminaljuyú around A.D. 400 when Teotihuacán influence was felt. The model is in the National Museum of Anthropology in Guatemala City. Compare with the photo on page 211.

sources of obsidian. Mayan lowland centers began about this time to take on importance as well. These included such great classic period centers as Tikal, El Mirador, Chichen Itza, Uxmal, Mayapan, Palenque, Copan, and Quirigua. Their roots of technology trace back farther in time to the golden era of the Nephites and Lamanites. Building upon the ashes of the Nephite heritage, the Mayas created a brilliant civilization.

A French philosopher once said, "Let us take from the ruins of the past the fire, not the ashes." In many respects this is what happened in Mesoamerica during the Classic period. The Nephites had abandoned God and all that was decent. It had been prophesied many times that if they should ever apostatize they would be destroyed. The prophecy was fulfilled. Using the Nephite knowledge and cultural attainments, those who survived managed to pull together a civilization that was remarkable in its own right.

Summary

1. There was an apostasy from the Church of Jesus Christ which began in about A.D. 200 and which resulted in the creation of very powerful false churches.

2. It appears that Teotihuacán may have been one of the centers of apostasy. Much of the Avenue of the Dead, the temples,

and the quadrangle with the temple of Quetzalcoatl were built during the period of apostasy.

3. Religion was the primary attraction of Teotihuacán. It reached a population of 100,000 during the period preceding the Nephite destruction. Teotihuacán may have evolved into a center for the secret society of Gadianton robbers.

4. Desired control over the Isthmus of Tehuantepec and the lucrative trade routes may have been a geopolitical factor that combined with Lamanite hatred of the Nephites to precipitate that last series of conflicts.

5. Teotihuacán was not controlled by the Nephites. It may even have conspired against them.

6. There is substantial archæological evidence for the expulsion of Nephites from the Land Southward at the beginning of the last wars. Around A.D. 300, many of the cities in the Central Depression of Chiapas, cities along the borders of Guatemala, and Laguna Zope in the Isthmus of Tehuantepec were abandoned.

7. The four-year period allowed the Nephites to prepare for their last battle was part of an ancient Mesoamerican pattern.

8. The Nephite army of a quarter million was destroyed in one day by a larger Lamanite army.

9. It is suggested that the "Lamanites" were the Mayas, and the "robbers" were Teotihuacános.

10. There are Mayan- and Teotihuacán-style settlements built near the Cerro Vigía just after the time of the Nephite destruction. This may be evidence of collusion between the two forces in destroying the Nephites.

11. Teotihuacán had considerable influence in Kaminaljuyú after A.D. 400.

12. The so-called "Classic" cultures began to really flourish coincident with destruction of the decadent Nephites.

10

CONCLUSION

> *. . . When my father saw all these things, he was filled with the Spirit and began to prophesy concerning his seed—That these plates of brass should go forth unto all nations, kindreds, tongues, and people who were of his seed.*
> 1 Nephi 5:17-18

Where has the search for Cumorah led us? In this book I have presented evidence that Mormon's Cumorah may be the Cerro Vigía. It is at the northern end of the Tuxtla mountain chain in the state of Veracruz, Mexico. There is always room for some doubt when dealing with such matters. Indeed, it has been said that in the realm of creative theorizing, absolutism is entirely out of place. It will be remembered that Joseph Smith set the example when he speculated on the location of Zarahemla, saying, "We are not going to declare positively that the ruins . . . are those of Zarahemla."

TESTING THE THEORY

What I have shown is that the candidate hill appears to fulfill all the criteria required in order to qualify as the last Jaredite and Nephite battleground. In Chapter 2, a geographic model was developed with thirteen specific criteria that had to be met. It met all of them. In Chapter 3, fifteen archæological and cultural criteria were developed. It met all of them reasonably well. Any candidate for the last Nephite battleground must pass through the screening to which the Cerro Vigía theory has been subjected.

It has been shown that there is nothing in either the Book of Mormon or in the statements by Joseph Smith which requires us to accept the hill now known as Cumorah, in upstate New York, as anything other than the place where Moroni buried the plates. As a candidate for the last Jaredite and Nephite battleground, it fails on most of the geographical criteria and almost all of the archæological criteria. Acceptance through tradition of that hill as Mormon's Cumorah has retarded progress in understanding Book of Mormon geography. An accurate geography is a prerequisite to meaningful correlation of the Book of Mormon with archæology.

A substantial case has been developed for the Cerro Vigía, which is surrounded by ruins dating to both Jaredite and Nephite times. However, more field research in the area of the hill would be helpful.

THE BOOK OF MORMON AND ARCHÆOLOGY

Within the context of Mormon's Cumorah being in Veracruz it is possible to gain a better understanding of Book of Mormon history through the eyes of archæology. We have been able to demonstrate that the archæological Olmecs were the Jaredites or rival lineages of the same times. The timing, location, and nature of the Olmec civilization is completely consistent with the last battleground being in southern Veracruz.

We have also been able to gain an understanding of how the Mulekites could have found Coriantumr, the last Jaredite survivor. We have examined evidence for the Mulekite migration to America and their subsequent movements. The significance of important ancient cities to the Book of Mormon has been briefly suggested. These cities include Kaminaljuyú, La Libertad, Chiapa de Corzo, Monte Albán and Teotihuacán. Understanding the development of such centers has helped to put the battles at Cumorah into perspective.

Geopolitical factors have been suggested as having a role in the Nephite destruction. Following the Nephite defeat by the Lamanites, whose traditional capital was in the highlands of Guatemala, Teotihuacános took advantage of the situation. Teotihuacán became a preeminent force in Mexico and extended its influence to Guatemala.

There is a significant amount of theorizing in this book. However, the reader will note that I have been careful to cite the actual words from the Book of Mormon so that the reader can draw his own conclusions. Those words, the words of Mormon and Moroni, are the first and foremost criteria against which any theory correlating the Book of Mormon with the outside world must be evaluated. The reader will have also seen a great deal of archæological data given herein which must be reckoned with. None of it appears inconsistent with the Book of Mormon. Some substantiates the Book of Mormon history directly, while other data helps us fill in historical gaps in Mormon's extremely brief abridgement.

THE RECORD REPOSITORY IN CUMORAH

It was shown in the Introduction that the word "Cumorah" means "arise-o-light" or "arise-revelation." It can aptly be applied to Moroni's Cumorah in New York, but what about Mormon's Cumorah in Veracruz?

One of Mormon's last and most important acts was to conceal within the Hill Cumorah all the sacred records that were not given to Moroni. He said,

> And it came to pass that when we had gathered in all our people in one to the land of Cumorah, behold I Mormon, began to be old; and knowing it to be the last struggle of my people, and having been commanded of the Lord that I should not suffer the records which had been handed down by our fathers, which were sacred, to fall into the hands of the Lamanites, (for the Lamanites would destroy them) therefore I made this record out of the plates of Nephi, and hid up in the hill Cumorah all the records which had been entrusted to me by the hand of the Lord, save it were these few plates which I gave unto my son Moroni. (Mormon 6:6)

The records buried by Mormon were the following:

1. **the Large Plates of Nephi** (the basis of Mormon's abridgement)—they were probably large in number as well as physical size, and were made by Nephi (1 Nephi 19:1-4);

2. **the Brass Plates of Laban**—probably the oldest and most accurate version of the Old Testament that may be recoverable (1 Nephi 5:10-19);

3. **the 24 Gold Plates of Ether**—they contained the record of the Jaredites. Moroni must have had access either to these plates or to Mosiah's translation of them when he abridged the record of the Jaredites (Mosiah 28:11-20);

4. **all the remaining permanent Nephite** records, which were no doubt very extensive (cf. Helaman 3:14-15).

The records given to Moroni were the following:

5. ***The Small Plates of Nephi***—a succinct account emphasizing religion rather than history, and terminating in about 130 B.C. These plates were made by Nephi (2 Nephi 5:29-34; Words of Mormon 3-11);

6. ***Plates of Mormon***—made by Mormon to contain his abridgement of the Large Plates of Nephi—they are the basis for most of the Book of Mormon (3 Nephi 5:8-12);

7. ***Plates used by Moroni*** to produce the section known as the "sealed portion" (Ether 3:27-28; 4:4-6; 5:1).

Why did Mormon bother to carefully conceal all the records not given to Moroni? Didn't the records possessed by Moroni contain all the knowledge essential to man's salvation?

The whole purpose of compiling the Book of Mormon history and carefully guarding the records for generation after generation was to bring a knowledge of the true gospel of Jesus Christ to the world, and especially to the descendants of Lehi. That is a commission given to The Church of Jesus Christ of Latter-day Saints, and it applies to carrying of the gospel to the entire world. Concerned with how that would be accomplished, President Spencer W. Kimball said to the regional representatives,

> If we do all we can, and I accept my own part of that responsibility, I am sure the Lord will bring more discoveries to our use. He will bring a change of heart into kings and magistrates and emperors, or he will divert rivers or open seas or find ways to touch hearts. He will open the gates and make possible the proselyting. Of that, I have great faith.   (Kimball, 1974)

I suggest that this prophecy will be fulfilled in many ways; it is indeed already being fulfilled. There will be even greater advances in communications which will permit more people to hear the message. Ways will be found to present the message in more effective ways. I also suggest that great documentary discoveries will have a role. Of particular impact will be discoveries which relate to the Book of Mormon.

New Discoveries Prophesied

In 1963, Spencer W. Kimball spoke on the Book of Mormon and suggested something which could be one mode of fulfillment of his later prophecy. "Archæologists may be excited as they read of ruins of ancient cities, highways, and buildings; and there may be yet hidden buried gold and priceless records." (Kimball, 1963)

The discovery of such records could do more to publicize the Book of Mormon and arouse people's interest in reading it than all of the other evidence combined. Though there may be other discoveries, Mormon's record repository lays in wait as potentially the greatest documentary discovery of all time.

An explicit prophecy that this record sanctuary would someday be discovered was made by an early Book of Mormon prophet, Alma. In doing so, he referred specifically to a portion of the records, the Brass Plates of Laban. As he entrusted these plates and other records to his son Helaman, he gave this exhortation:

> And now my son Helaman, I command you that ye take the records which have been entrusted with me; And I also command you that ye keep . . . all these things sacred which I have kept, even as I have kept them; for it is for a wise purpose that they are kept. And these plates of brass, which contain these engravings, which have the records of the holy scriptures upon them, which have the genealogy of our forefathers, even from the beginning . . . Behold, it has been prophesied by our fathers, that they should be kept and handed down from one generation to another, and *be kept and preserved by the hand of the Lord until they should go forth unto every nation kindred tongue and people that they shall know of the mysteries contained thereon.*[1] And now behold, if they are kept they must retain their brightness, yea and they will retain their brightness; yea, and also shall all the plates which do contain that which is holy writ. Now ye may suppose that this is foolishness in me; but behold I say unto you; that by small and simple means are great things brought to pass; and small means in many instances doth confound the wise. And the Lord God doth work by means to bring about his great and eternal purposes; and by very small means the Lord doth confound the wise and bringeth about the salvation of many souls.
>
> (Alma 37:1-7; see also Alma 37:8-14, 1 Nephi 5:19, and Enos 15-16)

The prophecy by Alma that the Brass Plates would be published to the world helps us to understand the almost matter-of-fact statement by Moroni in which he tells us that the gold plates of Ether will be found. As Moroni abridged that Jaredite history he said,

> And as I suppose that the first part of this record, which speaks concerning the creation of the world, and also of Adam, and an account from that time even to the great tower, and whatsoever things transpired among the children of men until that time, is had among the Jews . . . Therefore, I do not write those things which transpired from the days of Adam until that time; but they are had upon the plates, and whoso findeth them the same will have power that he may get the full account.

---

1. Italics are the author's.

The possibility of someday finding the complete Jaredite and Nephite accounts, not to mention the Brass Plates of Laban, prompted Dr. James R. Clark of Brigham Young University to make the following statement concerning the ancient Nephite library hidden by Mormon:

> My challenge then to us for new horizons—and this may sound strange—is to get enough faith on the part of the Latter-day Saints to ask the Lord to make that depository available to us. I mean it. I am serious about it. We will never do much with the textual problems and the linguistic problems of the Book of Mormon until that library of Jaredite and Nephite records—the originals, not the abridgement that we now have—is made available. The question is: Can we ever muster faith enough to ask for it?
>
> I would like to suggest to you these four things: We need exploratory faith. We need intellectual depth. We need dedicated service. In the last analysis, we need to be called of God.
>
> The Lord said to Oliver Cowdery, "You have not understood; you have supposed that I would give it unto you, when you took no thought save it was to ask me.   (Clark, 1959)

The prophet Nephi put it another way: "If my people desire to know the more particular part of the history of my people they must search mine other plates" [the Large Plates of Nephi]. (2 Nephi 5:33)

The impact that the promised discovery of that record repository will have has been alluded to in a number of prophecies. The Doctrine and Covenants (84:96-102) contains a prophecy about the future time when Zion will be brought to earth and says,

> The Lord hath brought again Zion!
> The Lord hath redeemed his people, Israel . . .
> The earth hath travailed and brought forth her strength
> And truth is established in her bowels . . .

This establishment of truth by discoveries in the earth will assist in ". . . proving to the world that the Holy Scriptures are true; and that God does inspire men and call them to his holy work in this age and generation. . . .Therefore, having so great witnesses, by them shall the earth be judged." (D&C 20:11,13)

Another prophecy in the Pearl of Great Price may refer to a time just preceding the Second Coming of Christ when it says,

> ". . . but my people will I preserve; and righteousness and truth will I send down out of heaven; and truth will I send forth out of the earth to bear testimony of mine Only Begotten; his resurrection from the dead; yea and also the resurrection of all men; and righteousness and truth will I cause to sweep the earth as with a flood, to gather out mine elect from the four quarters of the earth . . ."   (Moses 7:61-62)

FINDING THE RECORD REPOSITORY

It seems clear that Mormon's record repository will one day be uncovered. l expect that such a discovery will not be the result of a shepherd boy throwing a rock into a cave. Rather, it will probably be the result of concentrated research by those called to such an effort by the prophet of God.

The quest for understanding of where Mormon's Cumorah is located is just the first part of the effort. Correct location of Mormon's Cumorah cannot lead to a rapid discovery of the repository. In the first place, it simply will not be discovered until the timing is right. Secondly, if it were easy to find, it would have been found long ago. The hill Vigía is very large, and even a superficial survey would take weeks or months. The most modern and sophisticated detection methods will no doubt be required.

MEASURING UP TO THE CHALLENGE

We began this book with Joseph Smith's challenge, "It would not be a bad plan to compare Mr. Stephens' ruined cities with those in the Book of Mormon. Light cleaves to light, the facts are supported by facts, and the truth injures no one." I have tried to apply Joseph Smith's challenge to the quest for understanding the important area of Cumorah. I have not proven beyond a doubt that Cerro Vigía was Mormon's Cumorah. However, it does fit the geographic and archæological criteria remarkably well. It fits into the context of the times of the Jaredites, Mulekites and Nephites. The history of those people ties remarkably well into the ebb and tide of culture in Mesoamerica.

The subject of Book of Mormon geography is a subject of valid scientific inquiry. The great Mormon scholar B. H. Roberts wrote concerning the Book of Mormon,

> The Book of Mormon of necessity must submit to every test, to literary criticism, as well as to every other class of criticism; for our age is above all things critical, and especially critical of sacred literature, and we may not hope that the Book of Mormon will escape closest scrutiny; neither, indeed is it desirable that it should escape.
> (Roberts, 1906)

In these pages has been presented a careful scrutiny of some of the complex historical events which transpired and were recorded by Mormon. They have centered around Mormon's Cumorah. There is an amazing consistency in all this detail, and solid support for that detail from secular accounts and archæological data. It will ever be true that the deeper one probes, the more evidence one finds that the Book of Mormon is truly an ancient document written by ancient prophets.

Appendix A

Developing a Chronology for the Jaredites

Development of a chronology for the Jaredites is prerequisite to establishment of correlations between the Jaredite history and archæological remains. Unfortunately, the Book of Ether does not contain a single absolute date, and there is not even an internal count of years mentioned. Moroni had available on the plates of Ether an account from the fall of Adam to the time of the Great Tower. (Babel) Though he chose not to include that account in his record, the chronology which it contained was no doubt quite accurate, and certainly more reliable than that which we have today. Therefore, historical accounts by Ixtlilxóchitl which give 1,716 years from the fall to the flood, and another 416 years until the time of the dispersion, are given some credence. His record may be based on data going back as far as Nephite times.

We will therefore utilize a mixture of data from the works of Ixtlilxóchitl, the King James Version of the Bible, and the Greek Septuagint version of the Old Testament, in an effort to approximately date the flood and the tower of Babel. The date proposed for the tower of Babel is 2752 B.C. to 2697 B.C. The date proposed for destruction of the Jaredites is 550 to 600 B.C., based on the fact that the Mulekites landed in the general area of Cumorah and found that Coriantumr was the sole warrior to survive the Jaredite genocidal war. More argument concerning this latter date is given in Chapter 7. Nominally, therefore, I have used 2700 B.C. to 600 B.C. as the time span of the Jaredite peoples. The 2100 intervening years are divided between the 29 mentioned descendants of Jared, with addition of two more unnamed descendants between Riplakish and Morianton where intervening generations are implied. The table of dates developed is presented in Chapter 6.

Early Bible Chronology

It would be perhaps simpler if there were just one Bible chronology. Unfortunately, the King James version, based on the Hebrew Masoretic text for the Old Testament, differs from the

Greek Septuagint, which differs from the Samaritan Bible. How then, should we begin? I propose to start with the expulsion from the Garden of Eden and compare the King James, Septuagint, and Mesoamerican chronologies. Later, we will work in the other direction and give B.C. dates to the chronologies.

From the Fall to the Flood we have 1,656 years in the King James Version (KJV), 2,606 years in the Greek Septuagint, and 1,656 years in the Book of Moses (Pearl of Great Price). The Mesoamerican account by Ixtlilxóchitl gives 1,716 years. Though the time down to Adam from the Flood is not crucial to our chronology, I lean towards the Mesoamerican-KJV range of 1,656 to 1,716 years. That difference in age is just one percent, which is archæologically speaking of little consequence.

Another big difference between the KJV and the Septuagint is in the period from the Flood to the birth of Abraham. The KJV allows a mere 297 years while the Septuagint allows 1,172 years. Although the repetition of dates appears somewhat symbolic and may indeed hide a number of lost generations, I believe that the chronology in the Greek Septuagint is more accurate, for that particular period. (Such a position is not unorthodox, as the early apostles used the Greek Septuagint as their volume of canonized scripture.)

There are many problems with the KJV Flood to Abraham chronology. One generation, Cainan, is omitted. Shem lived over five hundred years after the Flood, so that in the KJV version he would have outlived Abraham. That is clearly out of harmony with the spirit of the Old Testament and the dispensation given to Abraham. Furthermore, synchronizations of the scriptural account with ancient history become hopeless. What are we to make of the founding of Egypt in 3100 B.C., the beginning of the Old Kingdom in Egypt in about 2700 B.C. (if the accepted chronologies are correct) or the development of the Mesopotamian civilization which was at a cultural pinnacle just when the KJV would require it to be destroyed by the Flood? For these reasons, and others, I cast my lot with the Septuagint for that period of time.

The total time span which I now calculate, down to the birth of Abraham, is 1,172 + 1,656 = 2,828 years. The Book of Abraham (Pearl of Great Price) suggests a possible error of a few years in the date of Abraham's birth as given in the KJV. However, using the accepted KJV date of 1996, the following results:

Adam's Fall	4824 B.C.
Noah's birth	3768 B.C.
Flood	3168 B.C.

Shem's death	2666 B.C.
Peleg's birth	2634 B.C.
Abraham's birth	1996 B.C.

Mesoamerican Sources for Dating the Flood

An alternative approach to dating the Flood is to turn to the Mesoamerican legends and calendars. The great Mexican calendar "Aztec calendar stone" shows four ages of the world which ended in destruction. These destructions were due to a flood, wild animals, great winds, and finally, a great earthquake. The Vatican codex gives the length of each of these ages. 1 associate the last with the great destruction by earthquake, etc., at the time of the Crucifixion in 34 A.D. Working backwards using those data gives destructions in 1372 B.C., 2336 B.C., and 3146 B.C., the latter being the Flood. This date is within just 22 years of the date I have reconstructed from the Bible, and which I would not claim to be that accurate. (See Ixtlilxóchitl, Vol. Il, p. 22, notes for discussion of Vatican codex dates.)

Another potential point of synchronization is the fact that the zero point of the Maya Long Count calendar system was August 12, 3113 B.C. (GMT correlation). Bernal (1969) has suggested that the beginning date may represent the time of the "birth of the gods," a description which would not be out of harmony with the concepts of the Flood. In fairness, however, this date could refer to the time of the tower or time of arrival in the New World. It is also possible that it was a totally fictitious number. However, it is sufficiently close to estimates of the Flood, from our other sources, as to lead us to suspect there might be a connection. If, for instance, one adds the time of 1,716, which Ixtlilxóchitl gives as separating the Fall from the Flood, to the Long Count date of 3113 B.C., the resulting estimate for the date of the Fall is 4829 B.C., five years different than we previously calculated.

The proposed time for the Flood in Noah's time was thus between 3113 B.C. and 3168 B.C., dates sufficiently early to solve a number of archæological and historical synchronization problems, though perhaps not all. However, fixing the date of the Flood does not completely solve the problem of dating the tower of Babel, since the Bible does not give any direct indication as to when, between Noah and Abraham, the dispersion took place. Therefore, I will turn to the Mesoamerican chronicles where more information is given concerning that span of time between the Flood and the Tower.

DATING OF THE TOWER

Ixtlilxóchitl states explicitly that 416 years elapsed from the Flood to the time of the dispersion. With the dates we have proposed for the flood this gives the following estimates for the dispersion at Babel:

	Flood	Tower
My biblical chronology reconstruction	3168 B.C.	2752 B.C.
Vatican codex reconstruction	3146 8.C.	2730 B.C.
GMT correlation—Mayan long count		
zero date: Julian Calendar	3113 B.C.	2697 B.C.
Gregorian Calendar	3114 B.C.	2698 B.C.

In developing my tables I have rounded off the date of the great tower to 2700 B.C., and hope that it is accurate to within a hundred years.

ARGUMENTS FOR EVEN EARLIER DATES

There could be a number of sound arguments presented which would make the time of the great tower much earlier in time. Some would place it at 3113 B.C., which would put it towards the beginning of the age of ziggurat construction, rather than in the height of such activity some centuries later.

Arguments have also been made to the effect that Abraham should be placed somewhere in the 2200 to 2500 B.C. time period. (Shanks, 1979) This proposal is rooted in the discovery of Ebla, a great city in Syria which dates from 2500 to 2250 B.C. Of importance to the question of dating Abraham is the discovery by Giovanni Pettinato (1976), that within the collection of some fifteen thousand cuneiform tablets discovered at Ebla, there is a language and some specific names which relate very closely to the Old Testament. Even more intriguing are the exact names of the five "cities of the plain" mentioned in the fourteenth chapter of Genesis. If the date for Abraham must be moved back to about 2300 B.C., it would coincide with the Muslim tradition which places the Abrahamic period at around 2300 B.C. (LaFay, 1978)

The entire issue of the date of Abraham, which of course influences the date of the tower of Babel, is being hotly debated. It is even having political as well as scholarly repercussions. This is an area that should be watched closely, but for the present I choose to stay with the traditional Biblical date for the birth of Abraham.

SUMMARY

A combination of Bible translations and Mesoamerican historical accounts has been used to place the time of the flood between 3113 B.C. and 3168 B.C. The Mesoamerican history helps to place the time of the tower of Babel, sometime between 2697 B.C. and 2752 B.C. These dates are subject to revision as new evidence develops. It is anticipated that if they are changed at all, it will be in the direction of earlier times for both the Flood and the tower of Babel. 1 have used the nominal dates of 2700 B.C. to 600 B.C. as the time span of the Jaredite civilization, based on the results of this analysis. The apportionment of time between the generations throughout Jaredite history is shown in a table in Chapter 6.

APPENDIX B
WHERE WAS NEPHITE NORTH?

INTRODUCTION

The Book of Mormon is replete with information about topography, travels, directions, and all the elements we associate with geography. Some authors of books dealing with the geography of the Book of Mormon have taken the position that Nephite north was the same as the north we use today. These writers include Simmons (1981), McGavin (1949), The Zarahemla Record, Allen (1989), and Hauck (1988). This rigid adherence to current understanding of the cardinal directions appears to present a significant problem in developing a geography of the Book of Mormon. What can be done with the Yucatan Peninsula which was sparsely populated during very early times? How can the various seas and lands be reconciled? Is it reasonable to assume that the Nephites used twentieth-century cardinal directions? A prominent Mesoamerican ethnographer, Evon Z. Vogt (1969:602) has raised the possibility that Maya directions were 45 degrees off of ours. In this appendix we will attempt to bring some evidence to show that the Mesoamerican directions were indeed not the same as ours.

HOW WAS TRUE NORTH DETERMINED?

North Americans live in a land where directions are not hard to find. The mountain ranges run essentially north and south. We can look into the night sky and find Polaris, today the practically stationary "north star."

True north represents an extrapolation of a line from the imaginary axis on which the earth spins. That may have been beyond the comprehension of common people in ancient times. Nevertheless, the Nephite leaders may have been fairly adept at astronomy. They knew that the earth rotates while the sun is relatively stationary (Hel. 12:15). The Europeans had problems with that concept many centuries later. Nephites noted the regular motion of the planets (Alma 30:44) and the appearance of a new star (3 Nephi 1:21). The calendar they developed at the City of Nephi, which we now equate with the ruins of Kaminaljuyú, Guatemala, began on March 21, 433 B.C. Gregorian (Edmonson,

1988:118). Their calendar reflects a knowledge that the true length of the solar year is approximately 365.2422 days.

The ancient Mexican histories also tell us that careful attention was given to astronomy. Various representations in the native painted books show later astronomers sighting stars using a special V-shaped instrument. Veytia (1836:31-32) reported that in the second century B.C. certain men dedicated themselves to a study of the regular movement of the sun, moon, and stars. These studies were used as a basis for a calendar correction in the first or second century B.C. at the city of Huehuetlapallan (Ixtlilxóchitl: 1952, 114).

WAS THERE A POLE STAR?

In the time of Lehi things were not as easy as looking for the pole star. In 600 B.C. Polaris was not a pole star. This is due to a 25,695 year movement in direction of the earth's pole. It describes an imaginary circle in the sky with a diameter of about 47 degrees. The reason for this is that the earth's spin axis is tilted 23.5 degrees with respect to its plane of orbit. The earth is not a perfect sphere, but has a slight bulge at the equator. The result of the gravitational tug of the sun and the moon is a torque which causes the earth to precess like tops sometimes do. This very slow directional movement with time causes the "Precession of the equinoxes," causing the direction of stars in the sky to change with the passage of the millenia.

A consequence of the precession is that Polaris described a circle in the sky with a diameter of 24 degrees at the time of Lehi. The closest star to the north was Kochab, the bright star at the end of the Little Dipper. It described a circle of eleven degrees. Thus, the average person would have had great difficulty in finding "north" from the night sky. This information was provided by an astronomer at the University of Indiana (Hollis, H. R., n.d.).

DIRECTIONS FROM SOLAR RISING OR SETTING?

Daytime direction determinations were likewise difficult. Where the sun rises and sets in Mesoamerica varies from 65 to 115 degrees clockwise from north for a determination of "east." Likewise, west could be anywhere from 245 to 295 degrees, depending on the time of year. The equinoxes, which occur with the sun actually rising in the east and setting in the west, might have been used. However, they were more difficult to determine than solstices, which are measured at the extremes of the sun's apparent movement during the year. Thus *direction determination became the province of early Nephite astronomers who appear to have used solstice readings.*

DIRECTIONS AND THE CALENDAR

The solstices occur on December 21 and June 21 of each year. The noting of those days had great importance as they impacted on calendar development and determination of directions. This is manifested in the many calendar stones which virtually always show directional symbols. Further, the solstice readings tie directly to the importance of the intercardinal points. The famous Aztec calendar can be easily observed to have the directional signs at the intercardinal points.

The Aztec calendar system had months of twenty days. Because of the structure of their calendar, only four of these days could begin the New Year. These days were referred to as "Year Bearers." These days were also associated with directions, namely: Reed = east, Flint = north, House = west, and Rabbit = south. The intercardinal points on the Aztec calendar stone do indeed carry these symbols. This fact can be supplemented with the ethnographic observation that the present-day Zoque people from the Isthmus of Tehuantepec believe that "the world is square, with its corners at the points where the sun rises and sets at the Solstices, that is, the 22nd of June and the 22nd of December" (Munoz, 1977:140).

Figure A-1 from the Codex Fejervary-Mayer shows that in the four quarters of the earth, there are personages flanking trees of life, each with a bird at the top. As with all Mesoamerican maps, the quarter designating "east" is at the top. However, notice the symbols placed between each of the tree of life panels. At the upper left hand corner, enclosed in a circle, is the symbol for "reed." Kelley states that all his sources associate "reed" years with the east, and he therefore identifies this intercardinal direction as east. He goes on to indicate that the symbol "flint" in the bottom left hand corner represents north. Symbols for "house" and "rabbit" in the other two corners represent west and south. These directions were probably obtained solstitially, while the principle earth quarters may have been obtained by the less obvious equinox readings. From this figure we can show not only that non-cardinal directions were in use, but also that the direction for north was skewed to the west, not to the east.

SITE ORIENTATIONS

Vincent H. Malmstrom (1981) has said that ". . . only recently has it begun to be appreciated that many of the architectural alignments found in Mesoamerica appear to be related to the religious and/or cosmological beliefs of the early civilizations which built them." *It would take an extremely liberal margin of error, say four degrees, to qualify more than a few sites or buildings from all of Mesoamerica as having been oriented to true north. This discovery is so unexpected that it merits further discussion.*

DIRECTIONS FROM SOLSTICE MEASUREMENTS

We will attempt to show in this very preliminary study that the Nephites used Solstice readings to determine their directions. The solstices occur on June 21 and December 21 of each year, where the sun reaches its extreme on the horizon. These are the longest and shortest days of the year. Those directions were quite easily observed. The solstice directions in Mexico are 115/295 degrees. That would imply a shift of "north" by sixty-five degrees counterclockwise. That conforms with the winter-sunrise—summer-sunset solstice.

The Nephites oriented their buildings and sometimes the sites themselves in a solstitial manner. In addition, the sites were themselves placed so as to obtain solstitial readings from nearby mountains. Those readings are in substantial variance with our current conception of directions. Furthermore, the painted documents and calendar stones of the natives indicate that true north was not called north.*

SIXTY-FIVE DEGREES WEST OF NORTH

Vincent Malmstrom (1978) has discovered that many of the important preclassic sites in Mesoamerica were deliberately placed so that the solstice could be measured when the sun passed over nearby peaks. Basically, he found that many, but not all sites in Mexico and Guatemala are aligned 65 degrees west of north. An example is the impressive ruin at Cholula where the largest man-made ancient pyramid is aligned 65 degrees west of north with the highest peak of the volcano Ixtaccihuatl. That corresponds to the summer sunset solstice. The temple face is at right angles to that direction. Other sites similarly placed relative to volcanic peaks with the 65 west of north direction are El Meson, Nopiloa, Remojadas, Tlatilco, and Tlapacoya. Tres Zapotes, Cerro de la Piedra, and Cerro de las Mesas are all reported to be lined up solstitially with the hill Vigía

---

*These comments do not apply to the Jaredites or to those who came after the Nephite destruction.

(possible hill Cumorah). The probable City of Nephi, Kaminaljuyú, had this solstitial orientation to its buildings. The important late preclassic site of Dainzú, near Oaxaca, has a 63 degree west of north orientation to its main facade. At Lambityeco it is 65 degrees.

Izpa is considered by its chief excavator, Dr. Gareth Lowe, ". . . to have been a 'Greenwich' and 'Mount Palomar' for its time . . . also something of a New World Athens or Alexandria in the critical intermediate era of pre-Classic Mesoamerican learning and artistic development (Lowe,1982:269)." It was a very important cultural center on the Pacific coast from roughly 300 B.C. to the time of Christ. Excavations of the site were made by the NWAF. Both Lowe and Norman who worked for the NWAF *confirm orientation of the site to solstitial directions, including alignment of some of the monuments.*

The previous readings were fairly firm. Less firm are the following identifications of sites: A protractor-aided study of the NWAF maps, correcting for use of compass north rather than true north, gives solstitial orientations for a great number of sites in the Central Depression of Chiapas (possible land of Zarahemla). These include La Libertad (possible Manti), Laguna Francesa, Sitio Colonia Ninos Heroes, Chapatengo, and San Francisco. Others are Santa Isabel, El Salvador, San Felipe, Laguna Dolores, and the possible site of Zarahemla, Santa Rosa. Overall, twenty-three sites have been identified so far which have the solstitial orientation. One reason why these readings are less firm than the others is that in the Central Depression of Chiapas there is a greater distance to mountains with which solstitial alignments can be made.

SEVENTY-FIVE DEGREES WEST OF NORTH

Malmstrom (1981) has also detailed many structures having an orientation of seventy-five degrees west of north. This began with the Pyramid of the Sun at Teotihuacán, Mexico. The great site of Teotihuacán was oriented about 15.5 degrees east of north, with the " Pyramid of the Sun" facing 75 degrees west of north. The archaeoasatronomer Aveni (1978:279) concluded that "Teotihuacán North" was more important than "astronomical north." The major pyramid at Edzna, which dates to about the same time horizon, also has the Teotihuacán orientation. Other spots having the seventy-five degree west of north orientation are Mound Y at Monte Alban and the Main Pyramid at Huamelulpan in the state of Oaxaca. It can also be seen as the side orientation of the "Sterling Acropolis and Plaza" at the ancient Jaredite site of La Venta (Malmstrom, 1981). This is in contrast to the overall La Venta orientation of eight degrees west of North.

NINETY DEGREES WEST OF NORTH

It appears from this partial study of directions in the early Nephite areas, that north was usually oriented at either 65 degrees or 75 degrees west of true north. This would certainly agree with the orientation on the coast of Guatemala where the Pacific Ocean was on the "west." It is also the alignment of the mountain chain that borders the coastline. This orientation is strongly reinforced by careful examination of the Mesoamerican calendars which note the actual named directions at the inter-cardinal points.

Thus, it is not at all clear that Nephite north was true north as we know it today. It is far more likely that the river Sidon went north in their directional system, the actual direction of the River Grijalva in the Central Depression of Chiapas.

However, there is also evidence that around the Isthmus of Tehuantepec the Nephite directions may have been shifted a full ninety degrees. Most serious students of Book of Mormon geography believe that isthmus was the "narrow neck of land." However, crossing it one goes due east or west in modern coordinates. The Book of Alma states that the adjacent Land of Bountiful was inhabited from the " . . . east unto the west sea."

Recent research indicates that the land of Bountiful was located with the River Tonala on one side, the River Coatzacoalcos on the other, the Gulf of Mexico on another side, and the Pacific on the other. The directional system in use at that time probably had the Gulf of Mexico as the East Sea and the Pacific Ocean as the West Sea. This would probably be for the lack of mountains to use as a reference along the Gulf Coast east of the Coatzacoalcos river. Thus, the "East Sea" became their "east" which results in a 90 degree rotation of coordinates.

NATIVE ACCOUNTS

One of the more important native accounts that speaks of the beginning of time is the *Popul Vuh* (Recinos, et al, 1950:68, 69, 207). Sorenson notes that "The Toltec rulers of the Quiche, along with other pre-Spanish groups, called the lowland zone bounding the Gulf near the Isthmus of Tehuantepec 'the East,' forcing the translators of the Popol Vuh into the bizarre statement, 'In the lands to the north, that is, in the East.'" Those same authors also stated:

The Gulf of Mexico, however it is situated in relation to land—eastward in northern Mexico, northward in the southern Gulf Coast area, or westward off the coast of Campeche—is the "East Sea," while in the same manner, the Pacific Ocean is the "West Sea." In the center of the land, then, around the Isthmus of Tehuantepec, west is on the Pacific side and east is on the southern Gulf coast area.

CITIES OF MULEK AND BOUNTIFUL

The City of Mulek appears to have been La Venta. This makes sense from many points of view. It was the most important Olmec city and had many monuments. Especially noteworthy is Stela 3. It appears to show the meeting between King Coriantumr, holding the baton of authority on the left, and bearded King Mulek, on the right-hand side. Stela 3 is reproduced in Figures A-2 and A-3. The location of La Venta is of importance in determining where the Land Bountiful and City Bountiful were located. The location, just east of the River Tonala, is in accord with its not being in the land of Bountiful but close to it (Alma 51).

The most likely location for the City of Bountiful appears to be at the modern village of Tonala. It is at the exit of the river to the Gulf, and it has a large lagoon protecting a third side. It is just within the boundary of the Land of Bountiful. Ancient ruins are abundant, but the site is not reported on archaeological maps. It is close to La Venta, though the river and some lagoons prevent a straight-line march.

The battle described in Alma 51 fits this scenario, as it is fourteen kilometers to the coast, and another six kilometers to the Tonala river. The strategy developed by Captain Moroni to tire out the Lamanite army, effortlessly capture the City of Mulek, and then defeat the Lamanites with fresh armies fits this geographic scenario. All of the directions given in this account are in accord with the Nephite scenario.

Location of the Nephite cities along the Gulf Coast between Coatzacoalcos and Villahermosa makes all of the battle action plausible. In the context of settlements on the Gulf Coast the trails are reasonable and certainly present practical distances. It all makes sense if the Nephites were calling the Gulf of Mexico the " East Sea."

SUMMARY

Hopefully, some of the abbreviated notes above will help to confirm the plausibility of the Nephite north being at about 65-

90 degrees west of north. In that context, it becomes much easier to understand the overall system used by the prophet Mormon, and those whose writings he abridged. This system fits the general direction of shorelines for the two seas. It fits the direction of the main mountain system along the Pacific Coast between the Isthmus of Tehuantepec and Guatemala. It also fits the general direction of the River Grijalva, possibly the River Sidon. It also helps to understand the directions described in the battle between the Nephites in the City Bountiful and the Lamanites in the City Mulek. They all appear to fit the model established.

Evidence from Mesoamerican calendars and other paintings is indicative of the ancient use of intercardinal points for directions. For example, the Codex Fejervary-Mayer shows that the directions were skewed counterclockwise. Replicas of the Aztec calendar stone, which hang on many living room walls, are vivid reminders of the possible change in directional systems.

Thus, from the supporting data presented here, it appears plausible that the Nephites might have used a directional system based in part on the solstice measurements. It is significantly different than that which we use today, with their north oriented sixty-five degrees west of true north to correspond with the direction of the solstices. In late Nephite history, as the Nephites moved northward, that may have changed to seventy-five degrees west of true north for some unknown reason. In the area around the isthmus of Tehuantepec, the land of Bountiful, it is probable that north became east, because they used the "east sea" as their directional reference. *With extremely few exceptions, true north appears never to have been used by the Nephites.*

References

Adams, Richard E.W.
1977a, *Prehistoric Mesoamerica*, Little, Brown & Co., Boston.
1977b, *The Origins of Maya Civilization*, University of New Mexico Press, Albuquerque, N.M.

Agrinier, Pierre
1984, *The Early Olmec Horizon at Mirador, Chiapas, Mexico*, Papers of the New World Archaeological Foundation, #48, Brigham Young University Press, Provo, Utah, p. 77.

Aharoni, Yohanan, & Michael Avi-Yonah
1968, *The Macmillan Bible Atlas*, Macmillan Publishing Co., N.Y.
1977, *The Macmillan Bible Atlas*, Macmillan Publishing Co., N.Y. Maps #82 and 85.

Allen, Joseph L.
1989, *Exploring the Lands of the Book of Mormon*, S.A. Publishers, Orem, Utah.

Anderson, Lawrence O.
1963, Joseph Smith: A Student of American Antiquities, *U.A.S. Newsletter* #85, Brigham Young University, Provo.

Aveni, Anthony F.
1979, Venus and the Maya, *American Scientist*, May-June, p. 274.

Aveni, Anthony F. (editor)
1975, *Archæoastronomy in Precolumbian America*, University of Texas Press, Austin, pp. 163-190.

Bennett, C. L.
1979, Radiocarbon Dating with Accelerators, *American Scientist*, 67, 450.

Berger, R., J. A. Graham & R. F. Heizer
1967, Contributions of the University of California Arch. Res. Facility, Berkeley, #3, August.

Bermant, Chaim, & Michael Weitzman
1979, *Ebla: A Revelation in Archæology*, Times Books, New York.

Bernal, Ignacio
1965, Archaeological Synthesis of Oaxaca, *Handbook of Middle American Indians*, 3:788-813, R. Wauchope ed. University of Texas Press, Austin.
1969, *The Olmec World*, University of California Press, Berkeley.
1974, *Teotihuacán, Historia de Mexico*, 1(12) p. 221, Salvat, Mexico.
1980, *A History of Mexican Archæology: The Vanished Civilizations of Middle America*, Thames and Hudson, Bath, Avon, Great Britain.

Bertin, Leon
1974, *The New Larousse Encyclopedia of the Earth,* Crown Pub., New York, pp. 151-166.

Blanton, Richard E.
1978, *Monte Alban: Settlement Patterns at the Ancient Zapotec Capital,* Academic Press, New York.

Blom, Frans
1926, Tribes and Temples, *Tulane University Middle American Research Series,* Publication #1, Vol. I, New Orleans, p. 29.

Bove, Frederick, J.
1978, Laguna de los Cerros: An Olmec Central Place, *Journal of New World Archaeology,* 11(3), January.

Breiner, Sheldon, and Michael D. Coe
1972, Magnetic Exploration of the Olmec Civilization, *American Scientist* 60(5), 566-75.

Brockington, Donald L.
1967, The Ceramic History of Santa Rosa, Chiapas, Mexico, *NWAF Papers,* #23, Brigham Young University, Provo.

Brodie, Fawn
1945, *No Man Knows My History,* Alfred A. Knopf, New York.

Brown, Kenneth L.
1977, The Valley of Guatemala—A Highland Port of Trade, in *Teotihuacán and Kaminaljuyú, A Study in Prehistoric Culture Contact,* W. T. Sanders and J. W. Michels, editors, Pennsylvania State University Press, State College, Pennsylvania.

Campbell, Lyle
1979, Middle American Languages, *The Languages of Native America,* Lyle Campbell and Marianne Mithun, editors, University of Texas Press, Austin.

Campbell, Lyle, and Terrance Kaufman
1976, A Linguistic Look at the Olmecs, *American Antiquity,* 41, 80. 1985, Maya Linguistics: Where Are We Now?, *Annual Review of Anthropology,* 14, 187-198.

Caso, Alfonso
1953, *El Pueblo Del Sol,* Fondo de Cultura Economica, Mexico, D. F.
1977, *Reyes y Reinos de La Mixteca, I,* Fondo de la Cultura Economica, Mexico, D.F., Lamina XXI (c).
1979, *Diccionario Biographico de los Senores Mixtecos,* II.

_____, **Ignacio Bernal, & Jorge R. Acosta**
1967, *La Ceramica de Monte Albán,* Memorias del Instituto Nacional de Antropologia e Historia XlII, Mexico.

Ceram, C.W.
1971, *The First Americans,* Harcourt Brace, Jovanovich Inc., New York.

Chadwick, Robert L.
1966, The Olmeca-Xicallanca of Teotihuacán, A Preliminary Study, *Mesoamerican Notes,* #7-8, Teotihuacán and After, Four Essays, John Paddock, ed. Dept. of Anthropology, University of the Americas, Mexico.

Chase, James E.
n.d., The Sky is Falling: The San Martin Tuxtla Volcanic Eruption and its Effects on the Olmec at Tres Zapotes, Veracruz.

Cheesman, Paul R.
1974, *These Early Americans,* Deseret Book, Salt Lake City.

Chimalpahin, Francisco de San Anton
1975, *Relaciones Originales de Chalco Amaquemecan,* S. Rendon ed., Fondo de Cultura Economica, Mexico, p. 169.

Christensen, Ross T.
1968, The Tree of Life in Ancient America, *Pub. of the Society for Early Historic Archaeology,* Provo.
1972, Perspectives on the Route of Mulek's Colony, *SEHA Newsletter,* #131, Brigham Young University. See also #111 and #118.

Clark, C.
1982, *Flood,* Time-Life Books, New York.

Clark, James R.
1959, Book of Mormon Institute, *Extension Publications,* Brigham Young University.

Clube, S.V. and W.M. Napier
1984, The microstructure of Terrestrial Catastrophism, *Mon. Nat. Brit. Astr. Soc.,* 211, 953-68.

Coe, Michael D.
1962, *Mexico,* Praeger Publishers, New York.
1965a, Archæological Synthesis of Southern Mesoamerica and Veracruz, *Handbook of Middle American Indians,* R. Wauchope, ed., Vol. 3, University of Texas Press, Austin, pp. 679-775.
1965b, The Olmec Style and its Distributions, *Handbook of Middle American Indians, Ill,* part 2, Gordon R. Willey, editor, University of Texas Press, Austin, p. 69, 679-715.
1966, *The Maya,* Praeger Publishers, New York.
1968a, America's First Civilization, American Heritage, New York.
1968b, San Lorenzo and the Olmec Civilization, *Dumbarton Oaks Conference on the Olmec,* Trustees for Harvard University, Washington, D.C.
1976, Early Steps in the Evolution of Maya Writing, *The Origins of Religious Art and Iconography In Preclassic Mesoamerica,* Nicholson, HB. editor, Latin American Center, Los Angeles, pp. 109-122.

Coe, Michael D. and Richard A. Diehl
1980, *In the Land of the Olmec, Vol. I, The Archæology of San Lorenzo Tenochtitlan,* University of Texas Press, Austin.

Coe, Michael D., Dean Snow, and Elizabeth Benson
1986, *Atlas of Ancient America,* Fact on File Publications, New York.

Corona Nunez, José
1942, Jiquilpan y el Lienzo de Jucutácato, *Boletín de la Sociedad Mexicana de Geografía y Estadística.* n.d., personal communication, Nov. 2, 1965.

Covarrubias, Miguel
1957, *Indian Art of Mexico and Central America,* Alfred A. Knopf, New York.

Cowdery, Oliver
1835, *Messenger and Advocate,* July, pp. 158-159.

Culbert, T. Patrick
1962, *The Ceramic Sequence of the Central Highlands of Chiapas, Mexico* Doctoral Dissertation, University of Chicago.

Damon, P.E., C.W. Ferguson, A. Long, and E.I. Wallick
1974, Dendrochronologic Calibration of the Radiocarbon Time Scale, *American Antiquity,* 39 (2), 350.

Davies, Nigel
1979, *Voyagers to the New World,* William Morrow and Company, New York.

De la Fuente, Beatríz
1972, *El Arte Olmeca,* Artes de Mexico, #154, Mexico.

Delgado, Agustin
1965, Archeological Research at Santa Rosa, Chiapas and in the Region of Tehuantepec, *Papers of the NWAF,* #17, Brigham Young University, Provo.

Dixon, Riley L.
1958, *Just One Cumorah,* Bookcraft, Salt Lake City.

Drucker, Phillip
1943, Ceramic Sequences at Tres Zapotes, Veracruz, Mexico, *Bureau of American Ethnology Bulletin,* #140, U.S. Govt. Printing Office, Washington, D.C.

Drucker, Phillip, Robert F. Helzer, and Robert J. Squier
1959, *Excavations at La Venta, Tabasco, 1955,* Smithsonian Institution, Bureau of American Ethnology, Bulletin 170, Washington, D.C.

Edmonson, Monroe S.
1988, *Book of the Year: Middle American Calendar Systems,* University of Utah Press, Salt Lake City.

Ehrich, Robert W.
1965, *Chronologies In Old World Archæology,* University of Chicago Press, Chicago, pp. 175-179.

Evans, C., and B.M. Meggers
1966, Transpacific Origin of Valdivia Phase Pottery of Coastal Ecuador, Atlas 36a, *Congreso Internacional de Americanistas, Sevilla,* Vol 1., Sevilla.

Fagan, Brian M.
1985, *The Adventure of Archaeology,* National Geographic Society, Washington, D.C.

Ferguson, Thomas Stuart
1947, *Cumorah Where?,* Zion's Printing Co., Independence, Mo.
1958, *One Fold and One Shepherd,* Books of California, San Francisco.

Ferreira, Jane W.
1976, Shell and Iron Ore Exchange in Formative Mesoamerica, with Comments on Other Commodities, *The Early American Village,* Kent V. Flannery, editor, Academic Press, New York.

Fishbein, Seymour L.
1986, The Sumerians of Mesopotamia, *Splendors of the Past, Lost Cities of the Ancient World,* National Geographic Society, Washington, D.C.

Flannery, Kent V., Anne V.T. Kirby, Michael J. Kirkby & Aubrey W. Williams, Jr.
1967, Farming Systems and Political Growth in Oaxaca, *Science,* 158 (3800), 445.

Flannery, Kent V. & Joyce Marcus
1976, Formative Oaxaca and the Zapotec Cosmos, *American Scientist,* *64,* 374.
1983, *The Cloud People: Divergent Evolution of the Zapotec and Mixtec Civilizations,* Academic Press, New York.

Franchi, José Alcina
1957, *Floresta Literaria de la América Indígena,* Madrid.

Friedman, Irving & Fred W. Trembour
1978, Obsidian, the Dating Stone, *American Scientist, 66,* Jan.-Feb., 44.

Garcia Payon, Jose
1971, Archæology of Central Veracruz, *Handbook of Middle American Indians,* Vol. II, Part 2, edited by Gordon F. Ekholm and Ignacio Bernal, pp. 505-557, University of Texas Press, Austin.

Garibay, Angel Maria
1956, 1969, Historia General de las Cosas de Nueva Espana, Bernardino de Sahagun, 10th book, chapter 29. Translation by M. Wells Jakeman.

Gay, Carlo T. E.
1973, Olmec Hieroglyphic Writing, *Archæology, 26,* 278.

Graham, John A.
1981, Abaj Takalik: The Olmec Style and its Antecedents in Pacific Guatemala, *Ancient Mesoamerica, Selected Readings,* John A. Graham, editor, Peek Publications, Palo Alto, California, p. 1.

Grove, David C.
1969a, Chalcatzingo, Morelos, Mexico: A reappraisal of the Olmec rock carvings, *American Antiquity, 33 (4),* 486-91.
1969b, The Pre-Classic Olmec in Central Mexico: site distribution and inferences, Appendix in *Dumbarton Oaks Conference on the Olmec,* edited by Elizabeth P. Benson, Trustees for Harvard University, Washington, D.C., pp. 179-185.

Grove, David C., Kenneth G. Hirth, David E. Buge, and Ann M. Cyphers
1981, Settlement and Cultural Development at Chalcatzingo, *Ancient Mesoamerica, Selected Readings*, John A. Graham, editor, Peek Publications, Palo Alto, California, p. 177.

Gruener, James C.
1990, *The Olmec Riddle: An Inquiry Into the Origin of Pre-Columbian Civilization,* Vengreen Publications.

Hammond, Fletcher
1959, *Geography of the Book of Mormon,* Utah Printing Co.,
Salt Lake City.

Hamner, C.V., H.B. Claissen, and W. Dansgaad
1980, Greenland ice sheet evidence of post-glacial volcanism and its
climatic impact, *Nature, 288,* 230-5.

Hauck, F. Richard
1988, *Deciphering the Geography of the Book of Mormon,* Deseret
Book, Salt Lake City, Utah.

Hawkes, Jaquena
1974, *Atlas of Ancient Archæology,* McGraw-Hill, New York, p. 149.

Heizer, Robert F.
1966, Ancient Heavy Transport, Methods and Achievements,
Science 153, 821.
1968, New Observations on La Venta, *Dumbarton Oaks Conference on
the Olmec,* Trustees for Harvard University, Washington, D.C.

Heizer, Robert F. and Phillip Drucker
1968, The La Venta Fluted Pyramid, *Antiquity, 42,* 52-56.

Henning, Paul
1912, *Tamoanchán, Estudio Arqueológico e Histórico,* Imprenta del
Museo Nacional de México.

Hess, Wilford M. & Raymond T. Matheny editors
1979, *Science and Religion: Toward a More Useful Dialogue,*
Palladin House, Geneva, Illinois, Vol. I.

Heyerdahl, Thor
1981a, *The RA Expeditions,* Doubleday & Co., Garden City, N.Y.
1981b, *The Tigris Expedition,* Doubleday & Co., Garden City, N.Y.

Hilton, Lynn and Hope Hilton
1976, *In Search Of Lehi's Trail,* Deseret Book, Salt Lake City.

Hunter, Milton R. & Thomas Stuart Ferguson
1950, *Ancient America and the Book of Mormon,* Kolob Book Co.,
Oakland Calif.

Irwin, Constance
1963, *Fair Gods and Stone Faces,* St. Martin's Press, New York.

Ixtlilxóchitl, Don Fernando de Alva
1952, *Obras Históricas,* Alfredo Chavero, editor, Editora Nacional, Mexico.
1985, *Obras Históricas,* Universidad Autonoma de Mexico,
Edmundo O'Gorman, editor.

Jakeman, M. Wells
1957, Review of Hugh Nibley, An Approach to the Book of Mormon,
U.A.S. Newsletter #40.
1959, "The Flood," The "Tower of Babel," and Other Studies; An Important
New Series in the Field of Biblical Archæology, *U.A.S. Newsletter, #56.*
1963, The Book of Mormon Civilizations: Their Origin and their
Development in Time and Space, pp. 81-88 in *Progress In
Archæology, An Anthology,* Ross T. Christensen, editor,
Brigham Young University.

Jessee, Dean C.
1971, The Writing of Joseph Smith's History, *BYU Studies,* 11 (4), p. 439.

Jimenez Moreno, Wigberto
1948, El Occidente de Mexico, *Sociedad Mexicana de Antropología,* IV Reunión de la Mesa Redonda, México, p. 156.
1966, Mesoamerica Before the Toltecs, *Ancient Oaxaca,* John Paddock, editor, Stanford University Press, Stanford, California.

Joesink-Mandeville, L.R.V.
Olmec-Maya Relationships: A correlation of linguistical evidence with archæological ceramics, *J. New World Archæology 3 (1).*

Kaufman, Terrence
1976, Archaeological and Linguistic Correlations in Mayaland and Associated Areas, *World Archæology, 8 (1),* p. 108, (London).
1979, Mesoamerican Indian Languages, *Encyclopedia Britannica, Macropaedia,* 11, 15th edition, Chicago.

Kelley, David H.
1966, A Cylinder Seal from Tlatlilco, *American Antiquity, 31 (5),* p. 744.

Kidder, A. V., J. D. Jennings & E. M. Shook
1946, *Excavations at Kaminaljuyú, Guatemala,* Carnegie Institution of Washington, Publication 561.

Kimball, Spencer W.
1963, The Book of Vital Messages, *The Improvement Era,* June, p. 490.
1979, *Ensign,* October, p. 13.

Kirchhoff, Paul
1981, Mesoamerica: Its Geographic Limits, Ethnic Composition, and Cultural Character, *Ancient Mesoamerica, Selected Readings,* John A. Graham, editor, Peek Publications, Palo Alto, California, p. 1.

Knowlton, Clark S.
1963, Review of "Just One Cumorah, " in *Progress In Archæology, An Anthology,* Ross T. Christensen, editor, Brigham Young University.

Kramer, Samuel Noah
1963, *The Sumerians: Their History, Culture, and Character,* University of Chicago Press, Chicago.

La Fay, Howard
1966, Gibraltar—Rock of Contention, *National Geographic,* July, pp. 102-121.
1978, Ebla, Splendor of an Unknown Empire, *National Geographic, 154 (6),* December, p. 730.

Larsen, Wayne A., Alvin C. Rencher & Tim Layton
1980, Who Wrote the Book of Mormon? An Analysis of Wordprints, *BYU Studies, 20 (3).*

Lee, Thomas A.
1969, The Artifacts of Chiapa de Corzo, Chiapas, Mexico, *NWAF Papers #26,* Brigham Young University, Provo.

Leet, Don
1948, *Causes of Catastrophe,* McGraw Hill, New York.

Leon, Nicolas
   1903, Los Tarascos, *Boletin del Museo Nacional de México,* Vol. I,
      Epoca 2, Agosto.

Leon-Portilla, Miguel
   1962, *Los Antiguos Mexicanos,* Fondo de Cultura Economica, México.
   1964, *Historia Documental de México,* Univ. Nacional Autonoma de
      México, Instituto de Investigaciones Historicas, Mexico, D.F.

Libby, W. F.
   1949, Age Determinations by Radiocarbon Content: Checks with Samples
      of Known Age, *Science, 110,* p. 678.
   1973, The Radiocarbon Dating Method, *Pensee,* Spring-Summer, p. 7.

Lindquist, Edward L.
   n.d., In Search of Cumorah: A Brief Study of the Possibility that
      Archæology can Elucidate the Problems of the Geography of the
      Book of Mormon, Brigham Young University.

Longyear, John M.
   1965, Archæological Survey of El Salvador, in *Handbook of Middle
      American Indians,* Vol. 4, Robert Wauchope ed., University of
      Texas Press, p. 32.

Lowe, Gareth W.
   1959, Archæological Exploration of the Upper Grijalva River, Chiapas,
      Mexico, *NWAF Papers #2,* Orinda, California.
   1977, The Mixe-Zoque as Competing Neighbors of the Early Lowland
      Maya, *The Origins of Maya Civilization,* Richard E.W. Adams,
      editor, University of New Mexico Press, Albuquerque.

Lowe, Gareth W., Thomas A. Lee, Jr.,
and Eduardo Martinez Espinosa
   1982, Izapa: *An Introduction to the Ruins and Monuments,* Papers of
      the New World Archaeological Foundation, #31, Brigham young
      University, Provo, Utah.

Luckert, Karl W.
   1976, *Olmec Religion, A Key to Middle America and Beyond,*
      University of Oklahoma Press, Norman, Oklahoma.

MacNeish, R.S.
   1972, *The Prehistory of Tehuacan Valley: Chronology and Investigation,*
      Vol. 4, University of Texas Press, Austin.

Malmstrom, Vincent H.
   1973, Origin of the Mesoamerican 260 Day Calendar, *Science 181,* 939-
      941, (September 7).
   1976, Izapa, Cultural Hearth of the Olmecs? *Proceedings, Association of
      American Geographers,* pp. 32-35.
   1978, A Reconstruction of the Chronology of Mesoamerican Calendrical
      Systems, *Journal for the History of Astronomy,* ix., 105-116.
   1981, Architecture, Astronomy, and Calendrics in Pre-Columbian
      Mesoamerica, *Archæoastronomy In the Americas,*
      Williamson, R.A., ed., Ballena Press, Los Altos, California.

Marcus, Joyce
   1980, Zapotec Writing, *Scientific American,* p. 50.

Matheny, Ray T. & Deanne L. Gurr
1979, Ancient Hydraulic Techniques in the Chiapas Highlands, *American Scientist,* July-August, p. 441.

McGavin, E. Cecil & Willard Bean
1949, *The Geography of the Book of Mormon,* Bookcraft, Salt Lake City, 2nd ed.

Mertz, Henrietta
1964, *The Wine Dark Sea,* Privately Published.

Meyer, Karl E.
1978, *Teotihuacán,* Newsweek Book Division, New York.

Michels, Joseph W.
1979a, A History of Settlements at Kaminaljuyú, *Settlement Pattern Excavations at Kaminaljuyú, Guatemala,* Pennsylvania State University Press.
1979b, *The Kaminaljuyú Chiefdom,* Pennsylvania State University Press.

_____, **& William T. Sanders**
1973, *The Pennsylvania State University Kaminaljuyú Project: 1969, 1970 Seasons Part 1, Mound Excavations,* Pennsylvania State University Press.

Miller, Mary Ellen
1986, *The Art of Mesoamerica from Olmec to Aztec,* Thames and Hudson, New York.

Millon, Renee
1960, The Beginnings of Teotihuacán, *American Antiquity, 26 (l),* p.1.
1964, The Teotihuacán Mapping Project, *American Antiquity 29 (3),* p. 345.
1973, *Urbanization of Teotihuacán, Mexico,* Vol. I, University of Texas Press, Austin.

_____, **& James A. Bennyhoft**
1961a, A Long Architectural Sequence at Teotihuacán, *American Antiquity, 26 (4)* p. 516.

_____, **& Bruce Drewitt**
1961b, Earlier Structures Within the Pyramid of the Sun at Teotihuacán, *American Antiquity, 26 (3),* p. 371.

Munoz, Carlos
1977, "Cronica de Santa Maria Chimalapa; en las Selvas del Istmo de Tehuantepec," Ediciones Molinos, S.A., San Luis Potosi, Mexico.

Navarrete, Carlos
1959, A Brief Reconnaissance in the Region of Tonola, Chiapas, Mexico, *NWAF Papers #4,* Orinda, California.

Nelson, Fred W.
1967, The Colossal Stone Heads of the Southern Gulf Coast Region of Mexico, *SEHA Newsletter* 103.6, Brigham Young University. n.d., Obsidian Exchange Networks in the Maya Lowlands, Brigham Young University.

Nibley, Hugh
1964, *An Approach to the Book of Mormon,* Deseret Book, Salt Lake City, pp. 338-363.

1952, *The World of the Jaredites,* Bookcraft, Salt Lake City.
1967, *Since Cumorah,* Deseret Book, Salt Lake City, Utah.

Norman, V. Garth
1973, Izapa Sculpture: Part 1, Album, *NWAF Papers #30,* Brigham Young University, Provo.
1974, "Book of Mormon Archæology Alive and Well," twenty-fourth Annual Symposium, Society of Early Historic Archæology.
1975, Izapa Sculpture: Part ll, Text, *NWAF Papers #30,* Brigham Young University, Provo, Utah.
1976, *NWAF Paper #30, Izapa Sculpture,* Parts 1 and 2.
1983, *SEHA Newsletter, #153,* June.
1980, *Astronomical Orientations of Izapa Sculptures,* Master's Thesis, Brigham Young University, Provo, Utah.

Nuttal, Zelia
1975, *The Codex Nuttal,* Dover Publications, New York.

Nuttall, Zelia
1901, The Fundamental Principles of Old and New World Civilizations, *Archæological and Ethnological Papers of the Peabody Museum,* Cambridge.

Paddock, John
1968, *Ancient Oaxaca: Discoveries In Mexican Archæology and History*, Stanford University Press, Stanford.

Palmer, David A.
1967, A Study of Mesoamerican Religious Symbolism, *SEHA Newsletter,* 103.61, Brigham Young University, Provo.
1976, A Survey of Pre-1830 Historical Sources Relating to the Book of Mormon, *BYU Studies, 17 (1),* p. 101.
1981, *In Search of Cumorah: New Evidences for the Book of Mormon from Ancient Mexico*, Horizon Publishers, Bountiful, Utah.

Parrot, Andre
1955a, *The Flood and Noah's Ark*, SCM Press Ltd., London.
1955b, *The Tower of Babel,* SCM Press Ltd., London.

Pasztory, Esther (editor)
1978, *Middle Classic Mesoamerica, A.D. 400-700,* Columbia University Press, New York.

Pereau, Francisco Beverido
1972, Las Ciudades, in *El Arte Olmeca*, Beatriz de la Fuente, editor. Artes de Mexico, Mexico D.F.
n.d., Personal communication, May 4, 1978.

Peterson, Frederick A.
1954, Women Warriors and Laughing Faces, *Natural History*, LXIII, pp. 210-215.

Pettinato, Giovanni
1976, The Royal Archives of Tell Mardikh-Ebla, *Biblical Archæologist, 39 (2),* May, p. 44
1981, *The Archives of Ebla: An Empire Inscribed In Clay,* Doubleday Co., Garden City, New York.

Plancarte y Navarette Francisco
1934, *Tamoanchán,* Editorial el Escritorio, Mexico, D.F.

Pratt, Parley P.
1975, *Autobiography of Parley P. Pratt,* Deseret Book, Salt Lake City, p. 55.

Press, Frank
1977, Volcanoes, *The World Book Encyclopedia,* Field Enterprises, Chicago, V-358b.

Putnam, Reed H.
1966, Were the Gold Plates Made of Tumbaga, *Improvement Era,* Sept., p. 788.

Ralph, Elizabeth K. & Henry N. Michael
1974, Twenty-Five Years of Radiocarbon Dating, **American Scientist, 62,** Sept.-Oct., p. 553.

Reader's Digest
1986, *Mysteries of the Ancient Americas, The New World Before Columbus,* Reader's Digest Association, Pleasantville, N.Y.

Recinos, Adrian, editor
1950, *Título de los Senores de Totonicapán, Anales de los Cakchiqueles Memorial de Sololá,* Fondo de Cultura Economica, Mexico D.F.
1952, *Popol Vuh, Las Antiguas Historias del Quiche,* Fondo de Cultura Economica, Mexico, D.F.

Reynolds, George
1905, *Improvement Era,* Vol. 8, 705.

Reynolds, George, & Janne M. Sjodahl
1957, *Book of Mormon Geography,* Deseret Book, Salt Lake City.

Ricks, Welby W.
1969, Possible Linear Script from Preclassic Mexico, **SEHA Newsletter,** #112, Brigham Young University, Provo.

Ritchie, William A.
1965, *The Archæology of New York State,* Natural History Press, Garden City, N.Y.

Rittman, A. & L. Rittman
1976, *Volcanoes,* Putnam's Sons, New York, pp. 57 & 81.

Roberts, B. H.
1906, The Translation of the Book of Mormon, *Improvement Era,* April, p. 435.
1951, *New Witnesses for God,* III, The Evidences of the Truth of the Book of Mormon Continued, Deseret News, Salt Lake City, pp. 501-3.

Rock, Fritz
1960, Chiuhnautecs y Cempoalteca, Las Antiguas Gentes del Nueve y del Siete, **Boletín del Centro de Investigaciones Antropológicas de México,** #9.

Roys, Ralph L.
1967, *The Book of Chilam Balam of Chumayel,* University of Oklahoma Press, Norman, Oklahoma.

Rust, William F. and Robert J. Sharer
1988, Olmec Settlement Data from La Venta, Tabasco, Mexico, *Science, 242,* Oct., 102.

Saenz, Cesar A.
1962, *Quetzalcoatl,* Instituto Nacional de Antropologia e Historia, Mexico.

Sahagún, Bernardino de
1956, *Historia General de las Cosas de Nueva Espana,* (Angel M. Garibay edition) Editorial Porrua, Mexico, D.F. *Códice Matritense de la Real Academia,* folio 191.

Sanders, William T.
1953, The Anthropogeography of Central Veracruz, *PMEA Xlll* -2-2:27-78.

_____, & Joseph W. Michels
1977, Excavations at the Palangana and the Acropolis, Kaminaljuyú, in *Teotihuacán and Kaminaljuyú, a Study In Prehistoric Culture Contact,* Pennsylvania State University.

Santley, Robert S., P.O. Caballos, T.W. Killion, P.J. Arnold, and Janet M. Kerley
1984, *Final Field Report, Matacapan Archæological Project, 1982 Season,* Research Paper Series #15, University of New Mexico, Albuquerque.

Schele, Linda, and Mary Ellen Miller
1986, *The Blood of Kings, Dynasty and Ritual In Maya Art,* George Brazillen Inc., New York, Chapter 5.

Sejourne, Laurette
1962, *El Universo de Quetzalcoatl,* Fondo de Cultura Economica, Mexico, D.F.
1956, *El Pensamiento y Religion en el Mexico Antiguo,* Fondo de Cultura Economica, Mexico, D.F.

Seler, Edward
1908, Die Alten·Bewohner der Landschaft Michuacan, *Gesammelte Abhandlungen,* III, pp. 33-156, Berlin.

Shanks, Hershel
1979, Syria Tries to Influence Ebla Scholarship, *Biblical Archæology Review,* May/April, p. 44.

Sheets, Payson D.
1977, *Radiocarbon, 19 (2),* 320.
1979a, Maya Recovery from Volcanic Disasters, Ilopango and Ceren, *Archæology, 32 (3),* pp. 32-42.
1979b, Environmental and Cultural Effects of the Ilopango Eruption in Central America, in *Volcanic Activity and Human Ecology,* Payson D. Sheets and Donald K. Grayson, editors, Academic Press, N.Y.

Shetrone, Henry Clyde
1930, *The Mound Builders:* A Reconstruction of the Life of a Prehistoric American Race, through Exploration and Interpretation of their Earth Mounds, their Burials, and their Cultural Remains, Kennikat Press, Port Washington.

Shook, Edwin M. & A.V. Kidder
1952, *Mound E-III-3, Kaminaljuyú, Guatemala,* Carnegie Institution of Washington, Publication 596, Contribution 53.

Shook, Edwin M.
1957, Lugares Arqueologicos del Altiplano Meridional Central de Guatemala, in *Arqueologia Guatemalteca,* Publicaciones del IDAEH, Guatemala.
1965, Archæological Survey of the Pacific Coast of Guatemala, Handbook of *Middle American Indians,* Vol. ii, p. 180, R. Wauchope Ed., University of Texas Press, Austin.
1967, The Present Status of Research on the Preclassic Horizons in Guatemala, in *The Civilizations of Ancient America,* Sol Tax, ed. Cooper Square Publishers, New York.

_____ **& Tatiana Proskouriakott**
1956, Settlement Patterns in Mesoamerica and the Sequence in the Guatemala Highlands, in *Prehistoric Settlement Patterns In the New World,* Gordon R. Willey, ed. Viking Fund Publications, New York.

Sidrys, Raymond, John Andresen & Derek Marcucci
1976, Obsidian Sources in the Maya Area, *Journal of New World Archæology,* 1 (5), pp. 1-13.

Silverberg, Robert
1962, *Lost Cities and Vanished Civilizations,* Chilton, N.Y., citing History of Greece by George Grote (1846).

Simmons, Verneil W.
1981, *Peoples, Places, and Prophecies: A Study of the Book of Mormon,* Zarahemla Research Foundation, Independence, Mo.

Sisson, Edward B.
n.d., Settlement and Land Use in the Northwestern Chontalpa, Tabasco, Mexico, A Progress Report, Harvard University.
1983, La Venta, Ubicacion, estrategica de un sitio Olmeca, *Mesoamerica, 4,* Junio Cuadro 5.

Sjodahl, J. M.
1927, *An Introduction to the Study of the Book of Mormon,* Deseret News Press, Salt Lake City, Utah.

Smith, Bradley
1968, *Mexico, A History In Art,* Doubleday, Garden City, N.Y.

Smith, Joseph, Jr.
1842a, *Times and Seasons,* Vol. III, #22, p. 922.

Smith, Joseph Fielding
1956, *Doctrines of Salvation,* Vol. 3, Bookcraft, Salt Lake City.

Smith, Ledyard
1955, *Archæological Reconnaissance In Central Guatemala,* Carnegie Institution of Washington, Publication 608.

Smith, Robert F.
n.d., Private communications, 1975.

Snow, Dean
1976, *The Archæology of North America,* Viking Press, New York.

Sorenson, John L.
n.d., *An Ancient Setting for the Book of Mormon.*
1971, The Significance of an Apparent Relationship between the Ancient Near East and Mesoamerica, in *Man Across the Sea, Problems of Precolumbian Contacts,* Carroll L. Riley et. al. editors, University of Texas Press, Austin.
1975, The Gates of God, *The New Era,* March, p. 18.
1976a,Instant Expertise on Book of Mormon Archæology, *BYU Studies 16 (3),* p. 429.
1976b,A Reconsideration of Early Metal in Mesoamerica, *Katunob,* IX, #1.
1977, Mesoamerican Chronology, *Katunob,* IX (February).
1985, *An Ancient Setting for the Book of Mormon,* Foundation for Ancient Research and Mormon Studies, Provo, Utah.

Sperry, Sidney B.
1968, *Book of Mormon Compendium,* Bookcraft, Salt lake City, p. 6, 448-451.

Stark, Barbara L.
1978, An Ethnohistoric Model for Native Economy and Settlement Patterns in Southern Veracruz, Mexico, in *Prehistoric Coastal Adaptions,* Barbara L. Stark and Barbara Voorhies, editors, Academic Press, N.Y.

Stephens, John L.
1841, *Incidents of Travel in Central America, Chiapas, and Yucatan,* First edition, Harper & Brothers, N.Y. Reprinted by Dover, N.Y. (1969).

Stirling, Matthew W.
1940, An Initial Series from Tres Zapotes, Veracruz, Mexico, *Contributed Technical Papers, Mexican Archæology Series 1.,* National Geographic Society, Washington, D.C.
1943, Stone Monuments of Southern Mexico, *Bureau of American Ethnology,* Bulletin 138, U.S. Govt. Printing Office, Washington D.C.
1965, Monumental Sculpture of Southern Veracruz and Tabasco, *Handbook of Middle American Indians,* Vol. 3, Part 2, Gordon R. Willey, editor, University of Texas Press, 716.

Taylor, R.E., D.J. Donahue, T.H. Zabel, P.E. Damon, and J.T. Zull
1984, "Radiocarbon Dating by Particle Accelerators: An Archaeological Perspective," in Archæological Chemistry III, J.B. Lambert, editor, *Advances In Chemistry Series #205,* ACS, Washington, D.C.

Tedlock, Dennis
1985, *Popol Vuh, Mayan Book of the Dawn of Life,* translation and commentary, Simon and Schuster, New York.

Teeple, John E.
1930, Maya Astronomy, *Contributions To Archæology and Ethnology,* #2, Carnegie Institution of Washington, Publication 403, Washington, D.C.

Temple, Wayne C.
1977, Mound Builders, *World Book Encyclopedia,* Vol. M, p. 776, Field Enterprises, Chicago.

Thompson, J. E.
1956, *The Rise and Fall of Maya Civilization,* University of Oklahoma
Press, Norman, Oklahoma.
1960, *Maya Hieroglyphic Writing, Introduction,* University of Oklahoma
Press, Norman, Oklahoma.

Thorarinsson, Sigurdur
1979, Damage Caused by Volcanic Eruptions, in *Volcanic Activity and
Human Ecology,* Payson D. Sheets and Donald K. Grayson, editors,
Academic Press, N.Y.

Treat, Raymond C.
1978, Wheat and Barley: Problem or Opportunity, *The Zarahemla
Record,* Sept., p. 7.
1979, Monte Alban, *The Zarahemla Record,* Fall.
1986, Mesoamerican Linguistics, *The Zarahemla Record,* #34.

Urrutia, Benjamin
1982, Shiblon, Coriantumr, and the Jade Jaguars, *SEHA Newsletter,*
#150.0, Provo, Utah.
1983, The Name Connection, *The New Era,* June, p. 38.

U. S. Naval Oceanographic Service
1969, *Oceanographic Atlas of the North Atlantic Ocean,* Washington, D.C.

Valenzuela, Juan
1945, La Segunda Temporada de Exploraciones en la Region de los
Tuxtlas, estado de Veracruz, *Anales del Museo Nacional de
Antropologia e Historia,* Vol. I, 1939/40, pp. 81-94.
1947, Informe Preliminar de las Exploraciones Efectuadas en los Tuxtlas,
Veracruz, *International Congress of Americanists,* 27th
Proceedings, VII, pp. 113-130, Mexico, D.F.

Veytia, Marlano
1836, *Historia Antigua de Mexico,* Imprenta Juan Ojeda, Mexico.

Vogt, Evon Z.
1969, *Zinacantan: A Maya Community In the Highlands of Chiapas,*
Harvard University Press, Cambridge.

Von Wuthenau, Alexander
1975, *Unexpected Faces In Ancient America—The Historical
Testimony of Precolumbian Artists 1500 B.C.-A.D. 1500,*
Crown, New York.

Warren, Bruce W.
1963, Further on the Claims of the Book of Mormon Characteristics of its
First Civilization, *Progress In Archæology,* An Anthology, *op. cit.,* p. 88.
1964, A Hypothetical Reconstruction of Mayan Origins, *Sobretiro del
XXXV Congreso Internacional de Americanistas,* Mexico, p. 292.
1978, *The Sociocultural Development of the Central Depression of
Chiapas, Mexico: Preliminary Considerations,* Doctoral
Dissertation, University of Arizona.
1983, A Cautious Interpretation of a Mesoamerican Myth: Reflections Upon
Olmec-Jaredite Roots, *SEHA Newsletter,* #154, July, Provo, Utah.

Warren, Bruce W., and Thomas Stuart Ferguson
1987, *The Messiah In Ancient America,* Book of Mormon Research Foundation, Provo, Utah.

Warrick, Richard A.
1975, Volcano Hazard in the United States, A Research Assessment, *Environment and Man Monograph,* #NSF-RA-E-75-012, University of Colorado, Boulder.

Washburn, J. N.
1974, *Book of Mormon Lands and Times,* Horizon Publishers, Bountiful, Utah.

_____ **& J. A. Washburn**
1939, *An Approach to the Study of the Book of Mormon,* New Era Publishing, Provo, Utah.

Weaver, Muriel Porter
1972, *The Aztecs, Maya, and their Predecessors,* Seminar Press, N.Y.

Weiant, Clarence W.
1943, An Introduction to the Ceramics of Tres Zapotes, Veracruz, Mexico, *Bureau of American Ethnology Bulletin,* #139, U.S. Govt. Printing Office, Washington, D.C.

Whitecotton, Joseph W.
1984, *The Zapotecs: Princes, Priests, and Peasants,* University of Oklahoma Press, Norman, Oklahoma.

Widstoe, John A.
1959, Is Book of Mormon Geography Known? in *A Book of Mormon Treasury,* Bookcraft, Salt Lake City.

Wilkerson, S. Jeffrey K.
1980, Man's Eighty Centuries in Veracruz, *National Geographic, 158(2),* August, p. 214.

Willey, Gordon R.
1971, *An Introduction to American Archæology,* Prentice Hall, N.Y.

Williams, Howell & Robert F. Heizer
1955, Sources of Rocks Used in the Olmec Monuments, *Contributions of the University of California Archæological Research Facility,* 1. Sept. p. 4.

Wittorf, John H.
1970, Joseph Smith and the Prehistoric Mound-Builders of Eastern North America, *SEHA Newsletter,* #123, Brigham Young University.

Zeitlin, Robert Norman
1979, *Prehistoric Long-Distance Exchange on the Southern Isthmus of Tehuantepec, Mexico,* Doctoral Dissertation, Yale University.

MAP SECTION INDEX

.

MAP 1
Relative Positions of Mormon's Cumorah and Moroni's Cumorah

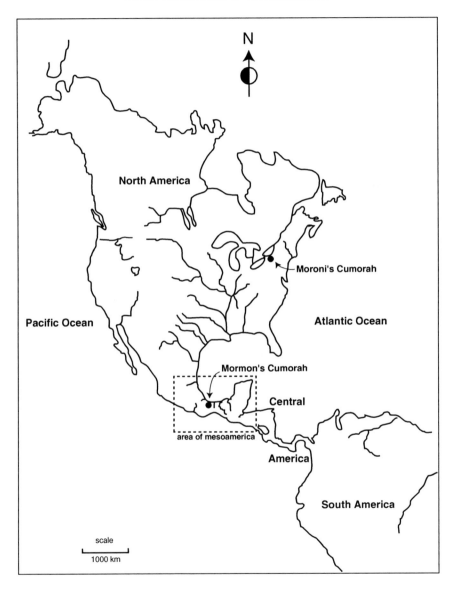

MAP 2
Modern Political Divisions in Mesoamerica

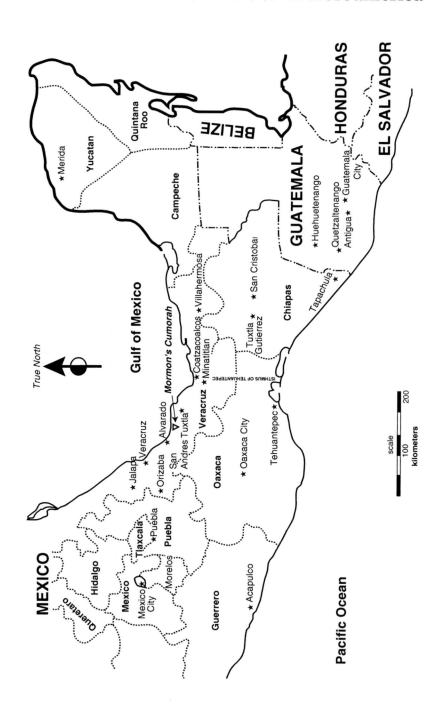

MAP 3
Book of Mormon Geography

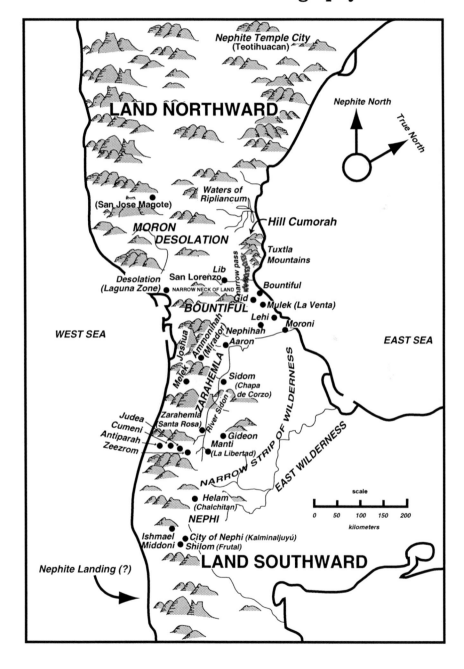

MAP 4   Narrow Neck of Land Region—

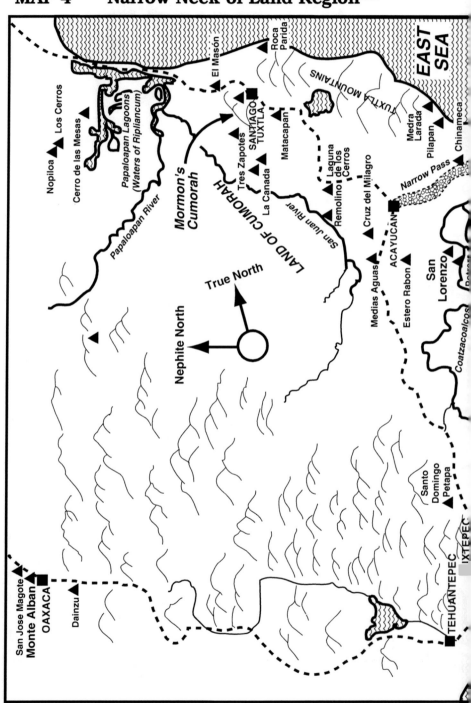

Archæological Sites Dating to the Book of Mormon Period

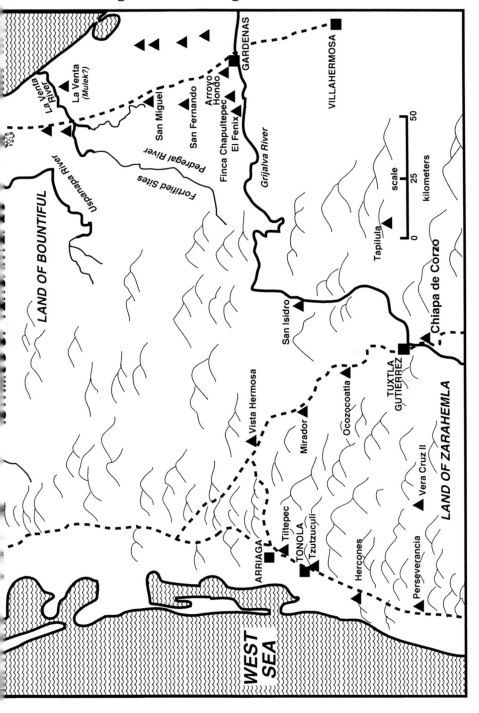

MAP 5
Suggested Route of the Limhi Expedition

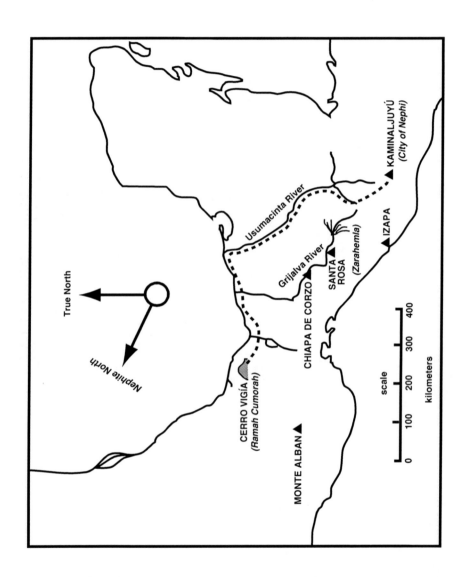

MAP 6

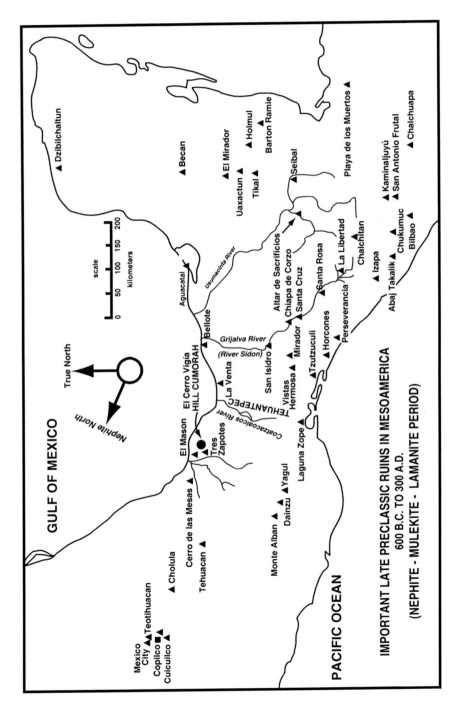

IMPORTANT LATE PRECLASSIC RUINS IN MESOAMERICA
600 B.C. TO 300 A.D.
(NEPHITE - MULEKITE - LAMANITE PERIOD)

MAP 7

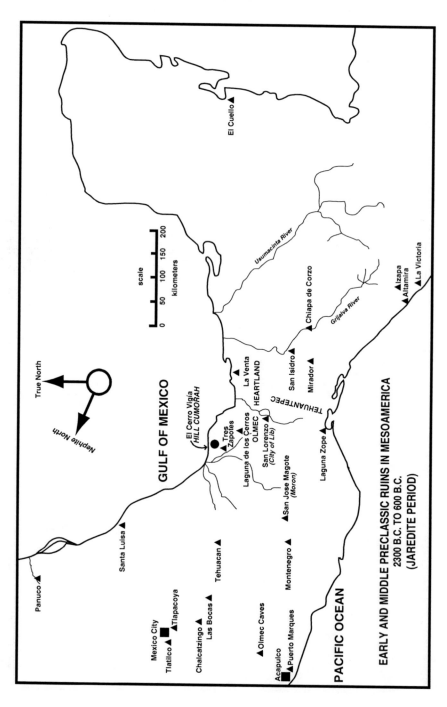

EARLY AND MIDDLE PRECLASSIC RUINS IN MESOAMERICA
2300 B.C. TO 600 B.C.
(JAREDITE PERIOD)

MAP 8
Movements of the Mulekites

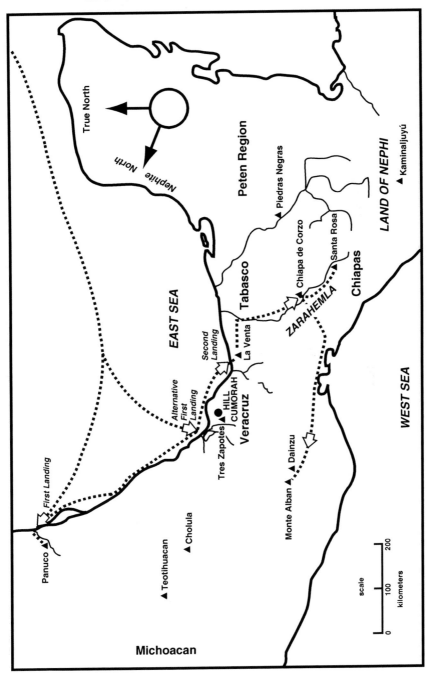

MAP 9
PreClassic Ruins in the Land of Nephi

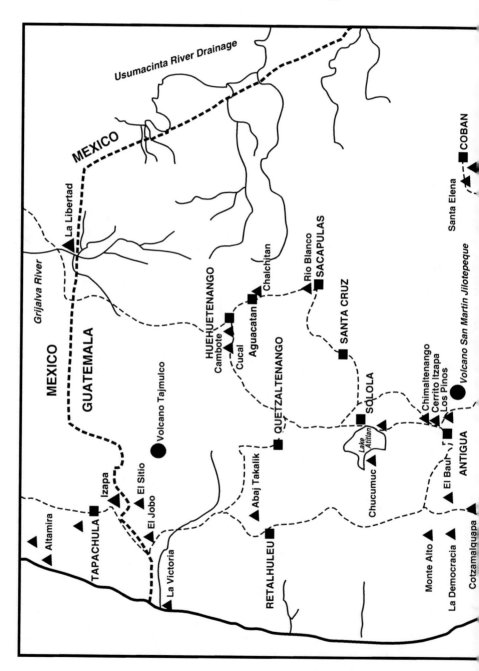

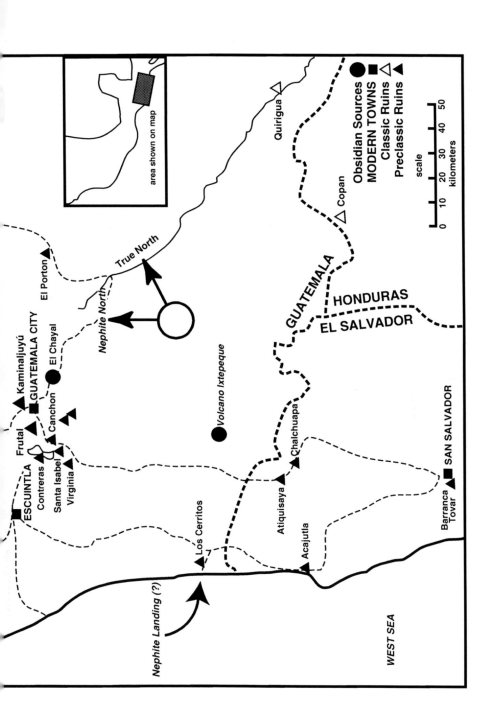

MAP 10

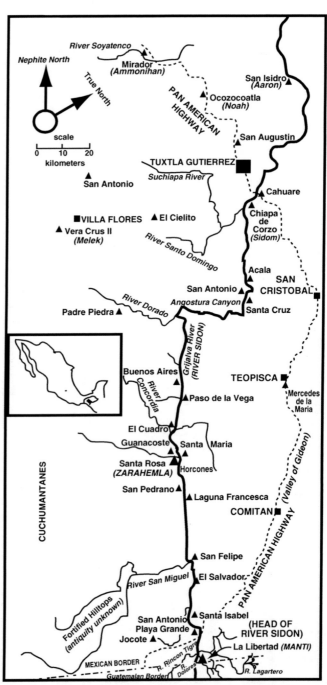

The Central Depression of Chiapas
Archaeological Sites Dating to Preclassic
(Book of Mormon) Period

INDEX

V